CW01499998

Introduction

To a small girl my father was a giant. It wasn't just his size, 6' 4¹/₂" tall and weighing 17 stone. His personality was also giant-sized. When he swept me up to ride on his shoulders I felt 10 feet tall. Riding on the front of his skis down the gentle Surrey slopes was like travelling with seven league boots. When, in rarely privileged moments, I visited him in his study (the holy of holies where children were not allowed), and sat on his massive knee in the chair that was always his, life suddenly felt wholly secure. He would tell me stories, talk to me about his 'teacher' (a signed photo of C.G. Jung hung on the wall above his desk), or sing me the song of the 'Mourning Dove'. This song was a particular favourite. He would begin it in a tiny, soft voice and his face was that of a dove in mourning: 'Sometimes I feel like a moooourning dove', repeated four times. Then suddenly, in a voice like thunder which made me jump out of my skin, he continued: 'Sometimes I feel like an eagle in the sky', and with each of the four repeated phrases his fortissimo grew to a sound that both thrilled and terrified me. To me, as a tiny child, his voice also was that of a giant.

His singing had always played an important part in his life. He had a fine baritone voice which could be infinitely tender, and it gave me great delight when he came every night to sing me to sleep in my cot.

In the dining room of the house where I grew up hung a print of Michelangelo's 'Creation of Eve' from the ceiling of the Sistine Chapel. In this well-known fresco God is seen floating in the sky, surrounded by a cloud, with flowing hair and beard which seem to melt into the cloud. Under his right arm peeps a frightened Eve who is looking apprehensively towards the naked figure of Adam reclining at his ease on the ground below. I used to confuse this old man, who represented God, with my father. My father seemed equally large and certainly appeared through my child's eyes to be quite as 'Almighty'.

I have other memories of him. Maybe I also confused him with Father Christmas, though that was more understandable. I remember when I was three, I had sent a request to Father Christmas for a torch.

It was war-time and my yellow cot was in my parents' bedroom as the rest of the house was filled with friends who were taking refuge from the bombing in London. On Christmas morning I opened my stocking while my father looked on from his bed. My disappointment when I had opened all the parcels and found no torch must have been heart-rending! My father was sympathetic and made suggestions as to where it might be. He asked if I had thought of looking in the fireplace where Father Christmas might have dropped it when he came down the chimney. And there it was, wrapped in now somewhat sooty Christmas paper, a beautiful silver torch. My joy knew no bounds. Somehow I wasn't quite clear about whether it was he or Father Christmas who had found his way into our bedroom through the chimney, nor was I too much concerned as to how a giant-sized father (or Father Christmas), could have fitted into that very narrow opening!

They are joyful memories, the times I spent with him. Gardening beside him with my tiny wheelbarrow and earning sixpence for my help. Creating my own rock garden beneath the kitchen window, while he gave his advice. Gathering mushrooms with him in Devon, at dawn: holding his great hand in mine as we walked over the dew-drenched fields; then after a breakfast of fresh field mushrooms (to me they still taste like food for the gods), the walk of a mile or so down to the seashore. When I could no longer keep up with the rest of the family I would ride high on his shoulders and for a short time have the satisfaction of looking down at my two brothers walking way below.

These memories shine out from my childhood like fragments of gold dust. Like the gold cigarette lighter my father had lost, which I dug up one day months later from the compost heap. I remember his delight at my discovery and my reward.

But it was not an easy time. War broke out when I was two. Just after my first birthday our house, which had a thatched roof, was burned to the ground. To re-build the house took a whole year and during that time we were refugees in other people's homes and in rented houses. My father's time was taken up with writing his books, with starting a Jungian training school in London and with his busy practice as a Jungian analyst, both in Mansfield Street and in West Byfleet. When the bombing in London intensified, friends and colleagues of my father's came to stay in our large house. The pre-war luxury of a live-in cook and maid as well as a governess, a nanny and

JUNG'S APPRENTICE

A BIOGRAPHY OF HELTON GODWIN BAYNES

DIANA BAYNES JANSEN

Helton Godwin ("Peter") Baynes, towards the end of his life (1943)
The ring on his left little finger was given to him by Jung.
It was made by the Navaho Indians.

Jung's Apprentice

A Biography
of

Helton Godwin Baynes

Diana Baynes Jansen

DAIMON
VERLAG

The author and the publisher would like to thank the following publishers and individuals for permission to quote from their material in this publication:

Bax, Arnold, *Farewell My Youth – and Other Writings*. Scolar Press, Hants, 1992.
Bax, Clifford, *Inland Far*. PFD (Heinemann) London 1925.
Baynes, Chloë & Thornycroft, Rosalind, *Time Which Spaces Us Apart*. Private Publication, 1991. (Permission granted by Chloë Baynes)
Cabot Reid, Jane, *Jung, my Mother and I*. Daimon Verlag, Einsiedeln, 2001.
Clayton, Ann, *Chavasse Double VC*. Pen and Sword, York, 1997.
Farjeon, Eleanor, *Edward Thomas – The Last Four Years*. Oxford, 1958.
Fordham, Michael, *The Making of an Analyst, A Memoir*. Free Association Books, London, 1993.
Foreman, Lewis, *A Composer and His Times*. Scolar Press, Hants, 1983.
Garnett, David, *The Golden Echo*. Chatto & Windus, London, 1954.
Hannah, Barbara, *Jung, His Life & Work: A Biographical Memoir*. Chiron Publications, Wilmette, Illinois, 1998.
Hislop, Francis Daniel, *Dr Jung, I presume. The Journal of Her Majesty's Overseas Service*. Corona, London, June 1960. Published in McGuire, William and Hull, R.F.C., *C.G. Jung Speaking*. Pan Books, London, 1980.
Jaffé, Aniela, *Memories, Dreams, Reflections by C.G. Jung*. Fontana Press, London, 1995.
Kirsch, Thomas B., *The Jungians*. Routledge, London, 2000.
Nicoll, Maurice, *In Mesopotamia*. Hodder & Stoughton, London, 1917.

A special thank you to the Jung Family for permission to reproduce the correspondence from Jung to H.G. Baynes and also for permission to reproduce the painting by Jung on the cover flap.

ISBN 3-85630-626-9

Copyright © 2003 Daimon Verlag, Einsiedeln

Letters by C.G. Jung and Emma Jung and painting by C.G. Jung
© The Estate of Emma and Carl Gustav Jung

All rights reserved. No part of this publication may be reproduced, stored in a retrieval system, or transmitted in any form, or by any means, electronic, mechanical, photocopying, recording or otherwise, without prior written permission from the publisher.

Contents

Part One
Childhood and Youth

Part Two
Zurich and C.G. Jung

Part Three
A Separate Path

HELTON GODWIN BAYNES was a man of unusual stature, both physically and in the breadth and scope of his personality. He spanned widely different aspects of life and counted among his friends some of the leading men and women of letters, as well as the outstanding personalities, of his generation.

He was a close personal friend to C.G. Jung during the later part of his life. He worked as his chief assistant in Zurich for many years, and was also the pioneer for Jungian psychology in Britain.

two full-time gardeners, disappeared and my mother was left holding the fort. The bombing came closer and we frequently had doodle-bugs sailing overhead. There was a time when three incendiary bombs landed in our garden, one on the roof of the house and two on the lawn. My father was tired and my mother became ill. Her illness lasted between six months and a year. To me it seemed an eternity and someone was employed as a house-keeper in my mother's absence. It was only later that we three children, my two older brothers and myself, realised how close our mother had come to death. She had developed septicaemia and at that time there were no antibiotics available. Her life was saved by the newly discovered sulphonamide drugs. The situation at home was difficult, the house-keeper was not a success, and my father became exhausted.

When my mother eventually returned from hospital, still hobbling about on crutches, it was clear that my father was mortally ill. He was struggling to keep his practice going and was having increasing difficulty with speech. Eventually a brain-tumour was diagnosed, in the speech area of the brain. Soon after my mother's return home my father was taken to hospital and he died there on the 6th September 1943. I was just six years old.

So the golden memories and the dark ones are intermingled. My last memory of him was just before he was taken to hospital. My brothers and I were being sent away to stay with my elderly God-mother in Camberley so that my mother could remain with my father in hospital. I was reluctant to go. I had that certain feeling, which children have, that something was in the wind. My father held me in his great arms and rocked me like a baby, looking at me with a face full of love and with tears in his eyes. He wasn't able to speak but somehow he conveyed to me a comfort and a sense of being held in his great and loving warmth, and I felt profoundly comforted. It was the last time I saw him.

Acknowledgments

I would like to thank all those people who have enabled me in the writing of this book.

First of all my father, who has come alive for me again as I rediscovered him through his letters and journals.

My sister, Chloë Green, for her help and advice and for allowing me to use material from her mother's memoir.

My daughter, Nicola Sutherland, for her professional editing skills and warm encouragement.

My nephew, Jonathan Baynes, for doing a splendid job with the editing of the final edition.

Joe Fisher, who read and corrected the manuscript and gave me confidence to continue when my courage faltered.

My sister-in-law, Ann Baynes, who has generously supplied me with material and with photographs for the book.

Ean Begg, who has supported, encouraged and enabled me in the long process of writing.

My brother, John Baynes, who has generously contributed towards the costs.

My cousin, Sir Robert Horton, without whose generosity the book could not have been published.

My publisher, Robert Hinshaw, who has gently encouraged me throughout and patiently awaited and prompted the final result.

The Jung family, who have given me their support and allowed me to print the correspondence between my father and Jung.

The Hon John Jolliffe for his encouragement and professional advice.

My stepson Justin Jansen, for reproducing many of the photographs.

My friend, Lindsay Molineux, for his technical support and scanning of many of the photographs.

Finally, a very big thank you to my husband, Christopher Jansen for his unfailing support, encouragement, advice and patience, throughout the writing of this book.

Part One

Childhood and Youth

Chapter One

Early Life

The same that oft-times hath
Charme'd magic casements, opening on the foam
Of perilous seas, in faery lands forlorn.

                    Keats, *Ode to a Nightingale*

Godwin's childhood is spent in a village near Reading, in the
South of England, in a family of strict puritan background. He is
the fourth of five children and often rebels against the narrow
horizons of his home. He has a need to explore a wider world
than that offered by the family business in timber, which the
three sons are expected to join. Helton Baynes' increasing disabil-
ity due to agoraphobia acts as a catalyst for Godwin's early fasci-
nation with psychology.

The sun was rising over Hampstead Heath and the St Stephens
Church clock in Pond Street was chiming 4:00 a.m., when Mary
Baynes gave birth to her third son. He was a big baby, nearly eleven
pounds, and already he had a shock of dark hair. It had been a long
and difficult labour and Mary was tired, but also relieved to see how
alive and vigorous her new baby appeared to be. Her husband's
neurotic illness over the last six months had led both Mary and her
husband Helton to believe that the baby would somehow be similarly
affected; that this sickness would inevitably sap the child's vitality and
affect his ability to live. The baby seemed to defy these fears, and his
loud and lusty cry brought tears to Mary's eyes. This was to be the son

she felt most passionately about, as though all the travail of the past months and the extended labour had bonded her more totally with this new life which she had created.

Helton Godwin Baynes (known as 'Godwin') was born in Hampstead on the 26th June 1882. The Baynes family originated in the Highlands and later came to settle in the south of England, near to Reading, which is where Godwin spent his early years. He was the fourth child of Helton A. Baynes and Mary Foster. The family consisted of an older sister, Muriel, two older brothers, Arnold and Jack, and a younger sister, Ruth. Godwin's father had a successful business in timber which was situated in Reading.

On both sides of Godwin's family there was a strong and even distinguished puritan background. The family attended Trinity Chapel in Reading and their lives revolved around the life of the chapel. The social life at home consisted of the odd visiting relation or missionary.

The Baynes family home was a large Victorian house called Briar Lea. It was in the village of Mortimer Common, in Berkshire, a quiet village with a scattering of houses along the main country road. On either side of the road were green fields edged by hedges which in summertime were white with may.

The woods near Briar Lea were resplendent with mature hardwood trees and in front of the house itself grew a small grove of tall wellingtonias. Nothing now remains of the old house but many fine old trees in the garden are still there as well as the surrounding brick wall.

Like so many of the spacious houses of that era, Briar Lea was pulled down and replaced by a number of small modern houses. However, the walk which the Baynes children used to take and their favourite spot for picnics are still partly there. The route takes one along a right of way, which ran beside the Bayneses' garden, over the lush, buttercup-studded meadows, through some mature woodland, with beech and oak trees, and continues until it reaches the river. One could imagine Godwin with his brothers, biking along these quiet country lanes, discovering his delight in wild flowers, butterflies, moths and birds, which were to become such an abiding interest in later life. He enjoyed ranging far afield over the somewhat flat countryside and climbing the tall impressive trees which surrounded the garden.

Godwin's interest in butterflies and moths would subsequently become a passion in his life. His butterfly collection, which was neatly arranged in three glass-fronted cabinets, was later to stand on the landing of his home. On rare occasions these would be unlocked and the children could admire the delicate shapes, the iridescent blues and every imaginable colour in this amazing collection. Every known species of British butterfly and moth was there together with many of the African species.

The Bayneses were a well-to-do, hard-working and philanthropic family; in trade, and yet living like gentry. Their spacious brick, Victorian house was neither beautiful nor luxurious but was certainly affluent, and it was surrounded by a large garden with vegetables, an orchard and an extensive lawn. The family had three or more servants as well as two gardeners.

Godwin's mother, Mary, was a tall woman with a warm and generous personality. She was involved in many charitable pursuits, taking an active part in village life. Her lively mind and natural generosity of spirit seemed to expand beyond the limitations imposed by the strict nonconformist atmosphere of their home. There is a portrait of her sitting at a table arranging flowers in which one sees a vivacity and animation which seem to positively light up her face.

Godwin's mother, Mary,
arranging a vase of flowers

Mary's maiden name was Foster, but through her mother's family she was distantly related to William Godwin and to Mary Shelley. It was from his mother that Godwin inherited his adventurous spirit and also his creative energy. It was also because of this connection that he was christened Godwin. William Godwin had begun his life at Wisbech in the Fens, which is where the Godwin family originated, and this is also where Godwin Baynes lived and worked for the first years of his marriage.

Godwin's father was a man with a keen business sense and high ideals, and he was a devoted husband and father. He ran the family timber business successfully until his agoraphobia made the journey to and from work impossible. He was a profoundly introverted man, shy and conscientious and deeply devout. He cut a somewhat sombre figure, with his long beard, his skullcap and dark clothes and appeared, perhaps, a little forbidding to a young child. His life revolved around the activities of the chapel near their home, sometimes taking the services and also 'receiving' people, including his own son, Godwin, into the chapel.

Perhaps Mary, with her strong personality and extraversion, accentuated Helton's extreme cautiousness. Certainly, he was a man who was dominated by his fears. These fears ruled his life from the time of his breakdown, when Mary was pregnant with Godwin. The agoraphobia increased in severity and ultimately, it became almost impossible for him to leave the house. In the late nineteenth century there was only limited knowledge of this condition and no known treatment or cure could be offered to Helton. Godwin, as a young child, was keenly aware of being somehow different. After all, other people's fathers didn't have to avoid open or crowded places. It seemed to become a challenge for him which was to shape his later life.

It was assumed, then, that daughters would remain at home to look after their parents. As a result of this, much of the onus of their father's illness was born by Muriel. Godwin later expressed the belief that Muriel's 'life had been spoilt by the grim evangelical atmosphere and close paternal dependence on her'. He spoke of the pious home milieu and of their narrow circle of friends: the 'only visitors were relatives (needy) and missionaries'. He said of Muriel that she 'probably had a hysterical bias and her whole interest was for years based on missionaries and mission work in distant lands. It was her passion.' This led to her increasing isolation and Helton, perhaps selfishly, encouraged this passion because it kept her within the family circle; he needed her as his prop and in a way, condemned her to a life of domesticity. She was committed to her father and to tending his illness from her early life, and was, as a result, never really free to marry. She devoted her later life to caring for her elderly parents and bought herself a three-bedroomed house named Wisley, in Mortimer Common, to be near them in their old age. She remained unmarried and led a life of unselfish devotion to others. A beautiful gossamer-like, hand-embroidered silk scarf survives, which was given to Muriel by Godwin, after the First War, in appreciation of her care of their parents; so he was aware and grateful, even though he was, in his life, to take a very different path from theirs.

Ruth was the apple of her father's eye, the child of his later years, and she remained with her parents until she eventually married, in her late thirties. She was a gentle and lovely person with a soul of great sensitivity and a rare artistic talent. She was gifted with her hands and could weave beautifully. But she was shy and timid and this was accentuated by a deafness which increased with the years. Like all the Baynes family, she was large, over six feet tall, and powerfully built. This gave her a somewhat ungainly and masculine appearance which, added to her lack of confidence, meant that she didn't manage to break away from home and its difficulties till late in her life.

Eventually Ruth was able to train as an occupational therapist. While working in the psychiatric unit of a London hospital she met her future husband, Bill Poulter, who was a psychiatric nurse in the same hospital. After they married, they set up house in Felixstowe and ran a post-office together. However, it wasn't a fulfilling relationship for Ruth. Bill invited his Polish friend, a man called Jan who was to become his lover, to come and live with them. In effect, Ruth became the housekeeper for the two men and all her love was lavished on Dan, her beloved golden retriever. When he died, she lost her best friend in the world. Within this somewhat bizarre household where Ruth uncomplainingly held the fort, she lived a rich, secret and totally hidden inner life. She expressed this in her writing, her paintings, her music (she was a fine pianist) and also in her weaving.

She devised a colour scale, taking the colours of the spectrum with sky blue as middle C. She then discovered that there was a correspondence between the harmonising of notes and the harmonising of the colours which represented those sounds. Harmony of sound could be translated into harmony of colour, and likewise, the discords in sound and colour also correspond. For Godwin's family she wove aprons and curtains which were also musical ditties!

Jack was also a huge man. He was a gentle giant and of the three sons, he was the steady and dependable one who could be relied on to give help and support when it was needed. Helton wrote of him: 'Jack is a dear boy and has never given us a moment's worry' – something that could certainly not have been said about Godwin. Jack ultimately took over the family timber business, known then as Baynes and Co., but later to become Gabriel Wade and English. The firm was well known locally and supplied timber to most people in the neighbourhood. Jack must have taken over responsibility for the business early in life because by the time Godwin left his public school, Leighton Park, Helton was finding it almost impossible to face the six to eight mile journey by horse and carriage to and from work.

Jack was to spend the rest of his working life, until his retirement in the 1950s, running the family business. He was a kind and benevolent employer and under his directorship the company grew and flourished. During the Second World War, he was to become a leading figure in the timber world, and received the MBE for his directorship. He married young but soon after the birth of his son, Norman, his wife died. He married a second time and never moved far from his birthplace, making his ultimate home with his second wife, Dorothy (with whom he had four more children), only a few miles from Mortimer Common in a large and beautiful house, Box Cottage, in Bucklebury.

Arnold, the eldest son, was the dark horse and he seemed to withdraw from the rest of the family. He married unhappily, a woman who wouldn't give him a divorce, and he lived the rest of his life in Wales with a partner he was never able to marry. This, together with 'Godwin's free and easy ways' (to quote his father's journal), must have caused Helton, with his strict religious scruples, immeasurable grief.

In spite of the restraints imposed upon the family by Helton's illness, Godwin enjoyed a happy and free-ranging childhood. He had the freedom of the woods and fields; he roamed far and wide on his bicycle, and they had an old white pony called Pat whom Godwin loved to ride. This pony pulled their carriage when the family travelled into town. She was a favourite with Godwin and he loved to gallop her over the fields. The exhilaration he experienced, when as a small boy he raced across the meadows astride Pat's ample girth, Godwin was later to associate with the possession of powerful and streamlined motor cars. He also had a certain empathy for Pat, and the restraints she suffered when harnessed behind a carriage. There was a time when she ran away, dragging the empty carriage behind her. After a wild chase she was eventually caught when her harness became entangled with a post. Often in later life, Godwin's need to escape from the shackles of whatever bound him made him think back to the pony, as he, also, longed to be free.

There were joyous times when the winters were severe, and Godwin would go skating with his brothers on the great and smaller lakes at Whiteknight Park in Reading. Gliding across the ice with snow-covered banks and the white snow-laden trees beyond, the boys, with brightly coloured woollen hats and scarves would shout and chase one another, with laughter and cries of delight. Above, an ice cold, cloudless sky and thin winter sun gave Godwin the sensation of being sharply and keenly alive, as he skimmed over the smooth frozen surface, with a swing and rhythm and effortless motion.

The ease, grace and poise which gave rise to such keen excitement and delight contrasted with the sense of confinement he felt within the family home. His close attachment to his mother appears to have been a part of this: he spoke later in life of the 'captivity, the constant domestic scrutiny (and) the overwhelming feminine attachment that crushed me to revolt' a feeling that had probably begun in early childhood.

As a result of her husband's illness, Mary, whose passionate nature and physical needs were not satisfied by her husband, became too heavily attached to her sons. This affected Jack and Godwin in particular. They both had difficulty in freeing themselves emotionally and had, unconsciously, tried to satisfy some of their mother's emotional needs. Perhaps Godwin, being the more adventurous one, and also the favourite, carried this more than Jack, and in his unusually free style of living, was living out some of his mother's unfulfilled emotional life.

Godwin's adventurous spirit also led him to explore forbidden pursuits as a young boy. He often used to climb onto the roof of the house where they lived for a time in Reading, a house called Southern Hill. He would sit hidden there, watching the entrance into their garden, surprising people as they approached. The tall trees in their garden at Mortimer Common which he loved to climb, were a challenge to his daring and courage, and a challenge too to his father's fears: it was as though he needed to prove to himself that these fears were not inherited. It was this same instinct for irresponsible devilry which brought him into conflict with authority at school and, time and again, resulted in disgrace as he was caught and punished.

Godwin remembered especially a childhood friend from school days called Howard Smith. He attended the same junior school as Godwin in Reading and he lived with his family, in a large house, just across the road from Southern Hill. Howard had a pretty little 'vixenish' sister called Ethel. She used to come and play together with her brother, in the shrubbery in Godwin's garden. These two were first cousins to Godwin's schoolboy hero, Tona Wallis, and his brother, Basil. They were all 'good Quakers'. Godwin remembers how

> ... we had a splendid time together. We had a torture tree in a secret part of the shrubbery and there we tortured the spirits of our enemies. No one was actually tortured in person but we all believed we had tortured those large inimical people like Rufus Morris, against whom we waged war. Their initials were cut in the bark of the tree to signify this humiliation. Basil was our poet and he wrote:

> > Morris minor I declare
> > He has got bright scarlet hair
> > And his temper is so hot
> > As bright scarlet hair he's got.

> This was put in Morris' letter-box and we pictured gleefully his rage. Howard Smith was never actually at school with me, I think. He had left before I went, but when we met at old boys' meetings, Howard's recitals of the humorous escapades of this time made noteworthy anecdotes. The naughty things he told and the excellent stories of nagging masters were exquisitely funny and exaggerated.

> When we were 12 or 13, we found a large packet of black, coarse tobacco lying on the road to Pangbourne and we made a gigantic cigar with brown paper and so made our first uncomfortable attempts at smoking.

Another account of this 'devilry' features a failed escapade involving Godwin and four friends from Leighton Park, whose names were Richardson, Alan Hill, Shrimps and Holdsworth. All senior boys, they had plotted together to hold a grand nocturnal feast in the catacombs under the school house. Finally the night arrived, and all the food for the feast was safely stowed away in the bike sheds. The friends had arranged to sneak out of the dormitories at midnight and meet at the agreed rendez-vous. However, in the darkness, Godwin had the misfortune to bump against a large object in the changing room, which created a fearful clatter. Startled by the noise, he made a bolt for the lavatory and locked himself in the W.C.

One of the masters, Mr Little, came to investigate the racket and found Godwin in the W.C. Apparently, Godwin's explanation as to why he was down in the changing rooms in the middle of the night was not found to be satisfactory. Mr Little proceeded to make a round of the dormitories and found Richardson's bed empty as well as Godwin's, and he started a hue and cry. The whole escapade was discovered with dire consequences, the provisions were confiscated and the boys punished. After this, Mr Little became for Godwin the symbol for 'the avenging figure of authority'. This authority figure was one that he was to meet often in later life, and between Godwin and authority there was to be continual warfare.

Godwin was a gifted and highly intelligent child and was the only one in his family who was sent to public school. It was during his time at Leighton Park that he developed many of the interests that were important to him throughout his life. Among these were his interest in music, his gift for singing and his fascination for the natural world.

A Quaker naturalist, Tona Wallis, became one of Godwin's boyhood heroes. He lived in the same block as the Baynes family, during the time that they were living at Southern Hill, in Reading (where they moved for a time so that Helton could live closer to his place of work). Tona was considerably older than Godwin and took little interest in him, but he captured Godwin's imagination and Godwin 'longed to be brown and thin and agile like him'. Tona had an Italian mother, a gentle and beautiful woman, whom Godwin greatly admired. It was in an attempt to emulate Tona that Godwin persuaded his father to send him to the same school.

Tona later became a friend to Godwin, who remembered him as 'handsome, with a strong animal, and at one time, a brutal trait, in his character; but he was always on the side of the angels when he left school. He was a harmonious, gentle, charming, manly fellow; a good botanist and a loyal friend.' It was because of Tona's influence that Godwin later decided, after working for five years in the family business, to try for Cambridge to read Natural Sciences. Later, he decided to change to medicine; however he developed a specialist's knowledge in the world of botany and had a fascination for birds and butterflies which remained with him until his death. Tona's early influence on Godwin was to last throughout his life, but sadly Tona himself did not survive for long. He died soon after the end of the First World War from influenza, but he remained, for Godwin, a person whom he both 'revered and loved'; an early role model of manhood, who had the all-round attributes of manliness and courage together with beauty and gentleness. Perhaps Tona offered Godwin the possibility of emulating qualities that were very different from those of the men within his family.

Godwin found, after he left Leighton Park, that he was becoming suffocated within the narrow circle of the chapel and he set out to find a new and different world for himself. He felt restricted socially and intellectually. The artistic side of his temperament was stifled in this repressive atmosphere where dancing, theatre and music (unless with a religious flavour), were forbidden. Godwin's younger sister, Ruth, remembers him climbing through her bedroom window, late at night, after secretly paying illicit visits to the theatre and the opera.

Ruth and Godwin were close as they were growing up, although there was an eleven-year gap in their ages, and she later became deeply influenced by his pioneering outlook. She was an unfailing support and faithful friend to Godwin throughout the many ups and downs of his later life. She was the one who understood his need to find his own separate path in life and who supported him on his often difficult and lonely journey.

Chapter Two

Cambridge and Student Days

I only ask to be free. The butterflies are free.
Mankind will surely not deny to Harold Skimpole
what it concedes to the butterflies!

Dickens, *'Bleak House'*, Ch. 6

Godwin realizes that a career in the family business is not for
him. He manages to gain a place at Trinity College, Cambridge, at
first to study natural sciences, and later to study medicine. This
becomes possible through the financial help offered by the Bax
family. Godwin's friendship with the sons, Arnold and Clifford,
gives him an introduction to an artistic circle of musicians, poets
and writers. Through these friends he later meets the girl, Rosal-
ind Thornycroft, who is to become his wife. The influence of this
gifted group of avant-garde young people, so different in outlook
from his own family, is a profound one for Godwin.

Godwin fulfilled the expectation placed on all three sons to go into
the family business after leaving school. He worked in the timber
firm, as a clerk and later on the entrepreneurial side, for five years. It
wasn't an easy time for him. There was a certain awkwardness, while
he was still a junior clerk, in being the privileged son of the managing
director. He felt increasingly constrained in what seemed to him to be
an extension of the family circle that he was trying to break away
from. Finally, Helton also realized that it wasn't working and he
agreed that Godwin should apply for a place at Trinity College,
Cambridge, to read Natural Sciences. Godwin was successful in

obtaining a place, but at that time his father was unable to pay for him. It was Alfred Bax, a long-standing friend of Helton Baynes since their youth, who through the influence of his wife, Ellen, agreed to pay for Godwin's university education. The Baxes were keen philanthropists, and when Godwin later changed courses, to study medicine, they insisted on the proviso that he must spend one year, after qualifying, working with the poor.

After the small world of business and the rather severe home environment, Cambridge seemed to Godwin like paradise. He threw himself into every aspect of Cambridge life and became drunk with the freedom of the atmosphere he experienced there. The nonconformist restrictions of home were finally cast off and the artistic side of his temperament was able to blossom. He indulged with gusto in all the forbidden pursuits. It was as though the many-sidedness of his personality could, for the first time, be given free rein.

He was an impressive figure: he had the physique of an athlete and his strength was legendary. He was fine looking and with his massive size and somewhat classical features, he made a powerful impression on all who met him. He had thick dark hair and a neat, Kaiser-like moustache; a distinctive long straight nose, gentle brown and rather sad eyes and a mouth that often expressed puzzlement but more often an impish humour and infectious merriment. He had a generous nature and a warmth of personality which endeared him to everyone, both men and women. A description of him in David Garnett's autobiography, *The Golden Echo*, emphasises this somewhat heroic quality as it was experienced by his contemporaries: he was 'so broad-chested and strongly built that he did not seem a tall man but a well-proportioned hero of antiquity. He was indeed an athlete of some distinction – having rowed twice in the boat race. ... He had wrestled with Hackenschmidt, the Russian strong man, and had lasted for three and a half minutes against him.'

The atmosphere of Cambridge in 1904 was one of leisure and delight. The social life and fellowship with one's contemporaries was certainly as important as the exams. The sons of the moneyed classes went there to have a good time at their parents' expense, and it was there that one met the people who would remain friends throughout life. For Godwin, the medical exams did not pose a great problem, and in those days the volume of medical knowledge was considerably less than that of today. The medical books were consequently slimmer and the degree course for medicine lasted only two years.

For Godwin, the sense of freedom during his time at Cambridge was intoxicating; the chrysalis of his formative years was at last free to develop into the butterfly of his wider self which had been constrained until now in a family mould that was too narrow to contain him. His exuberant personality and unusual energy brought him into contact with students of very different worlds. As an athlete, he played football for Trinity and swam for the university, and he was also an excellent oarsman. He obtained 'blues' for both swimming and rowing; he took part in the Oxford and Cambridge boat race, rowing in successive Cambridge victories in both 1906 and 1907, and he was in the University boat that beat Harvard by two lengths in 1906. He was well known not only to the athletes of his day: through his love of music and his fine baritone voice he was a central figure in the musical and artistic scene of the time. In a most unusual way he managed to span these two widely different worlds, and was immensely popular in both.

It was at Cambridge that Godwin first developed an unorthodox view of medicine which was to determine his eventual choice of career. It was just before an important boat race in Cambridge that he became ill with gastroenteritis. The crew were unable to find a substitute. However, they had succeeded in finding a student who was a Christian Science healer and this man was persuaded to visit Godwin in his rooms in college to see if he could help. To Godwin's amazement, he was healed and was able to get up and row in the race. He was shaken by this experience and as a result he bought a copy of Mrs Eddy's[1] book of 1875, *Science and Health,* and also sent a copy home.

He recognised at this stage that conventional medicine didn't have all the answers; there were other, less explicable and less tangible aspects to healing. Godwin made many friends in the artistic world of Cambridge who remained close to him when he left to begin his medical training at St Bartholomew's Hospital. It was suggested to him by this circle of friends that he should develop his splendid voice and go to Dresden to study to become an opera singer. This idea was warmly supported by his friends Arnold and Clifford, the sons of Alfred Bax, in whose Hampstead home he was to spend an increasing amount of time when he wasn't studying. To Helton's grief and

[1] Mrs Mary Baker Eddy (1821-1910) who lived in the United States, was founder of the Christian Science movement.

despair, this is exactly what Godwin did, interrupting his medical studies. He remained a brief time in Dresden in the opera school, taking part in performances of Wagner and Mozart. He had the larger-than-life personality that was ideally suited to a career on the stage as well as unusual ability. But he found the singers he trained with too wrapped up in their own narcissistic worlds and he was sickened by it. He soon realized it wasn't the life he wanted and after six months he returned to Cambridge to continue his medical studies.

It is tempting to see in Godwin's passion for butterfly collecting a symbolic expression of his own sense of having been 'pinned down'. He recognized this connection himself, later on, when he first began his analysis with C.G. Jung. Perhaps it was through his singing, which he was for the first time able to develop and study, that he discovered his own true voice and could experience the liberation of the butterfly which is at last free to fly.

It is remarkable that there were enough hours in Godwin's days to achieve so much in so many diverse spheres; that he was able to succeed exceptionally well in his medical studies as well as rowing and swimming for Cambridge, which required long hours of training every day. He was at the same time spending many hours discussing poetry and ideas with the literary and artistic students as well as reading widely the literature of his day. But his singing was his great joy and besides his voice training he was taking an active part in the musical life of Cambridge. Arnold Bax, perhaps the most intimate friend of his student days, was later to write of Godwin that he was 'one of the most all round men of his time'.

Much of Godwin's energy at Cambridge was taken up with the discovery of women. He recognized his own need of women, but he also discovered how attractive he was to women of all ages. He was a frequent visitor at the house of his tutor, Professor Seagrave, whom he both liked and deeply respected. Godwin saw this professor of zoology as the 'gateway to knowledge', and the Professor's wife was in turn charmed by this heroic-looking young man and encouraged his visits to their home, treating Godwin with special kindness. They had a beautiful daughter called Daphne who, although still a child at the time, was fascinated by Godwin and flattered by his attention to her. He met her again later while she was having her coming-out season in London, and they became caught up in a whirlwind romance.

Godwin had many women friends during his time at Cambridge and was briefly engaged to a young woman called Isabel. He wrote of how important the friendship and admiration of women was to him, while reflecting on his student days later in life. He remembers being in the boathouse at Putney just before the boat race between the Cambridge and Harvard crews, in September 1906: 'The impressions of the day of the race are naturally very vivid and I remember we all stood (i.e. the crew) on the balcony and looked down upon the crowd, eagerly waiting for the faces of our friends and inamorata. At that time I was engaged to Isabel H. and was expecting her as well as other fair admirers, and I had to get places for them.' This memory evoked another of a Mrs M, for whom he had also reserved a seat, 'and when she arrived she was so warm in her manner that I almost neglected Isabel in my attentions to her and I bitterly reproached myself for this afterwards.'

These memories suggest that there were female admirers aplenty, and his difficulty then, as in later life, was in confining his attentions to only one.

Godwin was an ardent socialist during his student days and a letter survives dated 1905 addressed to a friend called Tiggie. Writing from his digs in 5 Manor Street, Cambridge. He begins;

> My dear old Tiggie,
> I haven't time for a letter, [he then proceeds to write a long one!] I should dearly love to get at you to try and put you right concerning the aims of Socialists. You dear old thing! You are grinding your teeth over a mythical and obsolete nightmare that no Socialist outside an asylum would attempt to defend.

He speaks of capitalism as:

> the cruellest system of industrial slavery that has ever ground mankind to despair. National and individual greed has made the primitive barbaric instinct for property into a colossal and merciless religion.

He continues in strong biblical language, slating the establishment:

> This god you bow before is the golden calf grown so monstrous that you actually believe it has a divine semblance. ... Your liberals and your Tories are Levites of the golden calf to a man.

He waxes lyrical as he warms to his argument in favour of Socialism:

The engine truth, that supplies the motive power of Socialism and which is making these obese Levites toss in their feather beds is this: *That the wealth of a Nation can only be truly estimated in the lives of her people.* That is the spring which pours passion into the Socialist, that is why I laugh you to scorn when you call Grayson a scene-making humbug.

The letter ends on a more cautious note:

I don't want a Socialist Regime. I am not looking for an Utopia. The movement has to plan an ideal edifice in order to organize the building of it, but I do not want blood to run. I only want to stop the disease and that can only be done by a government that, above all things, desires justice, and that sets the value of human life above all consideration of its monetary equivalent.

This letter suggests that he was also active during his student days on the political front, and that after the fat and prosperous years of Victorian England, the Socialist Ideal was, unsurprisingly, not a popular one amongst the moneyed classes.

After leaving Cambridge and obtaining his MB, Godwin went on to St Bartholomew's Hospital in London to study for his MRCS[2] and LRCP[3]. He lived in an attic room of the student quarters in Little Britain, close to the hospital. A new life began for him, and his time was divided between his medical studies and the Bax household in Hampstead, which became for him a second home. After qualifying in 1910, he became a house physician and then a house surgeon in his teaching hospital.

While Godwin was still a student at Barts, he met the girl who was to become his wife. This was Rosalind Thornycroft, daughter of the well-known sculptor, Sir Hamo Thornycroft whose sculptures included a fine figure of Oliver Cromwell which stands outside the Houses of Parliament, as well as one of Gladstone opposite the Law Courts and another of General Gordon which stands in the Embankment Gardens.

Rosalind was exceptionally lovely. Garnett described her beauty as 'cool and flower-like'. She had a fresh complexion, large and expressive brown eyes and thick brown hair which she wore long.

---

[2] Master of the Royal College of Surgeons.
[3] Licentiate of the Royal College of Physicians.

D.H. Lawrence, who later became a close friend of Rosalind, is thought to have used her physical appearance as his inspiration when describing Lady Chatterley. His description exactly corresponds to the Rosalind Godwin first admired: 'A ruddy, country-looking girl with soft brown hair and sturdy body, and slow movements, full of unusual energy. She had big, wondering eyes, and a soft mild voice.'

Rosalind took after her mother, Agatha Cox, whose beauty had so enchanted Thomas Hardy that he is said to have used her as his model for *Tess of the Durbervilles*.

Godwin and Rosalind met at a musical evening organised by Rosalind's uncle, George McCleary. McCleary was a Wagner enthusiast and he would invite young people to musical evenings at his home in Hampstead. Godwin not only found Rosalind lovely but he was struck also by her unusual personality. She was strong-minded and independent and at the same time possessed an endearing feminine grace and gentleness. She was intelligent, a gifted artist and she was freer in her ways than the women he had known. In her memoir Rosalind describes her first meeting with Godwin:

> By 1907, Uncle George had made me very familiar with the later Wagner and I spent much of my time playing the scores. He organised musical evenings before taking a group of enthusiastic young friends to a performance (at Covent Garden). At one of these, on 24th February 1907, I met Godwin Baynes. He had a splendid voice and took the part of Siegmund while I tried to do Sieglinde.

Rosalind and Godwin began to see each other frequently and in a fashion that was remarkably free and unconventional at the beginning of the century, when women's modesty was closely guarded. She would join him in his student quarters and sitting under the light of his oil lamp, she would draw while he studied. She did a fine pencil drawing of him, his long legs stretched out as he sits at his desk, absorbed in his work.

Godwin and Rosalind formed a small group with Arnold and Clifford Bax. Besides seeing Wagner operas they went nearly every week to sit in the gallery at Covent Garden to enjoy the Russian Ballet which had just come to London. Rosalind described the impact of the Russian Ballet in London in 1911, when 'Nijinsky and Karsavina with their astounding leaps and dramatic effects' took London by storm. The ballets they saw at this time included Prince Igor, Sherherazade,

Carnaval, Les Sylphides, L'Après-midi d'un Faune, Petrouchka, L'Oiseau de Feu and, of course, Spectre de la Rose, the ballet for which Nijinsky was most famous.

The four of them took a holiday together at Cloghane in County Kerry. This is a tiny seaside village under Brandon mountain. They stayed together at a 'humble inn', where they were tormented by fleas. When it rained they spent many happy hours making music together in the little parlour where Arnold managed to coax music out of a cracked piano, playing Wagner, Brahms symphonies and his own compositions. Rosalind writes of this time:

> We soaked ourselves in early Irish legends and climbed the mountains to faery lakes, talking about Cuchullin and Finn and the blackbird of Derrycarn Cumin, and plunging about in the quivering bogs. The local Irish were all one could desire with their Irish-English and charming friendliness.

Godwin and Rosalind were both frequent visitors at the Bax household at Ivy Bank, Haverstock Hill. A group of literary and artistic young people now began to have regular meetings. Many were members of a group who called themselves the Fabian Nursery (a young offshoot of the Fabian society, two of the leading members of which were Bernard Shaw and H.G. Wells). The group consisted of a several young men and women most of whom were still students. This group, who gathered around the two Bax brothers, included a number of people who were destined to become distinguished writers, poets, artists or musicians. They included, besides Arnold (composer) and Clifford Bax (writer), Rosalind Thornycroft (artist) and Godwin; Paul and Dolly Corder, Bertie Farjeon (writer) and his sister, Eleanor (poet), Myra Hess and Harriet Cohen (pianists). These Meetings took place on Sunday afternoons, often at the Bax home and at other times at the House of Paul and Dolly Corder's parents; their father Frederick was the translator of Wagner libretti and a teacher at the Royal Academy of Music. After tea they would repair to the snuggery in the Corders' basement and talk about everything under the sun, their discussions punctuated with laughter and with music.

Everyone in the group was a student of either literature, music or art.

Godwin, as a medical student, was the exception, although he could hold his own in the world of music. It has been said of him that

Gustav Holst once heard him sing and pronounced him the best amateur singer he had ever heard.

Rosalind remembered the Bax household as it was then. The parents were exceptionally wealthy and the two young men 'lived at home in irresponsible luxury and romantic dreams – Clifford somewhat theosophical, Arnold immersed in Celtic beauty'. Godwin, with his giant size and dynamic vitality was a great favourite with the whole family and acted as 'a great leaven to the rather pre-Raphaelite atmosphere of Ivy Bank'.

The relationship between Rosalind and Godwin was now firmly established.

> In March of this year 1907 there was a great snow storm and all the toboggans were got out from storage cupboards by us and our Hampstead friends. The best run on the East Heath was lighted with flares. Here came all the Hockey Club and the Garnetts (Edward Garnett and his family), with their superior flat Canadian toboggan. Godwin sent me a note to say that he would be at the gate of our house, One Oak, at nine o'clock, to fetch me. The snow was very thick all along the roads and we had a wonderful evening. By this time I was entirely in love with him and when he came home with me and lifted me up and carried me across a huge drift of snow my future was more or less decided.
>
> He had already tried to be a professional singer, but had given it up. ... He stood out among the others as the radiant, vital, blooming personality whom we all loved. ...
>
> My parents, however, were not so bowled over and at first were very alarmed. My father was particularly apprehensive for he realised that Godwin was not, like himself, the sort of practical man who enjoyed nature and objects in a realistic country way. In fact he found Godwin rather incomprehensible. However, in the summer when we gave our annual hay party at my parents' cottage near Chesham, Godwin proved himself to be a man after Father's heart by using the scythe in a romantic, vigorous and splendid style.

Perhaps Rosalind's parents were as baffled by Godwin and his strict religious background, in stark contrast to their agnosticism, as Godwin's parents were puzzled by Rosalind and her remarkably uninhibited manner and avant-garde ways. However, Godwin got on well with her parents and had a great respect and admiration for his father-in-law to be. The Thornycroft parents gave their daughter total freedom to do what she wished, even to go away camping with Godwin. The young couple did everything together, and when Godwin visited his family in Mortimer Common, he took Rosalind with him.

The following passage from Rosalind's memoir gives a vivid description of the Baynes family, as she remembered them:

> I was taken to be presented to them (The Baynes family) and afterwards stayed there for weekends. It was an austere household. The day started with prayers in the dining room, with Mr Baynes extemporising some rather maudlin prayers; and it ended in the evening with more prayers and Mr Baynes playing the harmonium. On Sundays they would go to chapel in a closed cab, drawn by a fat white horse. While crossing some open commons it was necessary for Mr Baynes to have the blinds drawn down so that he would not be upset by the wide view.

Whatever the constraints of the Baynes household, romance triumphed and Rosalind gives a picture of the times she and Godwin spent together:

> In spite of this depressing atmosphere, Godwin and I were excessively happy and a real loving pair. The woods stretched away in every direction and were very beautiful with lakes hidden in small valleys. We would get up at about six o'clock to the sound of pheasants calling, walk through the woods, bathe naked in the lakes; climb trees, Godwin reaching the topmost branches to sway in the wind. We would scramble through bushes of rhododendrons, or sail boats in the streams. In the evening we would walk again over heather commons to the purring sound of nightjars; and on one occasion we even found a nest. Or we would sing and read poetry. Godwin was an admirer of Walt Whitman, Thoreau, Robert Louis Stevenson, W.H. Hudson and Fletcher. He collected butterflies and he loved fishing and rowing. Camping, sleeping out under the stars, throwing the boomerang were more of his passions. And of course he sang splendidly. He was altogether an overwhelming person and I was completely absorbed in him. We built together a really lovely life, but it was – as I later realised – on my side too exalted and exaggerated, and bolstered into almost an

absurdity by will and romanticism. On his side, however, it was the exuberance of a natural spirit.

This exuberance also had its drawbacks. It was as though in his huge appetite for life, Godwin wanted to *do*, and to *have*, it all. To be universally talented, popular, and admired by all women, meant a scattering of his energies in a profligate way. He may have seemed god-like to those who knew him during his student days, but it was not the way he experienced himself. In this scattering of his energy, there was, perhaps, a fragmentation of himself and a growing uncertainty as to who this 'Self' really was. What he was acutely aware of was his need for popularity and outer affirmation: without this he was lost. He especially needed this affirmation from women – it was important for him to have numerous women in love with him, and to be aware of their admiration.

He knew with total certainty that he did not want to be, or become like, his father, ruled by his neurosis and fears. It was as though the heroic image he projected at this period of his life was a reaction to his own fear of becoming like his father. This was the deep-seated fear that he later had to confront.

Portrait of Arnold Bax for his 21st birthday,
painted by his tutor, F. Coleman, in 1905 (photograph by Hank Jansen)

Chapter Three

The Bax Circle

I have been so great a lover: filled my days
So proudly with the splendour of Love's praise
The pain, the calm, and the astonishment,
Desire illimitable, and still content …

Rupert Brooke, *The Great Lover*

Godwin completes his medical studies at Barts and after qualify-
ing he goes to Paris to study hypnotism. Rosalind accompanies
him there and attends the Julian Academy of Art. They continue
to be frequent visitors to the Bax household and to enjoy camp-
ing parties with the circle surrounding Rupert Brooke, known as
the neo-pagans.

It was in the year 1905 that Godwin's friendship with Arnold Bax first became an important part of both their lives. During that winter Arnold's brother, Clifford, set off on a seven month journey around the world. Bax's biographer, Lewis Foreman[4], writes:

[Clifford's] seven month absence left a considerable gap in Arnold's life. Into this stepped Godwin Baynes, who came from a poor family background, and who became one of Mrs Bax's protégés. She paid for Baynes's education and it was while he was an undergraduate that he dominated the young Bax's circle.

[4] Foreman, L., *Bax; A Composer and his Times.*

During the years following 1905, Godwin spent much of his leisure time at the Baxes' spacious and beautiful home. Their days were spent playing tennis and croquet as well as cricket, the game that was to bring the circle of friends together long after Ivy Bank was sold. During the intervals when they weren't involved in one of these games they would spend time together discussing the worlds of music, literature and poetry.

> The Baxes kept open house to all clever people. Grouped under the friendly spire of the old parish church could be found poet, painter, novelist, as well as musicians, and these included Ernest Rhys, Henry Holliday and May Sinclair at that time. The Baxes' young friends were drawn from local artistic and musical circles of varied background. It was never wealth that was the key to the clique, but rather the ability and inclination to participate[5].

At the centre of this group were the two Bax brothers, Godwin, and also Maitland Radford, who was to become a doctor as well as a writer.

Maitland was the son of Dollie Radford, a middle-aged poetess who kept open house to artists and musicians. Maitland and his mother hovered on the fringe of Bloomsbury circles and were both a major influence in helping D.H. Lawrence when he and his wife Frieda were in difficulties, especially during the Great War. Radford, together with Godwin, was the political conscience of the group, and turned the Baxes' circle into Fabians: they all became idealistic socialists, at least in theory. On the cricket field and as dinner companions, the two Baxes, Godwin and Radford called themselves 'the Four Just Men'[6] and they dined regularly together. Ivy Bank, in those 'spacious Edwardian days'[7] was indeed a paradise. The house in Hampstead was the size of a large country house and included in its grounds a cricket pitch, a tennis court and an apple orchard. Arnold Bax in his autobiography, *Farewell My Youth* writes:

> The long rambling house, standing back from the road behind a semicircular drive bordered darkly by laurel and ivy, was not old, and yet had all the air of being so. It certainly seemed to belong to

---

[5] Clifford Bax, *Inland Far*.
[6] A reference to a work by Edgar Wallace.
[7] Clifford Bax, *Inland Far*.

the country rather than to a London suburb, for the window of my small and distractingly untidy study looked out upon a density of trees and shrubs through which not a sign of a house could be seen, whilst the garden was big enough to permit the unconfined personality of each season of the year to make itself intimately felt.

Below the terrace steps at the back of the house was a large lawn screened from westerly winds by a noble row of chestnut-trees, ponderous with lamp-like blossoms in spring, and beyond these a second green whereon all the summers of our youth Clifford and I, our friends, with one or two gardeners and policemen, played cricket to the peril of the adjoining greenhouses. There was a third little visited lawn near the Belsize Lane fence, and we even boasted a small apple orchard – a lovely riot of pink and white in the early days of May.

Roses, hollyhocks, sunflowers, and sweet peas luxuriated in that heavy soil, and for me the whole place was an island pleasance peopled with all the phantoms of adolescent dream, and I recognise now that my long-vanished garden played a more important part in the world of my youth than I knew at the time.

Godwin became a central figure in this world of music, poetry and privilege and made, as always, a powerful impact on the talented men and women within it. In his autobiography, Clifford Bax describes Godwin in the somewhat eulogistic style of the time:

We found, indeed, that our circle had a new centre, that it was dominated by a man who was then at Cambridge, whose name was Godwin Baynes, and who by virtue of his gigantic physique, omnivorous mind, universal goodwill, and overwhelming vitality, became an object of hero-worship wherever he went. He, if any man, might have made me question my use of life. His appetite for joy was insatiable. Twenty-four hours gave not enough scope for his high spirits. He could 'make merry a golden gift'. He swam vast lakes, climbed perilous mountains, rowed in the Cambridge boat, trolled forth songs by the hour, heckled anti-socialists on the Heath, passed examinations painlessly, read half the new books that come out, lectured on Walt Whitman, and even listened with interest to my exposition of Oriental mysticism. ...

My friend's flamboyant personality drove the colour out of most men. As fishes flow by the hundred into a whale, so did men lose themselves in Baynes. People who had seemed to be distinct

became, at first shock, no more than his admiring adjuncts. Where
they could do one thing, Baynes could do twenty; and they revolved
about him like courtiers of old time who were happy for days if the
king had vouchsafed them a kindly word. It is through remembering him that I recapture a sense of the world that was about us in
the years from 1906 to 1910.

For Godwin those years before the Great War in the company of
these gifted young people, most of whom did not have to earn their
living, and the many happy hours and days spent at Ivy Bank, must
have seemed a kind of paradise.

To this group, others soon were introduced from families who
lived in the area. They included the Farjeon family, Harry, Eleanor,
Joe and Bertie, and also the Hess family, when Myra, later to become
a famous pianist, was still a young girl. The writer David Garnett
became another active member of the group. His father Edward was
a well known editor and one of the first people to discover D.H.
Lawrence, and his mother Constance was a translator of many of the
best-known Russian authors into English. There was also an Anglo-
Italian family called Antoniettis, who were all strikingly beautiful in a
dark southern style. Later, Stacey Aumonier (short-story writer and
artist) joined the circle.

Godwin was especially close to the Farjeon family and Bertie was
the friend he was most deeply attached to. They exchanged many
warm and confidential letters, full of expressions of affection and
love. This was not unusual between the literary men and women of
the era. Expression of emotion and affection was seen, like the
breaking down of sexual barriers, as a revolt against the strictures
that existed particularly strongly in Victorian England, which did not
allow men to express feeling, especially not to one another.

There was also a close friendship between Godwin and Bertie's
sister, Eleanor, who was already beginning to blossom as a poet. In
her biography of Eleanor, Annabel Farjeon (Eleanor's niece) writes of
her as she was at the age of 29, in 1910:

> And now Eleanor fell in love for the first time and wrote sonnets to
> the loved one. Who he was is not known, and those few who could
> have told are dead. Godwin Baynes is one of my many discarded
> candidates, who in any case was now a most important influence.
> In *Edward Thomas: The Last Four Years* Eleanor wrote of him as
> 'the sun-god of our brilliant circle. This giant rowing-blue from

Cambridge (six-foot-four in his socks), with a heart and brain to match his physical prowess, was the most popular man I have ever known. When he was talking to you he compelled you to feel that you were more interesting to him than any other person in the room, and I still think that at the given moment this was almost true.'

Many of the women in their group loved this 'sun god'. It wasn't only that he was somehow heroic in stature, but also that he was himself deeply fascinated by women. He wrote of preferring the friendship and companionship of women to that of men and this remained true throughout his life.

Annabel Farjeon writes of Godwin's effect on women:

Baynes, who loved and was much loved by women, went in for romantic paganism. One woman in love with him for years was a painter, Olive Hockin, with whom Eleanor now and then shared a lonely life in the Berkshire woods. Seeing how she lacked physical courage, Olive Hockin determined to get her friend over some of these fears.

She goes on to describe a visit Eleanor paid to the Baynes family home at Mortimer. Olive considered that Eleanor needed educating in country ways and she persuaded her to sleep with her out in the open in the Berkshire woods. In the early morning Olive stripped and swam into the lake calling to Eleanor to join her.

In the middle of the lake, quite far away, a flat stone rose from a hidden base, like a little altar. 'There's something on it!' called Olive: 'Someone has been there.' She swam out, and presently came back smiling. 'It's a crown of wild parsley. Godwin has been sacrificing to the deity. Swim out and see.'

Eleanor, however, was too timid to follow.

Worship of Pan was in harmony with Eleanor's sense of paganism at this time and accords with her sonnet, *Pan-Worship* which her niece ventures might, indeed, have been inspired by the 'sun-god'. The passion aroused in her at this time was the inspiration for thirteen sonnets, the best poems she had yet written.

> Be patient with me. This is still too new.
> Oh, if I fail to wear when you are near
> The early comradeship, to find the clue

To laughter, to change clouded eyes for clear,
Remember I am going in such a dream
As puts bewilderment upon my days,
And the old habits, an uncaptured stream,
Flow in some outer region seen through haze.
I will resolve this presently; will learn
Not to outwear you in this instant mood,
And loving you, with all my strength will turn
The loving of you only into good;
Will hear you laugh, and laugh with you as well,
And make the time that was, still possible.

In February 1911 the Bax family moved from the spaciousness of Ivy Bank, which had become unsafe owing to subsidence, to the less open and rural setting of 7 Cavendish Square. That same year Godwin became officially engaged to Rosalind, although they didn't marry until two years later. Clifford also married at this time and the pattern of life, of artistic searchings and luxury, which had gathered around the Bax brothers, gradually began to break up. However, a group of young artists and poets continued to meet together with the Bax brothers in their home in Cavendish Square, until the outbreak of war in 1914 'wiped away all youthful dreams'.[8]

Godwin had introduced a young poet to the group, who had come to see him soon after he set up in practice because of severe bouts of depression. This was the poet, Edward Thomas. He wrote that through Godwin he had, 'got to know Clifford and Arnold. ... and a new world of leisured people.' Bax was one of the brighter stars in a 'circle of young people who met regularly on the tennis-court and in the garden-studio of Frederick Corder' s house in Albion Road.' He continues to say that this brilliant group of young men and women were constantly together: meeting several times a week, they 'played games, invented entertainments, discussed life, and thronged the theatre galleries to drink in Wagner, dote on the Russian dancers, and adore the Irish players.'

Clifford Bax's interests extended to producing plays, together with his theosophical circle of friends, in a company who called themselves the 'People's Free Theatre'. They produced classical plays in East End Halls. This was in tune with Mrs Bax's philanthropic and

---

[8] Arnold Bax, *Farewell My Youth*.

Quakerly attitude of helping others less fortunate than themselves
and it was later due to her influence that Godwin was persuaded to
open his first practice after qualifying in Bethnal Green. Two of the
leading lights of this theatre company were Godwin and Gwendolen
Bishop, who was later to become Clifford's wife.

Clifford refers to the summer of 1911 as 'a procession of golden
days'. He had bought an 'old grey Manor House' in a rural part of
Wiltshire in a small village called Broughton Gifford. There for the
next three summers leading up to the war, a circle of literary and
artistic friends would meet for a series of 'cricket weeks'. Their team
would take on all the local villages and when not playing cricket the
gathering became a week-long intellectual house party. Clifford
describes the first of these meetings in *Inland Far*.

> They all took a train from London on the eve of the first match,
> and arrived at the Manor House when the maid was distributing
> lighted lamps about the rooms. Throughout the day I had done my
> best to prepare for their pleasure; hiring a small fleet of bicycles
> (but none that was strong enough for Baynes), rolling the tennis-
> lawn for hard use on Sunday, and superintending the emplace-
> ment of a cider-barrel in the ingle-nook. Four of the team could
> sleep in the normal bedrooms. In order to house the others we had
> turned the long loft under the gables into a dormitory.
>
> For once at least in our lives, anticipation, experience, and
> retrospect were to be equally delightful. I doubt if upon that
> August evening when we sat down to supper at a long table of
> cherry-wood, under the serried beams of the hall, there was any
> group of men in any part of the world that was happier than ours.
> We were young enough to feel an aggressive cricketing spirit; old
> enough to endure defeat and personal failure, if these were our lot,
> without the dejection of boyhood. We shared, that evening, a mood
> that must have resembled closely the mood in which a pair of
> young Vikings assembled on the coast of Norway with the excite-
> ment of a sea-raid before them. After supper, when we had
> adjourned to the music-room, the company indulged in a riot of
> insolent wagers. Farjeon would bet that Baynes, for all his huge
> build, would not hit a six. Aumonier, madly vainglorious, would
> stake five shillings on his ability to take more wickets than my
> brother. And presently we were prophesying, each in turn, the
> number of runs that the various players would make on the

morrow, the entire team asserting that Aumonier would be out first ball. As balsam for this injury, someone – I think it was my brother – produced a limerick that ran:

'With regard to our free-hitting Stacy,
It is safe to assert that we may see
A wire arrive
Saying 'Lords, Half-past five.
You are wanted for Test, F.E. Lacey.'

And in a few minutes Baynes, who, like Bully Bottom, could never be left out of anything, had celebrated Farjeon's prowess in the lines:

There was a young fellow named Bertie
Who never made fewer than thirty –
It's perfectly clear
We could rhyme without fear
If his father had called him Doherty.

Soon afterwards without suppressing the desultory talk of good friends who had not associated for months, my brother went to the piano and Baynes began singing, – singing ditties from Cecil Sharp's collection, Elizabethan lays, and eighteenth-century drinking-songs. Meanwhile, the cider went round, the pipes were knocked out and recharged, and we all became sleepy enough to wish for bed but too well-content to lead the way.

Clifford continues to describe a haphazard breakfast the following morning as the cricketers straggled down while the parlour maid was busy with the coffee. Outside, through the open window, he describes a garden in high summer:

The green shapes of the garden and the colour of innumerable flowers, now fresh from their nocturnal cooling and at their gayest in the new sunlight. Bees, too, were gloating over the roses on the other side of the wall. A spray or two, in the abundance of August, had flourished across the windows. I suppose it was not until ten o'clock that the whole team had breakfasted. ... At ten-thirty. ... the village wagonette had appeared outside the gates. Cricket bags were hoisted into it: and after some delay, with half the team on bicycles and the other half in the brake, we were off down the fragrant high-hedged lanes. As Hartly and I, free-wheeling down a hill, span past the wagonette we could hear Baynes trolling out in his warm baritone:

> A lawyer he went out one day
> A-for to take his pleasure,
> And who should he spy but a fair pretty maid
> So handsome and so clever.

Then the homeward journey, past the meadows and old elms in the evening light. And finally, after the rush for the bathroom, all the players assembling in the hall:

> As if by so doing we might hasten the coming of supper: for we were fatigued and hungry, and sometimes there was a choric ejaculation of delight when the parlour-maid set a line of candles down the long table and when the cook followed with the first of her dishes ... [Afterwards] the night being clear and the air still temperate, we would find our way, by twos and threes, to the little square lawns in front of the house, and slant our deck-chairs at the most luxurious angle, and there – with the sharp stars creeping above us and the lilies that bordered the lawns glimmering like ghostly sentinels – we would smoke our pipes and launch forward into the interminable discussions that arise so plentifully in youth.

Another member of the cricket team, David Garnett, gives us a portrait of Godwin in his autobiography. He first met Godwin while he was visiting the house of Dolly Radford, mother of Maitland, who also lived in Hampstead:

> One afternoon when I arrived with my mother at the Radfords a little late for tea, we found in the drawing room a very large man sitting on a small hassock in the attitude of Rodin's Le Penseur, captivating the company by his parlour tricks. Constance was greatly charmed by him, and I asked him to come down for a weekend to the Cearne and he at once accepted. ...
>
> Godwin had a big-featured, fresh-complexioned face with dark hair already touched with grey, a rather clumsily made mouth with a dark moustache, the points of which he was at that time inclined to twirl up like those of the Kaiser. His eyes were hazel and, like those of a large and kindly dog, often held a puzzled expression. ...
>
> His charm, like that of the mastiff and the St Bernard, was to a considerable extent the result of his size, his splendid health and

magnificent physique. He was open-hearted, warm, affectionate and generous. Having escaped from a strict non-conformist upbringing at home, with prayers muttered into the seats of the chairs before breakfast, he had become an enthusiastic neo-pagan and I myself was just ripe for the neo-pagan revelation. Who and what were the neo-pagans? Perhaps the best idea can be got from the following lines from Rupert Brooke's The Great Lover:

> These have I loved:
> White plates and cups, clean-gleaming,
> Ringed with blue lines and feathery faery dust,
> Wet roofs beneath the lamplight; the strong crust
> Of friendly bread. ... etc
> And oaks; and brown horse-chestnuts, glossy-new;
> And new peeled sticks; and shining pools on grass;-
> All these have been my loves ...
> Nor all my passion, all my prayers have power
> To hold them with me through the gate of Death.

Those lines give a truer picture of Godwin than of Rupert Brooke himself. But now and then, when the joy of life and the love of white plates and gleaming conkers flagged for a moment, Godwin looked puzzled, and when he discussed things seriously he left me puzzled too. He, who was so good at learning everything and was so universally successful, got into a complete and hopeless muddle when he tried to think. ...

Our friendship with him blossomed rapidly, and he became a very frequent visitor at the Cearne, and often we slept out in the wood with Harold (Hobson).

Later on, a tension arose between 'Bunny' Garnett, as he was known to his friends, and Godwin. Garnett was a pacifist and decided not to volunteer for service in the First World War, which caused a disagreement between them. Later, Garnett's proposal of marriage to Godwin's beloved sister, Ruth, which Godwin had felt was not serious and was therefore making her unhappy, created a rift between them. But while the friendship lasted, both men subscribed to the neo-pagan philosophy, which was about giving oneself to life and disregarding the conventions of the time.

The Garnetts' country home, The Cearne, was at Limpsfield near Oxted in Surrey, set in a beauty spot and surrounded by trees. It was built for the Garnetts by Cowlishaw, who was a disciple of William Morris. Here the Fabian socialists would meet and discuss their beliefs and principles. They were free thinkers and believed in fresh air, open relationships and co-education. Godwin was soon enchanted by a new group of friends who gathered there, among whom was H.G. Wells, whose ideas were to have an influence on both him and Rosalind.

Life was for living and youth to be enjoyed with an exalted intensity and joie de vivre. Nature, friendship, romance and life with a capital L, were the ideals embraced by this youthful group who had come to be known as the neo-pagans. Neo-pagan was a term applied somewhat derisively to the group when Virginia Woolf first encountered them in Cambridge. The movement was influenced by the liberal customs at Bedales School, a progressive co-educational school which encouraged all outdoor activities; camping, walking, climbing and bathing in the nude. Rupert Brooke and Jacques Raverat had been pupils there and the neo-pagans adopted their liberal ways as a reaction against parents and the rigidity of the Victorian era.

If one remembers that for the majority of 'well-brought-up' women at the beginning of the 20th century, it was impossible for an unmarried woman to accompany a man without being in the presence of a chaperone, the neo-pagans did enjoy an astonishing degree of freedom. Godwin and Rosalind's daughter Chloë describes the neo-pagan movement in the following passage[9]:

> The open road, youth, and every minute of life to be lived to the full – these were the things extolled by the neo-pagans. But there was also a more serious side exemplified in the Fabian summer schools, which many of them attended and through which they became imbued with socialist ideals. Godwin and Maitland Radford were both members of this group which besides Rupert Brooke, included the four Olivier sisters, Maitland's sister, Evelyn, Ka Cox, Dudley Ward, the Raverats, [Gwen and Jacques], the Cornfords, [Francis and Frances], Justin Brooke, the Pye sisters and Bill and Eva Hubback. Godwin was to be included in Rupert Brooke's fanciful scheme for a select few of his friends who were

[9] From Chloë Baynes' book which includes her mother's memoir, *Time Which Spaces Us Apart*.

ever young in spirit. The idea was that in twenty years time they should 'fling away the dingy wrappings of stale existence and plunge into the unknown to taste life anew'.

He wrote to Jacques Raverat:

'On the first of May 1933, at breakfast time, we will meet on Basle station. Did you ever hear of so splendid a place of meeting? We may have parted, lost sight of one another for years. But on that spring morning, in that mad place, whiskered and absurd and unrecognisable, we'll turn up. And then? Then Life! What else matters? Details else when.'

A wild romantic dream and in any case the coming war would see to it that only a few could keep such an odd appointment.

In the early days of the neo-pagan group, Godwin fell in love with one of the Olivier Sisters. The Olivier girls were known as The Four Beauties of their day, but Brynhild was not only exceptionally beautiful; she was also proud, inaccessible, and chaste. She enjoyed the adoration of the men of their circle but apparently did not allow anyone to come very close. Godwin and Rupert Brooke were, perhaps, her most serious suitors at that period. A collection of passionate love letters from Godwin has survived. He writes of his life at the hospital and of needing to 'keep my nose to the books', and therefore being unable to join the group of friends at their next camping expedition; but he will imagine her 'crashing about with ... hair down, submarine, pastoral and sylvan, according to mood.' Soon after this he sent Bryn a passionate hymn to the sea: 'From the sea and me to glorious Bryn ... I haven't felt the electric touch of the sea on my body since last September in Ireland and just now I have been mad with joy of it and that is why I am writing to you about it.' And then again, 'I shall not see you at camp. ... I can't leave my work except at weekends. I take it with me to the hospital and read at the ABC and forget to order my porridge for lunch.' At this stage he is studying hard for his finals. In another letter he is writing with equal admiration to three of the sisters at once, to 'Miss Brynhild, Miss Daphne, and Miss Noel'. The eldest sister, Margery, was away at the time, probably staying with her father Lord Olivier, who was then the Governor of Jamaica.

Later he relives the previous camp with all four sisters and others: 'I passed the most beautiful night of my life under those firs on a great mound of sun-dried bracken, with Bunny (that astute financier) by my side. The sunrise over those vast vistas was unspeakable. I think romance reaches its fairest heights in these nights of wide, starry solitude … I am glad you are not going back to Jamaica just yet.'

Soon after this he moved from Ivy Bank, which for a time during his medical studies had become his home, to a 14/– a week bed-sitting attic at 35, Doughty Street. His work was preventing him from joining in all the exploits of their group. 'I was on duty all Saturday night and most of Sunday in the surgery. From 6 o'clock till half past two an unbroken stream of fractures, bruises, cut heads and fists surged through my room. They were mostly in their cups and I spent an amazing evening with them. I had not realized till then what a harvest of fractures a wet Saturday night in London brings to our doors.' He goes on to say that 'there is talk of a weekend at Burghfield and Mortimer, the respective abodes of Olive Hockin and Godwin Baynes. That idea must be encouraged and you are all coming.'

A day or two later he writes again, a paean of praise to youth and how to avoid growing old: 'Age comes as the result of surrender. It is a disgrace. Peace without honour. It is necessary to dig up one's life and re-pot it every spring and then Pish Tush to age … It is easier to live on old emotions than grow, create and develop newer, bigger, nobler emotions … Senile decay then is not the result of longevity as is commonly supposed, but the result of emotional immobility.' He finishes in a hurry because 'I am just off to sing at a socialist club of working men at Hammersmith, just behind Kelmscott House. It is a delight to be allowed to sing to workingmen. They are so generous and open-hearted and they have never learnt the meaning of the word boredom.'

These letters follow each other in quick succession. The weekend at Mortimer is taking shape. Godwin plans that Daphne and Noel Olivier will stay with Olive, while Bryn, Margery and Bunny will stay at the Bayneses': 'My mother and eldest sister are away but my father and little sister and a kind of adopted sister [Ruth's friend Enid Overend], and an uncle, will be at home and will be ever so charmed if you will come … I am writing to Olive about it to-night. It is a dear place and I do want my woods to see you and we could have one long picnic all the time.'

Godwin had moved back to Ivy Bank to be with the Bax family for Christmas and writes to Bryn from there while 'the dear boy [Arnold], is pouring the *Meistersinger* into the air with his magic fingers.

In July 1909 there was a camping party near to Bunny Garnett's country home The Cearne and the Olivier's house in Limpsfield, Surrey. They found an ideal camping place close to the River Eden at Penshurst. Bunny set up the camp and was joined by Godwin and later by the Olivier sisters with Dorothy Osmaston; Harold Hobson (an engineering friend of Bunny's) arrived with Walter Layton, and finally, Rupert arrived with Dudley Ward.

It is possible that Godwin proposed to Bryn soon after this weekend and was turned down. Paul Delaney[10] wonders if Rupert's poem 'Jealousy' perhaps contains a reference to Godwin and Bryn.

> A girl whom the poet once admired for her coolness and wisdom is now 'gazing with silly sickness' on a fool, whose 'empty grace ... strong legs and arms ... rosy face' suggest Godwin Baynes. Godwin did propose to Bryn a couple of months after the camp, and, if they are models for the two lovers, the poet cast a sickly eye on their affection. He imagines them married: the husband's strength running to fat, their love sinking into habit until the last act.

Was there perhaps jealousy between Rupert and Godwin over the beautiful Bryn, who Delaney infers had turned down the proposals of both these admirers? Perhaps there was rivalry between the two 'deities': Rupert Brooke, 'The young Apollo golden-haired' of Frances Cornford's poem[11], and Godwin, Eleanor Farjeon's 'sun god'. These two men, beloved of all women, were certainly not used to being turned down!

Godwin speaks of his 'love of life' and perhaps this sums up the attitude of the group as a whole at this period. It was later that its members grew apart: there were jealousies, heartbreaks, and break-downs, but in the early days, life was still golden. Godwin writes again to Bryn: 'I have just come back from a sublime holiday in my woods at home with Jacques and Olive. I wonder how many times I have curled up in my bed at night with the profound certainty that I have never had such a day in my life ... A sturdy march in the eye of the wind along the banks of a grey and silver river where I have spent many eager days as a boy, amphibious, ravished by the river and the

---

[10] Delaney, P., *The Neo-Pagans*.
[11] Frances Cornford's poem about Rupert Brooke, 'Youth' (see Chapter 5, p. 80).

sunshine in turn ... the comradeship of three human beings in passionate love with life.'

During the winter of 1909, Godwin joined the group at Bethesda, near Snowdon, to walk and rock-climb and also to take part in some Morris dancing. This time, Rosalind was also a member of the party. The friendship between them had now developed into love and it was possibly while they were climbing together during this holiday in Wales that Godwin proposed to Rosalind and was accepted.

But before this there was an uneasy time of uncertainty and indecision, when he was in love with both Rosalind and Bryn. He writes to Bryn with extraordinary naivety: 'I am not disturbed when I think of Rosalind and then of you, I see you both so clearly and know I can be faithful to both. One cannot put a padlock to one's heart and give it to one woman. Love comes to one like light from the stars. No single star can blind one to the glory and wonder of the firmament.' This statement could well have become Godwin's epitaph! Such largesse of loving was to cause him endless complications and heartbreak in the future.

However, Bryn receded into the background once Godwin had made his commitment to Rosalind. Soon afterwards, Bryn became engaged to Hugh Popham, at that time still a student at Cambridge, and later to spend his working life in the Prints and Drawings Department of the British Museum where he eventually became Keeper.

A description from Rosalind's Memoir about this period in their lives gives a vivid sense of the freedom and exuberance experienced by this group of young people:

> Our group was taken up with the idea of the freedom of natural life, and we spent weekends walking over the Sussex downs. Godwin introduced – I think with David (Bunny) Garnett – the idea of carrying sleeping bags and sleeping the night on the ground 'under the starry sky' like Robert Louis Stevenson. The first time I did this I went with Godwin up to the top of Ashdown Forest and we sat ourselves down on the hard ground under the whispering fir trees. The idea developed further and more ambitiously with lightweight tents and a primus cooking stove.
>
> One holiday he and I and Paul Corder, a fanatical lightweight camper, went for a walking holiday on the East Riding Yorkshire moors. Paul was very strict and wanted us to walk at least twelve

miles a day and carry an absolute minimum of luggage in our rucksacks, but Godwin, notwithstanding Paul's disapproval, brought with him a fishing rod and gear to catch trout in the moorland streams and a catapult for grouse and rabbit. The general idea was to be self-supporting. Mushrooms grew abundantly that year and so did puffballs, which were recommended by Paul and proved not to be poisonous as we had supposed. And so we lived, with the help of a few potatoes and a bag of oatmeal, almost without recourse to civilisation. Godwin was unsuccessful in hitting a grouse with a catapult, but succeeded in killing a rabbit. It must have been a very old rabbit, because after cooking it for ages and almost using up our whole supply of paraffin, it was uneatably tough.

There was one gloriously exciting night when we camped on the hill overlooking Rievaulx Abbey. A great storm arose with alarming lightning and Paul got out his handbook on camping. Its advice was to stick potatoes on the metal spikes of the tent poles to prevent them from acting as dangerous lightning conductors.

Such descriptions give one a picture of a life and also a general atmosphere that seem to belong to an era of innocence and delight. But perhaps the carefree days of youthful exploits were, in retrospect, somewhat idealised as a result of the devastating war years that were soon to follow.

In the spring of 1912, on April 15th, 'the whole world was staggered and distressed at the news that the "Titanic" (White Star Line) had been rammed by an iceberg in the N. Atlantic and gone down in an hour or two ... The experts said she was unsinkable being so well provided with watertight compartments ...'[12] It was as though the total security and sense of an unbroken peace and prosperity, which prevailed in Britain at that time, had been shaken by this cataclysmic event.

Just a month before the disaster, on March 13th 1912, another piece of news filled the newspapers of the day. This was the beginning of the militant era of the suffragette movement led by Emmeline Pankhurst.

Helton records that 'the hysterical militant suffragettes chose this time of national trouble to organise a window smashing raid in the

---

[12] H.A. Baynes' Journal.

West End of London, doing damage to the tune of £4,000 odd. 152 were arrested, including Mrs Pankhurst who is sent to prison for two months …' The militancy of these early feminists managed to earn the movement a bad name.

While doing his house jobs at Barts, Godwin became interested in psychology and the more unconventional aspects of medicine. In the early summer of 1912 he went to Paris to study hypnotism at La Salpetrière, a hospital for mentally unstable women, and Rosalind accompanied him. Rosalind writes of this time in her Memoir:

> My parents, most surprisingly, allowed me to go with him and while there I went to the famous Julian's school of art, which was the only one that Father knew of. I think their 'free' attitude was based on an absolute belief in the pure and innocent behaviour of anyone brought up in the way I had been by them. I agreed with this view, but, convinced that we were a special case by virtue of our perfect love on the lines of German romanticism – (Wagner's *Ewig Einig ohne Ende*) – we felt we were justified in becoming complete lovers. I did not, however, confess this 'marriage' to Mother, although it was a way of life together that was lived by many of our contemporaries of advanced people among Fabians and students.

While they were living together in France the two lovers made an expedition to Rouen which was described by Godwin in a glowing letter to his friend, Bertie Farjeon. He wrote:

> Oh Bertie, you and you only are to know that we have just finished a real pelerinage that ended triumphantly beneath the Arc de Triomphe, from Rouen to Paris. We were invited for a weekend to a wonderful old country house at Pont-de-l'Arche near Rouen. It was a lovely place, and coffee (gracious heavens, such coffee) and rolls were brought to you in your lovely eighteenth-century (early) bedroom and then you sauntered about the orchards and played tennis with two brilliant Balliol men and one adorable Etonian. And now behold us starting off from this sumptuous atmosphere with rucksacks and camping kit to Rouen.
>
> Rouen is a darling place. You must come there with me quite soon. The route to Paris lay over vast table-lands, through ancient forests, over high and crumbling walls, through holes in fences, by edges of the splendid vigorous Seine, along crests of chalk downs

with verdant, spacious valleys far below expanding to an edge of light; through the gilded salons of Versailles and finally emerging from the Bois de Boulogne up the avenue to the Etoile of Paris.

160.5 km in six tremendous days. Oh my dear man! Such delightful evenings we had too in our little tent, pitched on the crest or in a hollow of steep declivities or in moonlit forests or wherever we found ourselves at dusk. Then the meals we devoured! One meal at Mantes stands by itself, an Epic! I will not attempt to tabulate its unparalleled bounties.

To this paean Rosalind added a postscript; 'O Lord, we have a wonderful time here.'

Rosalind returned home while Godwin completed his studies at La Salpetrière, and she continued to enjoy the companionship of their group of friends. David Garnett, who through his closeness to Godwin had grown fond of Rosalind, writes about their friendship in his autobiography:

Not long after our first meeting he [Godwin] told me he had fallen in love with Rosalind Thornycroft, a cousin of the Oliviers. Their marriage was delayed for some time, until Godwin had qualified and settled down in practice. But I soon met Rosalind and became great friends with her. Her beauty was cool and flower-like and it seems to me that it has changed little in the last forty years ...

In the early summer of 1912, Godwin Baynes went to Paris to study hypnotism at La Salpetrière. Rosalind and I saw something of each other in his absence and when Ursula came back from Moscow for a visit to England, I persuaded both of them to come for a boating holiday with me on the Severn. With us came a Creole boy of my own age, a Jamaican of pure British ancestry, called Theodore Williams.

There follows a description of their double scull and the days of rowing upstream, camping in lovely meadows, and the laughter and harmony between the four of them, ending finally with a description of Rosalind, suggesting that she like Godwin evoked love and admiration in all who knew her:

Rosalind's laughter was thin and a little fastidious in comparison (to Ursula's) and sounded like a spoon ringing against a china cup. She was a lovely creature – a russeted apple in face, cool, delicate and critical in spirit. I was linked with her by my love of Godwin and felt a fraternal pride in her beauty. I remember, however, once, while we lay sunning ourselves upon a willow trunk hanging over the river after our bathe, wondering whether she was not almost too perfect a creature for Godwin, whom I saw momentarily, in a flash of realism, as an old bumble-puppy.

If this was indeed a 'flash of realism', it stands virtually alone amongst these descriptions of the Elysian days of youth of this group of artists, writers and poets – when there was time to reflect on life and play all day long and the need to earn a living was still only partly necessary for the talented young people who gathered around the Bax household. These carefree days were in stark contrast to the years of turmoil and horror that were to follow throughout the Western World. This upheaval and despair was to be reflected in Godwin's personal life as the passionate love between him and Rosalind, that was in 1912 at its zenith, failed to be sustained within the ordinariness of everyday life and the absences that were to follow.

Chapter Four

The Balkan War

Peace shall go sleep with Turks and infidels.
Shakespeare, *King Richard 11, iv.i. 139*

*Godwin volunteers for service in the Balkan War (1912 – 1913).
He reorganizes the military hospitals in Constantinople and
establishes a small hospital at San Stefano for refugees from the
Balkan countries. He is decorated by Enver Pasha and returns
home to a hero's welcome.*

Godwin's time in France came to an abrupt end in November 1912,
when he volunteered for service in the Balkan war. Helton Baynes
records in his journal on October 20th 1912: 'Alas! War has broken
out in the Balkans to free Macedonia from the cruelties of Turkish
misgovernment; and Montenegro first, then Serbia, Bulgaria and
Greece began the fight against Turkey ...'

Godwin was appointed as surgeon in charge of the Red Crescent
mission to Turkey. While he was there he reorganised the military
base hospitals in what was then Constantinople and he dealt with a
cholera outbreak.

When the fighting broke out once more he established and main-
tained a small hospital at San Stefano for the care of the Armenian,
Syrian and Russian refugees. For this he was decorated by Enver
Pasha who was a powerful figure during the Balkan War and later,
during the First World War, was to become the virtual ruler of
Turkey.

Red Crescent Mission Hospital in San Stefano
run by Godwin Baynes during the Balkan War (1912)

In his 'commonplace book' Helton Baynes made infrequent comments about his youngest son; often with incomprehension and with apprehension but also sometimes with admiration. He wrote with fatherly pride about Godwin's mission to Turkey.

30 November 1912

Now I can record that Godwin left Victoria on the 13th with two other doctors, Barton and Miller, and after two hours in Paris they went on to Marseilles, taking the SS Niger there for Constantinople. It was a slow boat, calling at Naples, Athens and Scutari, but Godwin enjoyed that, and we have had cards … Some 600 Greeks going to join their brethren, and seeing the doctors' Red Crescent emblem, tried first to throw them overboard and then to knife them, and had to be pacified; and now Godwin writes that he has bathed in the Aegean Sea! Wednesday's 'Standard' told us of the doctors' arrival, presumably on the 26th and on Thursday the 'Daily News' said they had volunteered for 'dangerous cholera service', and had gone to the San Stefano camp. Godwin is doing Christian work and God will take care of him! I trust it may help him to find his way back to a simple and strong Christian faith, such as he had when I (as we had then no pastor at Trinity) had the joy of receiving him as a church member. He has noble ideals, but religiously I don't know where he stands, and I doubt if he knows himself. Like Goethe, he probably longs for 'more light'.

On the following day the family received a letter from Godwin in the Dardanelles. There was an exciting story about a Greek destroyer that had shot across the bows of their boat, the Niger, which was carrying the Red Crescent Mission to its destination. The passengers, including Godwin, were taken prisoners of war and the Greek captain demanded Godwin's passport and then confiscated some of the boat's cargo of coal and oil as contraband. Luckily, they escaped unscathed and that night, Godwin and one of the other doctors, Barton, were bathing in the Aegean by moonlight and from a rocky outcrop on the island of Lemnos they made a spectacular dive from a height of thirty foot, which caused a sensation among the crew. A sudden gale delayed their arrival but they were eventually given a warm reception by the Turkish Governor when they arrived at their destination at Suyrud. In contrast to their rough treatment by the Greeks, the Turks were welcoming and gentle and showered the doctors with hospitality.

The Bayneses received another dispatch from Godwin on December 6th, relating the conditions that prevailed when they eventually arrived at their destination in San Stefano. They found a desperate situation with thousands of wounded Turks lying out in the melting snow and mud. Godwin and his two companions set to work immediately and with the help of the British and American ambassadresses, Mrs Lowther and Mrs Rockhill, they set up and equipped a seventy-bed hospital, and this they managed to achieve in only three days. Helton is full of admiration for the work Godwin is doing, and he notes in his journal that Godwin and his 'assistants are doing grand, heroic work, and volunteers are rallying to him. Godwin is showing the very best in himself.'

This was a period of intense action for Godwin. It was his first major medical experience since qualifying from Barts. Was there a part of him that needed the action and practical medical experience after the somewhat unreal and emotionally charged atmosphere of the group of friends, whom Godwin refers to in his letter to Bertie Farjeon from Constantinople as, 'You dear folk who pace the slopes of Parnassus.' During Godwin's absence, Rosalind, abandoned back at home, received an affectionate letter from Arnold Bax, commiserating with her grass-widowhood.

Oh how happy I would be if I could have you all to myself this week, little girl, for this west even, streaming with storm as it is today, would cover you over with its own world-old enchantment and ease the anxiety of your heart. AE thinks it is simply splendid about our boy[13]. I would like you to have heard how he spoke about it, and Balfour too says he has the greatest admiration and respect for what Tiny is doing[14]. Indeed I know that every friend of his feels the same way and we shall all honour him as well as love him all his life for this noble deed.

Godwin soon writes to his dear friend Bertie, giving a picture of his work and his new responsibilities at the mission hospital:

> I am a changed man for the present. I hardly can see myself through it all. We keep no Sabbaths here and we are the slaves of our own routine. All day I am directing, giving orders, giving people the sack or engaging them, trying to soothe ruffled tempers and foreseeing storms on the horizon, thinking ahead – tasting in short all the triumphs and ignominies of a responsible position …
>
> I am writing to Eleanor [Farjeon] very soon. I know I shall love the poems or she would not have sent them to me, for she knows how I love and I trust her choosing for things to delight in …
>
> You must know I am starting a wonderful new hospital in nine splendid pavilions specially constructed in Germany for a hospital. We are putting them up now and tomorrow I go to Stamboul to buy all the beds and bedding and the countless necessary stores and provisions. It is going to be the finest hospital in the field and we shall have 160 patients in by the end of the week.
>
> Bless you for your loving care of my Rosalind, my beautiful lady, from your friend, Tiny.

Godwin was home again from Turkey by March 1913 and on 25 March a dinner was given by the 'friends' in celebration of the returning hero.

Eleanor created the menu for this dinner and to accompany each course, one of the company was invited to make a satirical speech:

---

[13] AE refers to George Russell, an Irish writer and painter, and friend to Arnold Bax in his Irish period.

[14] Tiny was the nickname Arnold and his friends gave to Godwin.

MENU

***

Hors d'oeuvres Anastatique

Petit Marmit Empyema
Crème Mal de Mer

Filet Sole Pagani

Noisette de Cholera Germ
Haricot Gangrene
Pommes "Tiny"

Poulet passé aux Enfers
Salade

Peche Melba
Croute Notary

Scruts

Desserts: Hluss, Badajos, Hunkh, Oids, Djemli (with or without Djeli),
Djeli (with or without Djam), Djam (with or without Djemli)

WINES
Lymph, extra sec, 1863
Sparkling quinine

TOASTS

***

"THE KING"
Mr Paul Corder

"THE QUEEN"
Mr Herbert Farjeon

"THE ARMY AND NAVY"
Mr Arnold Bax

"OUR COLONIAL POSSESSIONS"
Mr Maitland Radford

"THE GUEST OF THE EVENING"

Mr Stacey Aumonier
Dr Godwin Baynes will retort

"THE COSMIC EQUATION"
Mr Lynn Hartley

"THE COMMERCIAL PROSPERITY OF THE BRITISH PEOPLE"
Mr Clifford Bax

"TURKISH WOMEN"
Mr Francis Colmer

"LADY W"
Major Ford

During the evening the Russian Ballet (engagements permitting) will dance 'Scheherazade', 'Prince Igor', etc. etc.

Soon after his return, Godwin paid a visit to his parents, taking with him Rosalind and Arnold. However, in spite of Helton's pride in his son's achievements in Turkey, this was not a successful visit. Helton is deeply disappointed at what he perceives as Godwin's arrogance and attitude of superiority towards his family.

I don't like any sad notes in this diary but truth compels me to say the visit of the trio has been most disappointing. We expected such a joyful home-coming, not having seen Godwin since August last and so much has happened in his life during these months; but we found it a sort of corkscrew process to get *any* news out of him; the trio lit a fire in the morning room and practically lived there (smoking and I fear drinking), while at meal times they sat together and whispered to each other, evidently thinking it a bore to listen to or join in our talk. As Jack said, they were so 'superior' that we felt de trop; and if I had waited at the end of the table for them to pass me anything, I might have starved. No courtesy, no attempt to please host and hostess, or to defer to their wishes, simply the selfishness which receives all and gives none. Their conduct sadly depressed me and troubled us all; if these are the boorish manners of London society, I bless our deliverance! As Edward White once wrote to me, 'Neglect of and indifference to Christianity soon shows itself in the character.' May God soon answer my daily petition and restore to Godwin his old faith in God, Christ and the Bible. After all we have done to give Godwin all the splendid educational advantages which have made him what he is, it is sad to see such *apparent* ingratitude and rudeness to the home ones who always give him a warm welcome. He has been flattered for years and suffers from a swelled head, regarding us probably as Puritan old fogies whose ideas and opinions are worth just *nil*. Still, there is time yet for him to recover and I gladly admit that he and Ros were better behaved when Dermid left[15]. Jack took Mary and the girls on some motor-rides; we had chess and bridge and singing. We all agreed we never saw Jack better or happier, he is such a dear, good fellow and has never given us a moment's pain or anxiety. Matthew Arnold says 'A gentleman is one who does not inflict pain.' True! Godwin's impulses and his heart are right, as he has abundantly proved in Turkey, but he is swayed by his companions, and still has much to learn.

Sad reflections from Godwin's father; the return of the 'Conquering Hero' was a disappointment, as Godwin seemed unable to disguise his impatience with his own family and his roots, who appeared on his return in such stark contrast to the brilliant Hampstead circle of friends. Perhaps it was an inevitable result of his growing away from them, a process that was possibly accentuated by his experiences in the Balkan War. But could he have become the pioneer he was in life unless he had broken with the strong puritan traditions of his past? In his later years in life he was able to return to some of his family's Christian values, but by then he had made the faith his own; it was no longer a faith and way of life imposed by a father he couldn't admire and who he certainly did not want to emulate. For Godwin, his father's faith and religious observance was too powerfully connected with his crippling fears – fears that hemmed him in emotionally and physically. It was as though, in every aspect of his life, Godwin was wanting to prove that he had not inherited his father's illness. Possibly it was because Helton's breakdown had coincided with Godwin's birth that he was the one out of the five children who was most deeply affected by it. Was it this that unconsciously led him to a career concerned with mental illness?

Perhaps he had felt compelled to distance himself from his family problems, leading him to live his life in an excess of extraversion which he later needed to balance with a more reflective attitude to

---

[15] Dermid was Arnold Bax's Irish nick-name.

living. Godwin's exuberance at this period was legendary. Frances Cornford, a gentle poet, one of the friends from his Cambridge days, and granddaughter to Sir Charles Darwin, spoke of an animal energy which emanated from him. She said that his presence in a crowded room could make itself felt the moment he entered, like a mighty gust of wind. To an introverted poet, as she was, he had an overwhelming effect. This may have been true for Eleanor also, but however much she may have loved and admired Godwin as a young girl it was Edward Thomas who aroused her deepest love. In her biography of Thomas[16] she describes her impressions of him at their first meeting in 1912.

> My first impressions were of his tall easy figure, his tawny colour, the grave pleasant tones of his voice, and a swift sidelong glance from his keen eyes when Bertie introduced us. Talk was rather diffident till we reached the tea-rooms, where Godwin's presence glowed on and put us at our ease. I don't remember anything he said, but to look at and listen to Edward was enough; he had a higher degree of beauty of person, voice and mind than I had ever known combined in anybody, or have known since.

However, it was Godwin's exuberance and joie de vivre as Eleanor Farjeon refers to it, that made him so universally popular. At one of the many evenings spent at Ivy Bank, the friends played a game in which each member of the party was allocated scores out of ten for particular characteristics. Eleanor kept the score sheets and on one of these are the results for all those present. Godwin's score reads as follows:

Pride	4
Vanity	0
Ostentation	2
Joie de Vivre	10
Christianity	5
Paganism	5
Will	9
Fire	7
Grit	8
Adaptability	8

[16] Farjeon, E., *Edward Thomas:The Last Four Years.*

Godwin achieved the highest scores of the seven included in this chart, in joie de vivre, will and adaptability.

But the heady student days were over and it was time for Godwin to begin leading the life for which he felt he was destined. He was ready to fulfil his promise to his Bax patrons to set up a practice for the poor. He chose a practice in the East End of London, in Bethnal Green.

Chapter Five

Practice in Bethnal Green

A young Apollo, golden-haired
Stands dreaming on the verge of strife,
Magnificently unprepared
For the long littleness of life

Frances Cornford, *'Youth'*

Godwin sets up in practice in Bethnal Green. Rosalind helps
with the practice and the housekeeping assisted by Ruth, who
also acts as chaperone.

Godwin rented a small house and a surgery in March 1912. He put
up his brass plate and started work in his first practice. At that time
conditions were very bad in Bethnal Green and doctors in that part of
London were scarce. Godwin's sister Ruth remembers that 'many of
the people who came to the surgery were suffering from starvation
and nothing else.' Unemployment was high and the women took in
sewing to make ends meet. They would be paid half a crown for
making a shirt so could pay little for a visit to the surgery. Some could
pay nothing at all. After one day's work, Godwin returned with two
shillings and sixpence; 'It will pay the rent', he said.

As soon as Godwin was established he and Rosalind decided they
wanted to be together. In a manner that was quite unconventional at
the time, Rosalind joined him in Bethnal Green and they invited Ruth
to come and live with them to help keep house, for the sake of
decorum.

Helton was understandably concerned about this arrangement although he was making a great effort, on Ruth's account, to be broad-minded. He wrote in his commonplace book of his misgivings, after a visit from Godwin and Rosalind to look over the furniture Godwin's parents had been storing for them. While they were visiting his family at Mortimer, Godwin spoke of his and Rosalind's plans to be together and suggested that Ruth might like to live with them at the surgery as chaperone, 'so as to avoid all tongue wagging'. Helton presented his concerns about this arrangement at a family council. To his surprise, Ruth said she would really like to go, 'saying she wishes to see other kinds of life, more than is possible in a village, and that she can run down for Whitsun and weekends.' He overcame his worries in relation to the 'glamour of London life', and Godwin and Rosalind's 'bohemian ménage', and eventually gave his consent to Ruth, considering that her 'dignity, discretion and calm judgement' would enable her to deal with the more troublesome aspects of London.

Soon after Ruth and Rosalind moved into the little house at 30 Victoria Park Square, Bethnal Green, Helton received a long newsy letter from Ruth, describing her new London life and the six-roomed house which stood in a pleasant square, a small oasis in the London slums. She was enjoying her new life; on the first day of her stay Godwin had seen eight patients, she and Ros (despite never having cooked before) had made a wonderful pudding, and above all, she was happy! Helton's fears were somewhat appeased and he was even persuaded to pay them a visit.

For Helton, a visit to London was a major event and it demanded all his resolve and determination to overcome his crippling fears. It was for Godwin very important that his father should see for himself that after all his vacillation and youthful impetuousness, he was now a doctor, fully qualified and managing his own practice. It was also a practice that would satisfy Helton's philanthropic principles. Godwin had been advised by three doctors known and respected by Helton, Dr McCleary, Dr Addison MP and Sir E. Cornwall MP, to go onto the panel in Bethnal Green, so Godwin was at last doing something of which his father fully approved.

Helton and Mary caught a morning train on 11th July 1913 and their son, Jack, joined them in Reading. The three of them arrived at Paddington station at a platform that was not the familiar one. Because it was an island platform it was acutely upsetting to Helton:

[text continues p. 81]

Godwin as a baby sitting on his mother's lap.
From left to right: Jack, Mary, Godwin, Helton,
Arnold and Muriel (1883)

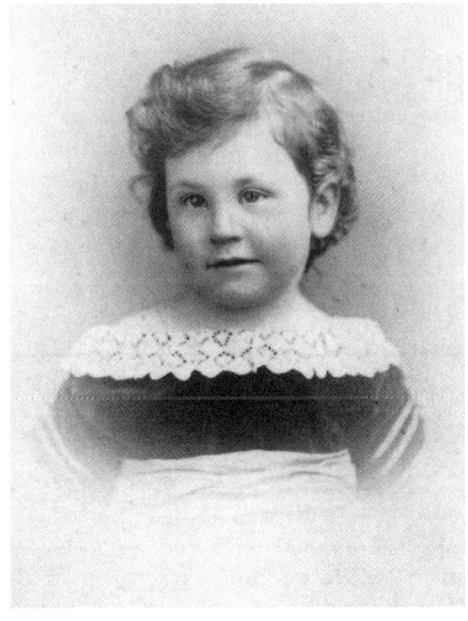

Godwin, aged about two years

Godwin as a small boy

*Baynes family. From left to right: Muriel,
(unknown), Helton, (unknown), Godwin, Ruth,
Mary & Arnold. (Godwin, aged eight or nine)*

Godwin's mother, Mary

68

Father, Mother & Ruthie.

*Godwin's parents, Helton and Mary, reading in the garden
with baby Ruth*

Godwin as a young clerk in his father's timber firm (ca. 1903)

Family picnic near Mortimer Common
Left to right: Mary, Helton, Ruth, Muriel, Jack, Arnold,
Godwin (with the mischievous grin!)
(Woman with hat in background, unknown)

Godwin at Cambridge, the rowing blue, with his Leander jacket

Cambridge crew (1905)
HGB is the tall one at the back.

The Cambridge crew (1907)
with Baynes rowing (number four)

Godwin, the giant rowing blue

*Setting sail for Turkey to set up a hospital
for the Red Crescent Mission during the Balkan War (1912)
(Godwin is third from the top)*

Captain Baynes, RAMC, First World War

Rosalind Thornycroft, at the time of her marriage to Godwin

Godwin, as a newly qualified doctor

Godwin, the rowing blue (1906)

Ruth's drawing of their mother, Mary

Helton and Mary Baynes, in their old age

his agoraphobic fears overcame him and he was thrown into a state of panic. He immediately put up his umbrella, grasped hold of Mary and Jack, and together they dashed up the stairs and on to Bishops Bridge Road. Jack found Ruth, who had come to meet them, and they travelled with her by underground to Liverpool Street and from there they took a 'motor bus' to Victoria Park Square. After a three-minute walk they reached the surgery, at Number 30, and there, Rosalind was waiting to welcome them.

Helton describes the situation of the house, with Bethnal Green Museum immediately opposite full of treasures from natural history, and to the left of the museum, some lovely gardens, bright with flowers. He is delighted with everything in this modest home, 'the newly done up state of the old house [giving] a bright air to everything', and he comments favourably on the original taste, 'simplicity and unostentation being the ruling virtues'.

What they saw and experienced in Godwin's first home reassured both his parents and also relieved their anxiety in relation to their youngest daughter. Ruth was eighteen years old, but she had led a sheltered and protected life and this was her first real experience of life away from home. Helton was also reassured about Rosalind, whose outlook and background was so different from theirs. Both he and Mary felt more accepting of the unconventional aspect of Godwin and Rosalind's relationship, and were reconciled to Ruth being a part of their household. He confided to his journal: 'Mary and I feel pleased and thankful about all we saw and heard, and believe that Godwin and Rosalind may hope for many years of good, noble work among the needy East Enders.'

They went along the road to fetch Godwin from the surgery at noon. This meant a ten minute walk and Helton managed it without difficulty. The surgery was in an old corner shop which Godwin had converted into bright and convenient consulting rooms. He had found large railway posters and hung them on the walls to make the surgery look more cheerful. The other rooms in the building he had let to a couple called Mr and Mrs Hammond, who were full of praise for the young doctor. They told his parents: 'He is so kind and nice, just the doctor we wanted.'

Godwin's total earnings so far, that week (it was now Friday), had been £3.15. After their lunch, prepared together by Ruth and Rosalind, Godwin did some visits and later returned to have a 'long, happy and confidential talk about his success hitherto, his prospects, expenses etc. in settling in, date of his marriage etc., the best filial outpouring I have enjoyed for many a day.'

Helton records one month later that Ruth had returned home, after three and a half months of housekeeping together with Rosalind. She was looking well and happy and had been a very great help to her brother. He became aware that as a result of the plays, concerts and ballets she had enjoyed in London, and the friends of Godwin's she had met, that her outlook and sympathies had been widened by the experience.

The Bethnal Green practice, with its poverty and hardship, also had another side. There was a constant stream of visitors; all the friends belonging to the Bax circle continued to meet and to socialise together, and the simple establishment at Bethnal Green became the centre for evenings of poetry, of literary talk and of music. Arnold Bax and Godwin spent many an evening making music together, Arnold accompanying Godwin in opera and German Lieder, as well as his own compositions. Ruth recalled one afternoon, in particular, when Arnold played through a piano rendition of the whole of the 'Meistersinger' overture, to his appreciative and captive audience. The group of friends were still fanatical devotees both of Wagner operas and the Russian Ballet. They would go most weeks to queue outside Covent Garden gallery in order to get good seats to see Pavlova and Nijinsky dance, as that was the year when Diagileff's ballet had a season in London.

Eleanor and her brother Bertie were also frequent visitors and Eleanor remembers it as being:

> Far afield from most of Godwin's friends, but nothing kept them from flocking after him to the shabby old-fashioned, scantily-furnished house warmed by his presence. Rosalind dispensed prescriptions (quite illicitly surely, but who cares now?) in the dispensary on the street level, and hunted the Caledonian Market for cheap attractive crockery to help out the bits given them by their families. I chiefly remember a lovely old shawl which she got for half-a-crown, a curious trestle-bed apt to let its occupant down, and two loveable jerboas, who became dear to us all.

Another visitor to the little house at Bethnal Green was Bunny Garnett. He remembers being:

A continual and welcome visitor in the little house and there I got to know many of Godwin's friends, in particular Bertie Farjeon, who had fallen in love with Rosalind's sister Joan Thornycroft. I had also brought in friends of my own to Godwin's circle, perhaps the most important being Edward Thomas, who through Godwin, got to know Clifford and Arnold Bax and a new world of leisured people. I believe, indeed, that the friendships he formed at this time did more to liberate him as a poet than anything he had experienced before.

At Bethnal Green, Godwin was hard-worked, yet there was a feeling of gaiety and an absence of strain remarkable in a busy doctor's household. This charm and light-heartedness were reinforced by two tame jerboas which became playful as the evening wore on. One night Godwin, in pouring out some Chartreuse, spilled a few drops upon the floor. One of the jerboas tasted the precious liquid, found it agreeable and tasted again. Suddenly it leaped up on the divan bed on which Bertie Farjeon and I were idly watching it. It jumped four feet in the air and fell back beside us with a flop. Presently it began wandering about. But when it reached the edge of the mattress it stepped blithely into space and tumbled to the ground. Godwin picked it up, reported it under the influence of drink, with blurred responses, and tucked it up in bed in its cage to sleep off the effects.

It is interesting to consider the two very contrasting, and possibly conflicting aspects of Godwin's personality. On the one hand he must have been experiencing a distressing inside view of the suffering and extreme poverty of many of his patients. Most of these patients were well below the poverty line at a time when there was no Social Security or National Health. Possibly it was the first time he had witnessed real hardship: at that time much of the ill health was caused by deprivation and unsanitary living conditions and, in the children especially, from under-nourishment. As a doctor, there must have been the added distress of being able to do so little, and often to be able to offer no more than palliative medicine.

On the other hand he was still entertaining, and was still very much involved with, the artistic circle of leisured people, many of whom would never need to earn a living. From Garnett's account of his many visits to the little house in Bethnal Green, it would seem that he managed to combine both these worlds, and to appear relaxed and at ease in both aspects of his life. Whatever the hours he was working, which must have included long days of surgeries and home visits as well as night calls, he clearly had enough energy to continue to join his friends in visits to the Russian Ballet as well as to pursue their youthful passion for Wagner's operas. He must, indeed, have been endowed with an almost super-human energy at this time in his life.

It was at this period of his working life that Godwin first became actively aware of the psychological aspects of medicine, recognising that healing wasn't solely dependent on the doctor's medical knowledge and the drugs administered. He realised that the doctor's personality could affect the cure and also that psyche and soma (mind and body) are inextricably linked and that one cannot be treated without recognising that both have a part to play, whether the 'illness' manifests with predominantly physical or psychological symptoms.

Godwin's understanding of, and intense interest in psychological medicine attracted patients to him who were not understood by more conventional doctors. One of these was the poet Edward Thomas who came to see him because he was suffering from periods of deep depression. These depressions are mentioned by his wife, Helen Thomas, in her book, *As It Was*, which describes, in a very intimate way, their life together. Eleanor Farjeon records that, 'The dark moods that had tormented him lightened with this release into self-expression.' She is referring here to his writing. These black moods and depressions haunted Helen and Edward's marriage and Helen, who was a woman of generous spirit, welcomed Eleanor's visits: with her love for Edward and the poetry they shared together, Eleanor was at times able to lighten Edward's dark moods.

Helen Thomas refers in her book to visits Edward paid to a doctor when these moods became intolerable; he would sometimes be away in London for weeks at a time. 'Rumour got about that Godwin Baynes was analysing a new patient who was suffering from depression', writes Annabel Farjeon, in her biography of Eleanor. 'When missed from parties and meetings he was treating this patient.' For a time Thomas became very dependent on his visits to Godwin. They helped him through and enabled him to gain some insight into the dark times which, he acknowledged later, became the source of his creative writing.

However, Thomas' feelings about Godwin were ambivalent. At one time Eleanor Farjeon took the risk of discussing Edward's emotional problems and commented that he was no longer seeing Godwin.

Thomas' reply was: 'Godwin can't help me. When he first came to see me he made me feel that I was the most important person in the world to him. As I came to know his world I found he gave the same impression to everybody – and I don't like being one of a crowd.'

Annabel Farjeon comments in her book on the close friendships; the intimacies with friends and children and with those in need, which were the very stuff of Eleanor's life:

> Eleanor loved the intimacy of these *tête-à-têtes*, but in them there was the very element of which Edward Thomas had complained in his relationship to Godwin Baynes. For the time each individual was made to feel the most important person in the world, and for the time this was probably true: there was no trickery, no disloyalty in the emotional response between the protagonists. Yet to the fastidious there was the knowledge of being one of a crowd.

Perhaps it was this quality in Godwin that enabled him as a doctor to give himself wholly to whoever was with him at the time. He was remembered long after he ceased to be a GP for being an exceptional doctor and this was also an essential quality in his work as a psychotherapist later in life.

Chapter Six

Marriage

Let me not to the marriage of true minds admit impediment.
Shakespeare, *Sonnet 116*

Godwin and Rosalind are married in Galway.

On September 11th, 1913 Godwin and Rosalind were married at noon in the cathedral in Galway. It was an unconventional and quiet wedding and the only family members present were Rosalind's parents, Sir Hamo Thornycroft and his wife Agatha. There is a somewhat rueful entry in Helton's diary, and it is clear that Godwin's parents were not included among those who were invited, though no doubt a journey to Ireland would have been out of the question for Helton when even the journey to work was becoming increasingly impossible. Helton was happy that the wedding took place in a Protestant church and that the marriage received God's blessing. Whatever his misgivings may have been about Rosalind, the unconventional aspects of their lives together and this most unusual wedding, he is thankful that Godwin is practising a 'noble profession', that he has endeared himself to the people of Bethnal Green, and that Rosalind delights in his work. He adds that: 'In an engagement of four years (I think) they have rarely been separated from each other, except during the five months he was at San Stefano and their mutual love has been well tested. They know one another through and through, and no foolish conventions have blocked the pathway to their love. I believe their ideals are noble and good, though they do not use our spectacles, and our prayers and longings for them will be answered. All our three boys have good wives.'

Considering Helton's religious principles and the conventions of the time in relation to a physical relationship before marriage, his comments on their pre-marital relationship seem remarkably broadminded.

Like everything that Godwin and Rosalind did together, their wedding was both unconventional and romantic and also quite in keeping with their neo-pagan philosophy. In Rosalind's memoir she gives a full and poetic description of their wedding and honeymoon:

> In the summer of 1913 Godwin and I decided to get married and that we wanted the wedding to take place in Galway. So I went out there with a bicycle to domicile myself in order to get a marriage licence, while Godwin remained in Bethnal Green. My sister Joan came with me and we had a happy time together, boating and painting in water-colours. Then Mother and Father came, and finally Godwin. We stayed at the Eyre Hotel in Galway. In strange ignorance of all things religious I called on the parish priest and asked him to marry us. I was quite astounded that he peremptorily refused when I said that we were not Roman Catholics and turned me away forthwith. I then tried the Church of Ireland and here, at the Protestant church of St Nicholas we were accepted. Having arranged with the organist to play obligingly a very secular Elizabethan love song – 'Fain would I change that note' – for the ceremony, we all turned up at the church. I was wearing a traditional Galway grey shawl. But somehow or other, through another muddle, we hadn't got the licence! This time the Church of Ireland took a firm line and said we must get it from Clifden, fifty miles away. So leaving Father and Mother in Galway, Godwin and I hired a motor car and drove off at high speed to Clifden in order to get back the same evening and be able to go to the church early the next morning. By the time we had been given the licence by the Canon and taken tea with him, it was getting late, so we drove off in the dark along the mountainous road. Suddenly we were stopped by some obstacle which proved to be a donkey asleep in the middle of the track. Screams and yells came from the tinkers who owned the donkey and who were sleeping by the roadside. As the animal was not lying across the road but lengthwise, the wheels of our car passed neatly on each side over him without injuring

him in any way. The tinkers hauled him out and after some argument and hard words we managed to make our getaway.

The next morning, 11 September 1913, we went again to the Cathedral and this time we were married. Father and Mother went on to stay at Recess by the Clifden railway, while Godwin and I mounted our bicycles and rode about eight miles along the east side of Lough Corrib. Here we saw a small fishing boat moored to the shore just opposite a little stony and bushy island; so rowing ourselves across to it we spent the night on the ground – and very rocky ground it was. The morning was lovely, the sky pale thin blue and very Irish. Remembering Synge and the Abbey Theatre Players, Yeats, Cuchullin, Finn and Brah-na-Boyne, we rode gaily back to Galway in order to take the steamer to the Aran Islands. We had decided to go to Inisheer, the smallest of the three Aran Islands and which we had been told was the wildest. As it had no harbour the steamer was obliged to anchor some way out and we were then rowed ashore in a curragh. This boat is about twenty-five feet long and six or seven feet wide. The wooden frame is covered tightly with tarred canvas. The boat is therefore very light and able to skim comfortably and gracefully over the crests of enormous waves. The island was divided into numerous fields, only about twenty feet square. The walls some six-feet high were built with the stones which had been collected when clearing the patches of ground. In this way the cattle were protected and potatoes and cabbages were grown. Godwin and I had brought light-weight camping equipment with us and, having put up our tent in one of these grassy enclosures and started to cook some food, we became aware of people whispering and shuffling outside the walls. We soon discovered that a large number of the islanders had come to us and were deeply interested in our primus stove and saucepans of aluminium, a metal they had never seen before. They became very friendly and said they would give us a party during the evening. So later we assembled on a grass dance-floor in front of the house of Mr. Powell. About forty people had come and were all very merry and ready for a dance. The men wore bright blue trousers made of hand-woven tweed and grey woollen waistcoat jerkins. On their feet they wore pampooties, which were shoes made of cowhide with the hair still on and laced up with a thong over the instep. The young men were very agile, vaulting silently over the high walls. The women wore bright scarlet long full skirts and tight bodices. The skirt was in two layers and when it rained hard the upper skirt could be pulled up from the back right over the head to shelter the face and shoulders. Only the men danced, and the music was not made by a fiddler but by a whistler with an extraordinary gift. For more than half an hour he whistled reels or jigs loudly and continuously, while the rhythmic soft patter of the boys in pampooties on the lawn was beautiful to hear. After the dancing was over an old man started story-telling. He appeared to be clearly recognised as the established best local comedian and made his audience wild with laughter. But as the stories were told in Irish, their natural tongue, unfortunately we could not understand the jokes.

The next day it rained hard and we were very glad to be invited to stay the night in Mr Powell's house. He seemed to be the head man of the village. He was most hospitable and courteous, and spoke and enunciated the most perfect English. When at a loss for a word in English he would appeal to his little ten-year-old daughter, Biddy, who had learned a better command of our language at school. The house was of the usual cottage plan: one large central living-room with one small room at either end. These were the bedrooms and we were given one with a bed that had a curved wooden canopy reaching from head to foot. The evening was spent by the turf fire, over which hung a huge cauldron that seemed to have bread baking inside it. Lying in front of the fire was an enormous pig who evidently was a much loved member of the family. The two little girls were using her as a sofa.

When it was time for bed the turf fire was banked up with ashes. Mr Powell presented us with a bottle of porter to take with us as a night-cap and we settled comfortably under a large thick patch-work quilt in the curious bed. The next morning was fine and after exploring the beautiful lonely little island, we went down to the shore with our friends the Powell family in time to be rowed in the curragh to the steamer waiting in the offing. It was market day in Galway and many people were taking their cattle to be sold. The animals were urged into the sea with much shouting and beating, hauled by ropes into the curragh and then to the steamer. As the steamer was about 200 yards away from the shore, some of the poor creatures had to swim, and they were finally hoisted up on board in slings round their bellies.

After a few days in Galway it was time for us to return to Bethnal Green and Godwin to his surgery.

It was as though the wedding and honeymoon, and their life together at this time, was like the fulfilment of a romantic dream which Rosalind and Godwin had woven and enacted together. But as Rosalind herself commented, perhaps there was a sense of creating a romantic Irish idyll, turning their very lives into the music and poetry they had enjoyed together; perhaps the romantic ideal couldn't cope, in the end, with the monotony of ordinary life. As Frances wrote of Rupert Brooke, maybe both of them were in a way, 'Magnificently unprepared for the long littleness of life.'

Another description of their marriage was written by Rosalind's mother, Agatha Thornycroft, in a letter to her daughter Elfrida, which gives a somewhat more prosaic account of the wedding with more emphasis on the discomforts and difficulties than the romantic aspects. The rain, together with the discomforts of an Irish wedding were more apparent to the Thornycroft parents!

Agatha describes the actual wedding ceremony very briefly: 'Ros put on her Irish shawl which is a sort of fawn colour with a white pattern as a border round the edge, and we went to church in a sidecar, all four of us together. There were only about half-a-dozen other people in the church and the organist played some sweet rather sad music before and after the service and we went into the vestry and all signed our names and then it was over.'

Chapter Seven

Wisbech

We are the music makers,
We are the dreamers of dreams,
Wandering by lone sea-breakers,
And sitting by desolate streams.

O'Shaughnessy, *We are the Music Makers*

Godwin and Rosalind move to Wisbech where he becomes the
first successful panel doctor, facing considerable opposition from
the doctors in practice there. Godwin and Rosalind continue to
entertain their London friends, who come to stay in Wisbech,
until the outbreak of war. Their first baby, Bridget, is born and
Godwin acts as accoucheur.

In the late winter of 1913 Godwin and Rosalind moved to Wisbech.
It was an inauspicious time to arrive when local riots were taking
place following the introduction of National Insurance. Perhaps
Godwin was appointed because of his large physique and intrepid
character. A report in the local paper said that the appointing
committee had voted unanimously for Godwin as there was no doubt
in their minds that he was the candidate who would be most able to
look after himself. They arrived at Wisbech station to be greeted by a
welcoming committee consisting of the entire town council and a
fanfare from the local brass band. Godwin and Rosalind were cere-
moniously marched through the streets to their house at number 27
Market Street to the rapturous applause of the locals.

Did he realise at the time how close he was living to the home of his namesake and distant relative William Godwin, who was born in Wisbech to an equally restrictive puritan family, in 1756? Like Godwin, William had also rebelled against the restrictions of his family roots; in his best-known publication, *Political Justice,* he wrote what was then a revolutionary document, promoting social equality. Later, in his marriage to Mary Wollstonecraft, recognized as the first woman feminist and certainly the first to write about the status of women[17], he also espoused equal rights for women. Together they had a profound influence on the social mores of the time, challenging the status quo which had left large sections of society feeling oppressed and largely unrecognised. However, paradoxically, they suffered considerable oppression from this very society themselves. By defying society's conventions, they became ostracised and were perpetually desperate for lack of money. Their unorthodox lifestyle was emulated by their daughter, Mary Shelley, wife of the poet, Percy Bysshe Shelley. She lived her parents' principles more radically than they did, eloping with Shelley when she was only 16, and suffering severe social isolation and later, as a widow, poverty.

Godwin Baynes was also a rebel to some extent and a pioneer, questioning both his family's religious beliefs as well as the repressive Victorian morals and the stark inequalities of the time. It was perhaps fitting that it should be Godwin who established a new practice in the Old Market, Wisbech, under the new National Insurance Act[18].

In the Wisbech Society 28th Annual Report in 1967, Dr C.K. Elliott, who was practising from the same house as the one in which Godwin and Rosalind had lived, published an article on the history of the town. He writes that the first doctor who was appointed as panel doctor under the new legislation was a local man called Dr Dimmock. He was very popular with his patients but was resented by the other doctors in the town who, for the most part, supported the British Medical Association in opposing the Act.

After a time Dr Dimmock began to receive threatening, anonymous postcards with vague allegations of malpractice and impropriety. Legal proceedings against him brought him to a state of disillu-

[17] In her book *A Vindication of the Rights of Women*
[18] The National Insurance Act 1911, enabling people below a certain income level to obtain free medical treatment while the government supplemented the doctor's income.

sionment and despair and a few days later he was discovered dead, having taken an overdose of veronal and morphia. About five thousand people gathered outside the Dimmocks' house in the Market Place to support the family. Things got out of hand and stones were thrown through the windows of the houses and surgeries of the other doctors. The Mayor of Wisbech read the Riot Act and in a contemporary account there is a lively description of the event: 'A portion of the town was virtually given over to the mob, stones hurled through the air ... and pandemonium raged ... people rolled over like ninepins and the dull thud of truncheons could be heard.' Godwin was appointed soon after these events on account of his enormous size. It was thought that he would be able to survive the heckling.

The Bayneses' new home at 27 Market Street remained as the address for the Wisbech medical practice until 1983. Dr Elliott, who had lived there for many years, gave a picture of the house as he knew it, and one may assume that things had changed very little. He described it as a large Georgian house. There was a big room situated to the left of the hall with three windows overlooking the Market Place and this became the waiting room. The centrepiece of this room was a fine carved fireplace. The consulting room was beyond the waiting room and from it a veranda projected out into a spacious walled garden. Beyond the garden there was a pigeon loft containing tumbler pigeons which Rosalind remembered with delight: 'turning on their backs and somersaulting before returning' causing Godwin, 'almost ecstatic pleasure'.

Godwin's fees for non-panel patients was six shillings a year and there was an extra charge for medicines. For the panel patients (who constituted the majority of his patients), there was no charge. Godwin would do his rounds on a bicycle, rather than using the more usual pony and trap, and one cold winter he was even seen doing his rounds on skis.

His passion for natural history was still very much in evidence. The willow trees in the garden harboured willow hawk moths which would emerge from their cocoons in unexpected places and Godwin would spend his free time searching for butterflies and exploring the Wicken Fen for rare species.

The two lively gerbils, bought at the Caledonian Market in London, were still a part of the establishment and had the run of the house, to the great delight of his younger patients.

Rosalind, writing about the early days in Wisbech in her memoir recalls:

> It was difficult at first to make the practice a success because the reigning doctors were very much against the new system which obviously trespassed on their private ground. However Godwin, with his great charm, soon became very popular and the practice built up. Eventually we became financially quite well-off. I had a cook who taught me to cook a little, as I had never done any cooking at my parents' house. Then Godwin employed a dispenser, a young lady who worked in a little pantry-like room next to his consulting room and the waiting room. We even had a small 'buttons boy' to open the door to patients during surgery hours.

The following year after their arrival in Wisbech, Godwin and Rosalind decided to return for a holiday to their beloved Ireland. Taking the advice of Arnold Bax and Arnold's great friend, the Irish poet, George Russell, they went this time to Glencolumbkille, in Donegal. This was another idyllic time together when they recaptured the magic and romance of their honeymoon. They fished for trout in the lakes and streams, drinking in the beauty of that green and wild landscape, and together they climbed the nearby hills, though more slowly than before, as Rosalind was due to have a baby in July.

Bridget Rosalind was born on 18th July 1914. Godwin was there to help bring her into the world and he remembered her arrival with great fondness later in life, after the marriage had broken down. He wrote of her: 'Bridget is my love child. She represents the happiest days of my life. When she was born, 10 months after our marriage, our love was cloudless. I myself acted as accoucheur. R would have no one else to attend her. I received my Bridget into the world and I have adored her ever since. R always consults me when she is ill because strangely enough, although she does not trust me as a husband she does as a doctor.'

Bridget was born at home. All went smoothly and Rosalind insisted on nursing the baby herself. She was a beautiful child and seemed to possess, from the outset, an amazing zest for life. Rosalind was a natural and devoted mother and Godwin was totally enchanted by his little daughter. Rosalind, using her artistic gifts, 'threw herself into the decoration of the nursery, a small room at the head of the stairs, overlooking the Old Market. Here painted figures from a wide range of fairy tales peered out from the walls and roof.'[19]

But the romantic dream of their marriage began now to fade somewhat, as the realities of life superseded: the demands of patients, interrupted sleep with night calls and a baby who needed to be fed. Meanwhile Rosalind was increasingly distressed by Godwin's roving eye; although it never went beyond a mild flirtation, her pride was hurt. The immediate object of dissension between them was the young woman who was acting as dispenser for Godwin. During the vulnerable time after the birth of their first baby, Godwin's admiring glances caused Rosalind intense unhappiness and in some way fractured their romantic idyll. As Rosalind later recognizes in her memoir, for Godwin it was no more than 'the exuberance of a natural spirit'.

Eleanor Farjeon was one of the many friends who visited the couple in their new home and she writes[20] about her recollections of her stay at 27 Market Street.

> Godwin and Rosalind had flitted from Bethnal Green to Wisbech. Their going was a blow to us all; and to them, I think. Why did they go? Godwin wanted to 'find himself'. He told me that in London he was pulled in too many directions, by too many interests, among too many well-loved friends. He was running away from his devastating popularity. The Wisbech practice was a favourable one, under the aegis of the famous Misses Peckover of that town, well out of reach of the distracting attractions of the Russian Ballet (then at fever-heat), of Beecham opera, of multitudinous parties arranged and impromptu. But what then? Once more he had acquired a roomy old house, on the market square, with ample space for the friends he drew after him. Radfords, Garnetts, Farjeons and Baxes flocked north when they could and would. Almost on arrival Godwin and Ros planned a spring gathering, at the time of the Wisbech Fair, when all their friends should be with them. They spoke of it as The Millennium. Meanwhile we sallied to Cambridgeshire in twos and threes.

Later in her book she describes The Wisbech Millennium party to which she came in March 1914. It was:

[19] Dr C.K. Elliott: Article in the Wisbech Society Annual Report (1967).
[20] Farjeon, E., *Edward Thomas – The Last Four Years*.

A hurly-burly of gaudy nights and days: 27 Old Market faced on to the Market Place, and we stepped from the front door straight into the Fair at its thickest, into the hum and bustle of the booths and side-shows, and the pandemonium of the giant roundabouts. At night their coloured lights glared into the first-floor room where we assembled, when we were not spilling out into the streets to buy each other still more trumpery, gape at the sword-swallower, and bring home still more coconuts. Our party numbered too many crack shots to be popular with the gypsies who ran the shies. Nut after hairy nut succumbed to Bertie's deadliest Yorkers, and Godwin's balls slew seven at one blow. He returned half his spoils to the disgruntled showman before, laden with trophies, we piled into the cars of the most raucous roundabout, and started the switchback journey through nether Hell. When Bertie dropped a coconut into its bowels he sprang to his feet, demanding excitedly of the attendant demons as we whirled past that the machine be stopped instantly, and his property restored. The altercation waxed hotter at each round, but the *casus belli* never came to light.

On Sunday a paper-chase was organised. Joan, fleet as Atalanta, was one of the hares, and Godwin, who knew the district, was the other. After ten minutes we hounds were up and away. The trail led out of Wisbech, far afield into the private market-gardens cut across and across by a network of dykes. The pack cried havoc through a maze of apple-orchards. Godwin eluded it by leaping dyke after dyke, a feat beyond the rest of us. Presently I found myself within a stone's throw of Joan, inaccessible because of the ditch between. As we dodged back and forth, she seeking a way out and I a way round, our ears were assailed by angry shouts, two or three dykes away. One of our pack was in trouble: Bunny [Garnett], dodging an irate fruit-farmer, also trying to find a way out or round. Hares and hounds turned tail and sneaked home, hoping that Godwin's scutcheon was not blotted. It would never do for the respected Misses Peckover to identify their new young doctor with a Sabbath breaking rabble summonsed for trespassing. But the incident blew over without result, except that the Old Market house party behaved circumspectly for the rest of the Millennium.

This was to be the last of these carefree gatherings. After the Millennium party in Wisbech, so enchantingly described by Eleanor Farjeon, the group of friends began to disperse and go their separate ways. Marriage and the war took them in different directions, and many did not survive. It was the end of an era not only for this group of privileged young people but for the country as a whole. It marked the final chapter to a way of life that would never come again but also heralded the beginnings of a fairer and more democratic society – one that was more in keeping with Godwin's egalitarian principles.

In August of that year Godwin and Rosalind were peacefully rowing a boat on the River Ouse at St Ives, when they heard the news that war had broken out. The news was unexpected and they were taken completely by surprise. They quickly went ashore and returned home. But there was no sense, at the time, of emergency or panic. People believed that the war would be over in two or three months. However, Godwin took the precaution of buying a great bag of lentils, in case they should encounter food shortages.

The war suddenly put a different complexion on life in Britain. The sense of security and comparative affluence which was dominant among the privileged classes, as a result of nearly 100 years of peace, was suddenly shattered. Godwin no longer felt able to ignore what was happening at the front, and like almost every young man at that time, he was overtaken by the burning sense of idealism and the need to fight against the oppression of the Kaiser, for the Mother Land.

Having continued to practice for a while after the outbreak of war, he decided, finally, to sell the Wisbech surgery. In July 1915 he wrote to his friend and fellow doctor, Maitland Radford, who also held strong socialist principles, offering him a half share in the practice. He told him this would bring in about £1,400 a year, which at that time was a very comfortable living. Godwin wrote: 'I think I shall sell it for a song if I cannot find anyone, as I feel I cannot stand out of this bloody business any longer. I feel dirty.'

Maitland, who like Godwin joined the RAMC later, didn't take up the offer; but by October Godwin wrote to him that the practice was sold, adding that he wanted a good long talk with him before volunteering. Maitland remained one of Godwin's closest friends and they continued to correspond throughout the war.

On 28 December 1915, Godwin joined the Royal Army Medical Corps. On that day he was ordered to Aldershot, and in January 1916, he crossed to France. It was hard for Rosalind to accept Godwin's need to join the army. He was not, as a doctor, under any obligation to fight in the war and Rosalind must have felt a sense of betrayal and abandonment, finding herself suddenly alone with Bridget, who was now a year old, and with their second daughter on the way.

It was a difficult time for those who were left behind and although Rosalind was a remarkably independent young woman it was unusual, then, for a woman to have to fend for herself. She could neither understand Godwin's ardent sense of duty and patriotism, nor his need to leave his family and his secure practice. It was a patriotism that seduced all the young men of that era: those who did not subscribe to this overwhelming fervour to fight for their country, or who called themselves pacifists, were branded as cowards. Maitland also shared Godwin's desire to go to the front, and he also spent many months with the RAMC in France, but their paths didn't cross. However, in June 1916, when Godwin was with the British Expeditionary Force in France, and before Maitland left for France, Godwin wrote to him asking if he would send a copy of D.H. Lawrence's *The Rainbow* which had recently appeared; he continued, perhaps a little ruefully, that 'bully beef and a tent together is good stuff for comradeship'. Maitland was to spend many months in France, and their friend, Stacey Aumonier, another member of Bax's cricket team, wrote sympathetically to Maitland while he was serving at the front saying that, 'Even Tiny found three months enough in Turkey, and he doesn't know what nerves are.'

Chapter Eight

First World War

I'm back again from hell
With loathsome thoughts to sell;
Secrets of death to tell;
And horrors from the abyss.

Siegfried Sassoon, *To the Warmongers*

Godwin joins the RAMC and is posted to France. He is wounded in the Battle of the Somme, and is sent home on six months' leave. He is posted to the Far East in October 1917 and returns from Bombay in January 1919 to find Rosalind has given birth to a third daughter. This daughter is by another man and Rosalind is wanting a divorce.

Godwin was posted to France at the beginning of 1916 and during his absence, Rosalind, who was expecting her second baby in March, moved back to Hampstead to be near to her family. Bridget remembers the Zeppelins in wartime London, as they were chased by searchlights in the night sky. She recalls 'Being carried in blankets to a safer cellar next door and seeing the sky criss-crossed with moving beams.'

London was not a good place to be with small children. As the air-raids intensified, Rosalind decided to leave with her two small girls, Bridget, now three, and Chloë, who had been born while Godwin was away in France, one year before. They moved to the comparative tranquility of Pangbourne where Godwin's parents had found a house for them called The Myrtles, not far from their home in Mortimer Common.

Rosalind managed on her own in a way that was unusual for a woman of her generation. She had help, of course, as all middle-class women did. A nanny called Ivy for the children and a woman 'for the rough' (which in the days before hoovers and washing machines meant hard physical work). Godwin's periods of leave were infrequent and brief. Rosalind was to become increasingly self-reliant and was later, in the course of the divorce proceedings, to be dubbed as a 'feminist'.

In Bridget's reminiscences of The Myrtles she writes of a small village with a green, and nearby the Thames with river steamers providing entertainment on their afternoon walks. The two little girls shared a bedroom and a secret staircase led from the room, inside a cupboard, up to an attic with sweet-smelling apples. She writes:

> And I have a picture of our splendid Daddy, home on leave, regaling us with the magnificent sound of his powerful baritone voice as he sang the Italian air Caro Mio Ben with the intention of lulling us to sleep. But I feel sure we would have been roused rather than lulled by this bedtime performance.
>
> As a treat we were sometimes allowed into Daddy's study, a sanctuary which contained books and treasures of all kinds. There was a particularly lovely book with full-page illustrations of birds. My favourite was the corncrake. I don't think Chloë was old enough to join in my attempts at polishing the solid brass fire-stand which was as big as a stool, and which was my pride and joy. But my greatest wonder was the carved ivory model of the Taj Mahal in which there were successive interiors. The last of them could never be seen but of course I knew it must be as perfect as all the rest. On the wall was a reproduction of Leonardo da Vinci's Head of Christ. This was explained to me with the minimum of reverence because my parents were unashamed pagans. There was a richly beautiful carpet on the floor, brought back probably by Godwin from his service in the Red Crescent expedition to Turkey in 1913. And on his desk were the pipes which he always smoked, their smell seeming to pervade the whole study.'

About Godwin's war years there is little that has been recorded. We only know that he served in France and Mesopotamia and that he was mentioned in dispatches. He was posted to France on 2nd January 1916. He was then told to go to Boulogne and he crossed the following day, going on to Etaples about 20 miles further south on the coast.

There is no record of Godwin's time in France and only two of his letters survive from that time, both of them to Rosalind. The first is from the Somme, on 8th August 1916. It is addressed to: Rosalind Baynes, 11a Park Hill Rd, Haverstock Hill, London, NW. The post-mark is dated 8th August, '16, and stamped on the envelope is the official stamp saying 'Passed Field Censor.' He writes:

My Sweetheart,

We have come to a country where dust clouds hang in the air and cover everything dead and alive. The transport in August is a grand dust-raiser. The men have changed wonderfully in a week. In the train yesterday they were irrepressibly musical. We had a concert in an orchard the night before last and I listened to songs whose origin is as dark and obscure as Stonehenge. Really Tommy Atkins[21] is an astounding creature. When we arrived at 1 a.m. this morning the whole horizon East of us was flashing with the big guns like summer lightning.

All our movements are very obscure and we never know where we are going till we get there. My contour maps are beautiful but I have not enough colours. Will you remember to send me a box of nice coloured pencils of 10 or 12 colours that won't rub off easily. At present we have only red and blue and green. Another thing I want badly is an electric torch, a nice cylindrical one with say 6 re-fills. I should like the torch as soon as possible, but if it is very difficult for you – don't trouble about it. I can't get anything here and my electric torch was broken en route.

The flies here are beastly.

Major Gull and I share a mattress and sleep out in the garden. He is really awfully nice. He writes bad poems, is a regular, only 26, started the war as a lieut, has a very charming wife who writes him innumerable letters. He had 6 to-day in one mail and nobody else had any and he lives at Yattenden where old Balfour Gardiner lives. He is magnificent to look at. Almost perfectly built and seems to have none of the vices of the regular soldier.

The Colonel wants me to join as a combatant officer. He says I could have a captain's commission in a month.

The Colonel is very funny and I like him awfully. He really believes that shells have two large eyes and a pair of antennae and they come loping along and when they catch sight of you down

---

[21] Another term for 'Tommy', the British soldier.

they come. If you pretend to be a carrot they go sailing on over-head.

I had to throw out a lot more of my kit as we all had to get down to 35 lbs and no more so I sent back the great kit bag.

The post is just going.

Darling, I do love you so much, oh so terribly. Kiss me my sweet and send me another sweet little letter.

Kiss my two darlings

I am your lover, your little James

[This nick-name must have been a private one used by Rosalind alone.]

One can't help noticing a somewhat rueful note in this letter as he comments on the number of letters his companion lieutenant is receiving from his wife while the rest of his fellow soldiers receive none.

A description from the First World War experience of Noel Chavasse in his biography[22] helps to give a picture of a doctor's set up in the RAMC and gives one an idea of what Godwin might have been involved with at this time.

The Regimental Aid Post would be the most forward position for emergency medical care and it was the stretcher-bearer's job to collect the wounded and escort and carry them there, where the doctor, in theory, would be waiting. After preliminary dressings the wounded went further back to the Advanced Dressing Station, then back again to the Main Dressing Station. Those in need of specialised treatment or an operation proceeded out of enemy artillery range to the Casualty Clearing Station, which was often the size of a large hospital. Right at the rear, in places like Etaples and Boulogne, were the enormous Base Hospitals and from there a man might hope to be evacuated to England.

So Godwin would have been serving at the rear in one of these large hospitals, in Etaples. The experience of the front line was for the younger doctors, who had only recently qualified. Having been qualified now for about six years, his greater experience put him further from the firing line. But the horrors of the front line were never far from his awareness. Noel Chavasse describes the state of the young men as they came out of the trenches at Ypres.

---

[22] Clayton, Ann, *Chavasse Double VC.*

Our men have had a terrible experience of 72 hours in trenches, drenched through and in some places knee-deep in mud and water. To see them come out, and line up, and march off is almost terrible. They don't look like strong young men. They are muddied to the eyes. Their coats are plastered with mud and weigh an awful weight with the water which has soaked in. Their backs are bent and they stagger and totter along with the weight of their packs. Their faces are white and haggard and their eyes glare out from mud which with short, bristly beards give them an almost beast-like look. They look like wounded or sick wild things. I have seen nothing like it. The collapse after rowing or running is nothing to it. Many, too, who are quite beat, have to be told they must walk it. Then comes a nightmare of a march for about 2 or 4 miles, when the men walk in a trance … and in about 3 days, they are as fit as ever again.[23]

Did Godwin ever see the young men in this state or were they already recognisable as young men by the time they reached him? One wonders also if he himself ever experienced the life of the trenches, as Noel Chavasse describes it in the following passage.

The trench was over the knee in mud, and I had great difficulty in moving the men along it. Several stuck fast and we had to dig them out … I had to run across the fire-trench in front as the communication trench was full of water. What a sight! I never realised what war really meant till I got up there. Our men were absolutely unfit to make an attack, having been sitting in water for two or three days. A stream of water ran the whole length of the trench, so I had to have every second man bailing out water. It rained all the time, and every ten minutes seemed an hour. We had a keg of rum, which I passed along the trench in two water-bottles at mid-day and again at night. It was very much needed, as we were all soaked to the skin and shivering. We were relieved at 6:30 p.m. in a terrible fog. The men had just to clamber out of the back of the trench and run. My greatcoat was so heavy that it toppled me over and I fell five times on my way back.[24]

---

[23] Ibid., p. 82.
[24] Ibid., p. 84.

There is an entry in Helton's commonplace book commenting that on September 4th 1916, Godwin had narrowly escaped being killed on the Somme: 'Godwin has trench fever and was knocked down, buried and bruised by a German shell at Delville Wood what a mercy he was not killed.' It was a narrow escape and although he was not badly injured he was severely shaken by this incident. He was sent home afterwards for some months, because of the trench fever, but also with what is referred to on a surviving army form, as 'debility'. Was this another term for shell-shock? It gave him a grand opportunity to spend time with his family and to escape, for a time, the terrible scenes of death and dismemberment, which were the doctor's daily experience. Had he not been sent home that September, he would certainly not have survived, for the doctors who were sent to replace him during his sick leave were bombed while working in the hospital and the whole team were killed.

Trench fever was a disease, common in the Great War, which had influenza-like symptoms, and it incapacitated men, at this time, in epidemic numbers. The cause of trench fever was eventually traced to the excreta of the body louse. Lice were an affliction endured by everyone during the war on the Western Front. Chavasse wrote of the lice: 'These cause [the men] great irritation, and rob them of sleep when off duty. The lice inhabit chiefly the shirt, pants and trousers, in which millions of eggs are laid in a very short space of time.'

Godwin was moved first to a hospital in Rouen on September 7th – visiting Rouen under rather different circumstances from the visit he described just four years previously, in his letter to Bertie Farjeon. From there he went to Le Havre and crossed over to Osborne where he is reported as having spent a night in the 'Kaiser's Room'. Helton writes: 'Now he can go home and recuperate on a month's sick leave. His is a marvellous escape!'

One of the few documents which survive from this period is an Army Form with the following information: Lieut H.G. Baynes R.A.M.C. is admitted to the Convalescent Home for Officers at Osborne House on the Isle of Wight on 4.9.1916. The Nature of injury or illness: Debility.

Godwin returned home to his family at their new house, The Myrtles, and perhaps this was his first opportunity to see his little daughter, Chloë, born on March 25th and now just 6 months old. One can imagine their delight at seeing him and also his relief, after the horrors of the Western Front, to be with his family again.

On September 14th Helton records: 'Godwin and Ros arrived Tuesday evening (12th), and as this house is full, we got them rooms at Haddon Hall Hydro, close by. We talked till 10:45 p.m. Tues, Godwin bright and *apparently* well; yesterday, a gusty, but fine opportunity, a big picnic on the hillside and in the evening music and dancing galore; and to-day they were off at 9 a.m. to Caragh Lake, Co Kerry, just under the MacGillicuddy mountains. They cross from Holyhead.'

While Godwin and Rosalind were enjoying a second honeymoon in Ireland, perhaps trying to recapture some of the earlier joy and romance together, Bridget and Chloë went with their nurse to stay at Mortimer with the grandparents. Helton describes the two little girls; 'Bridget talking more and very bright; Chloë a bouncing baby.' The pair returned from their brief Irish holiday, looking, according to Helton, 'grandly well' and bringing for his birthday a parcel of trout caught the previous day in Caragh Lake.

After having been seen by the medical board, Godwin was sent to the East Coast for two months, and then to the Royal Flying Corps, Ruislip, near Harrow; 'A happy easy post. Ros can easily go to him', writes Helton.

On March 26th 1917 he records; 'G. R. and Bridget here; he has to cross to Havre on the 29th after being at home. It was a happy little visit though G had a bad head-cold. I liked Ros better; she understands us. They lately spent a weekend with H.G. Wells in Essex.' This visit and Godwin's and Rosalind's friendship with Wells were to cause Godwin's father great concern and disapproval. He blamed Wells and his ungodly ways, and also his considerable influence on his son and daughter-in-law, for the subsequent breakdown of their marriage.

The other surviving letter to Rosalind from Godwin was written on April 1st 1917, from the Officer's Club, A.P.O. No 1 B.E.F., while waiting to cross to Le Havre. Godwin writes:

My darling little girl,
There is a great wind this day and I doubt if the ships will brave the crossing. Very cold it is too.
The list has just been posted and I am to go to that same district where I was this time last year. I shall try and get to No 20 if possible. The army has to take a long breath after making a decision like sending me from one base to another and I can hardly expect to leave here for two or three days, but it is very jolly here,

and where ever one walks one always comes to sea or docks. I like to go down to the harbour when the tide is high. It is such a romp with everyone shouting and throwing ropes and tugs churning the water and straining at ropes in any direction. There was one great ship with one tug pulling ahead and another slightly bigger tug pulling astern. It was a good contest but I believe the great ship was not being quite straight about it. Every now and then she would manage a twiddle or two with her own screw to encourage the little one in front. While this was going on the other steamers and destroyers and tugs all about, would cry 'pip-pip' or 'poop-poop' according to the exigences of their vocal apparatus. And the sun sparkled on the poppley water and dogs barked.

Ah! What a scene it was. I have been for a grand walk alone by the sea and on to the tops of the plateau (same old plateau), when I found hundreds of thousands of derelict automobiles of every description. They were all dismantled and dilapidated and not in any sense portable yet they were closely guarded by fierce men with fixed bayonets. As I walked along the edge of this strange park, I happened to stop for purely personal reasons and a bayonet was at my elbow in an instant. This surprised me more than I can say. I discovered later that these were all Belgian and represented a national industry ...

I find I have no scissors no gloves and only one pipe but I think it would be unwise to send them to me here as you know what the B.E.F. is like.

You must try and persuade Lloyd George to give votes to every soldier and then have an election. I tell you the demand for Peace candidates who would vote for an immediate and dishonourable peace would startle even *The Times*.

My lovely babes and how are they? Tell my curly-head that her Dadskin worships her and, oh my Chloëkins, my apple-cheeked king-cup I embrace you.

My darling adored wife, I enfold you in my arms and my heart bursts with fondness,

Kiss me my sweetheart

Your devoted, James.

The mention of 'dishonourable peace' referred to here must have echoed the feelings of so many gallant young men whose patriotic ardour had been disillusioned by the horrors and meaningless slaughter in this war. In Siegfried Sassoon's famous letter to *The Times*[25], published three months after this letter from Godwin, he writes about being 'a soldier, convinced that I am acting on behalf of soldiers. I believe that this war, upon which I entered as a war of defence and liberation, has now become a war of aggression and conquest.' In spite of the fact that he was awarded an MC for his extraordinary bravery during the Battle of the Somme, he continues: 'I have seen and endured the suffering of the troops, and I can no longer be a party to prolong these sufferings for ends which I believe to be evil and unjust.' How many must have agreed with Sassoon and yet, for this letter, he narrowly escaped being court-martialed. Instead, because of the influence of his friend and fellow poet, Robert Graves, he was sent to Craiglockhart War Hospital, in Edinburgh, to be treated by the well-known psychiatrist, Dr W.H.R. Rivers, for shell-shock.

Godwin may well have been aware of Sassoon's feelings about the war in 1917. Sassoon was a first cousin of Rosalind's (he was the son of Sir Hamo Thornycroft's sister, Theresa), and had been close to her in childhood. Godwin would certainly have known him and must have whole-heartedly supported this protest.

Godwin was back again on leave from France in August 1917 and Helton records (Aug. 7-9th 1917): 'Godwin (on leave) and Ros here, full of life and energy. Godwin is not only a *splendid animal*, but a thoughtful *man;* yet all the time he was coming in 1882 I was suffering from nerve breakdown and for 5 of the 9 months I was absolutely laid aside! He gave me excellent ideas for the Briary and pond.'

Godwin was back again on September 26th for a flying visit before being posted to the East. He and Rosalind went off to Dulverton, on Exmoor, to get a few days fishing before his departure, 'but the nightly raids over London', writes Helton, 'is driving them back to their babies, especially as he may have to sail any moment. So he stopped on the way back to say goodbye to us, and the memory of the 3 hours together is beautiful; he was full of earnest talk about Wells' discovery of God, and the shortcomings of the Christian Church. As the last words were said he whispered to me "God bless you." We feel almost relieved he is going to an unexciting front, for he says, anything is safer than France.'

[25] Sassoon, S., *A Soldier's Declaration*, an open letter published in *The Times*, 31st July 1917 in protest against the continuation of the war.

On October 9th 1917, Godwin sailed for the East, arriving in Bombay on February 2nd after a stay of six or seven weeks in Durban. It was while he was in Bombay that he received a letter from Rosalind informing him that she was expecting another man's baby. This news came like a bombshell and Godwin's reaction to it was to enter into a trajectory of, in his own words, 'reckless, heedless' living. He didn't return home again until January 1919.

Life in Bombay, when they were not on duty, centred around the typical soldier's life abroad: a lot of alcohol was consumed, lovely young women were plentiful, and for those who played, there was the opportunity to show one's skill at polo. This, however, was one sport that Godwin did not play. By the summer of 1918 he had left Bombay for Baghdad.

It was while Godwin was on the ship en route to Bombay that he met a fellow officer, Captain Meade, who was fascinated by Persia, and Godwin made a decision to volunteer to go as M.O. to the remotest town possible in Persia, an ancient battlemented town not far from Basra, called Hamadan. Captain Meade even undertook to teach Godwin some Persian during the voyage. This decision was made in reckless mood, as the distance between him and his family widened, both physically and emotionally. Perhaps he had become aware during his leave at home that all was not well with the marriage, that something was in the wind. In fact, Godwin sailed for the East on 11th October 1917 and Rosalind and the co-respondent in their later divorce, Kenneth Hooper, spent the night together at the Savoy Hotel on 13th October.

It was during his time in Persia that Godwin had an adventure which he often reflected upon later in life. He was climbing alone, feeling somewhat desolate, a high mountain which towered above the town of Hamadan. Near to the summit of the mountain he surprised a golden eagle on her nest. The nest had young in it hungrily awaiting the return of the male bird. As Godwin approached the eyrie the mother, startled by the intruder, flew from her nest and swooped down on him from above. Her claws, powerful beak and six foot wingspan were suspended threateningly above him and he found himself, for several minutes, locked in solitary combat with this magnificent bird. It was an experience that made a profound impression on him.

Having left his family behind Godwin was plunged into a very different life, first in the heat of Bombay and then in this remote, mediaeval Persian city. The following account by Maurice Nicoll of his experience in the RAMC in Mesopotamia in 1916-17, gives a vivid picture of the conditions they were working under at the time. Nicoll was a contemporary of Godwin's, who had also studied medicine at Cambridge and Barts. He too had a life-long interest in psychology; before the First War he was a close friend of C.G. Jung and had been deeply influenced by Jung's psychology. There had been a time when Jung had hoped that Nicoll would become a 'disciple' and introduce Jungian psychology to England. However, after serving in the war he came under the influence of Gurdjieff and then Ouspensky. He later formed his own community promoting Gurdjieff's philosophy as the connection with Jung became less central to his life. There is no mention of Godwin and Nicoll having met and yet it seems inconceivable that they didn't know each other. Nicoll writes in a letter to his sister, on 27th June, 1916, from Basra, and this description must surely have been much like Godwin's experience, just a year later.

> Dearest C
>
> It's hot! Nothing metal in the tent can be touched. Water in a pail is so hot you can't put your hand in it. Through these thin canvas roofs the sun cuts like a knife through butter. ... And sick – streams of ambulances all day. I see a hundred cases, I should think, each day – new ones – and have a ward i.e. a few temporary shelters, tents, sheds, filled with eighty others, just lying on the ground. Poor devils, it's terrific, heat-stroke, heat-exhaustion and malaria mostly. One staggers round. We go to Amara next week. The new lot of doctors is gradually taking over ... I give quinine and salts and milk and soda to all my patients and never any fancy mixtures. That and opium. The exhausted men need opium here and they sleep for two days and wake new men. Use the drugs of the country. ... The rest is a matter of cold water, wet sheets, rest and shade, and electric fans and diet. *We have no fans yet after two years occupation.* 'Not foreseen', etc. So the ward gets stifling at night with all the mosquito nets hanging and heat cases get bad again.

Nicoll describes the intense heat, reaching 110-120°F in the shade by midday. The men were dying like flies from heatstroke.

A typical hot day begins with a dawn that comes as a sudden hot yellow behind the motionless palms. A glittering host of dragonflies rises up from the swamps, wheeling and darting after the mosquitoes. In the glowing light, mysterious shapes slink past. They are the camp dogs returning from their sing-song. ... After midday, the world is a blinding glare and the intake of air seems to burn the lungs. A comparative stillness descends on the scene. On the plain, activities cease. Through the double canvas roofing of a tent, the sun beats down like a giant with a leaden club. The temperature in the wards increases. At the worst moments, you feel distinctly that it would be possible, by giving way to something that escapes definition, to go off your head ... It was during the afternoon and evening that heat-stroke occurred in the main, when the humidity of the air began to go up. A great many of the new troops had no idea of the danger of the sun. The Tommy does not estimate a situation very quickly. The attempt to change the main meal of the day to an evening hour did not meet with success and during the afternoon the men would sit bucking away in their tents and refuse to adapt themselves to the idea of a siesta. Moreover, the Tommy is obstinate by nature and does not like to give in. He goes on marching in the sun, even though he feels bad, and the collapse is swift and fatal.[26]

Godwin returned to Durban and there he was admitted to hospital to have his appendix removed on January 5th 1918. He remained in the East until his final return home on January 5th 1919, having sailed home, via the Suez Canal, from Bombay.

During Godwin's time in the East, Rosalind was feeling abandoned and unhappy. He had left just four months before the birth of her second daughter and she could not understand his strong need to fight, as doctors were not compelled to join the forces.

There had been a growing strain in the marriage before he joined up. Rosalind was finding Godwin's 'free and easy ways' increasingly intolerable. During this long period of absence, when Godwin was in India and Mesopotamia, Rosalind had met again a young man called Kenneth Hooper, a friend and admirer from her Hampstead days. They had a brief affair with the result that Rosalind was again pregnant. Jennifer Nan was born in July 1918. One can only imagine how Godwin must have felt on hearing this news, which was accompanied by Rosalind's intention to separate from him.

[26] Nicoll, M., *In Mesopotamia*.

Chapter Nine

Return from The War

And doth not a meeting like this make amends,
For all the long years I've been wand'ring away?
                    Thomas Moore, *Irish Melodies*

Godwin returns home from Bombay at the beginning of 1919.
The marriage has ended and Godwin is shipwrecked. He works
for the Ministry of Pensions, treating patients for shell shock, first
in Cambridge, where he coaches the Trinity rowing eight, and
later at the Denmark Hill Military Neurological Hospital. His
interest in psychology leads him to study psychiatry at the Maud-
sley Hospital. While working there he meets the Swiss psycholo-
gist, C.G. Jung and this meeting is to change the course of his
life.

Godwin's homecoming in January 1919 was a desolate one. He had
been away for most of two years, experiencing the horrors of the front
in the Somme, the magnitude of the loss of life, and coping, as a
surgeon and doctor, with a situation that must have been appalling,
draining, and seemingly hopeless. Then, in Mesopotamia and in
Bombay, different circumstances, but also gruelling, with the mad-
dening heat and desperately inadequate conditions and medical
provisions. One can imagine his exhaustion and disillusion compared
with the young hero who had returned to such welcome and festivi-
ties after the Balkan War. Now there was no welcome and no
reception committee. His second daughter, Chloë, was two years old.
Apart from the six weeks he spent on leave with his family at The
Myrtles, between August and September 1916 he had hardly seen her.

In addition to this, Rosalind had a new baby daughter by another man, and was determined that the marriage should end.

Godwin had been away from his family for fourteen months, from October 1917 to January 1919. The marriage had been rocky before he left with Godwin's roving eye being an increasing bone of contention between them. Rosalind had decided during Godwin's long absence that it was no longer possible for her to continue in the marriage. As a forthright and independent-minded young woman, she was not prepared to accept a relationship in which she was not given Godwin's loyal and undivided attention. Godwin's irrepressible nature was to blame. The break-up was to leave him shipwrecked. He would happily have continued the marriage and would have accepted little Nan as his own daughter, but it was not to be.

Godwin returned home on January 5th. Helton recorded this memorable day in his journal:

> Mary's 68th birthday and she is vigorous and able to do much. Her most welcome present was a marvellous surprise visit at 4 o'clock from Godwin!! We had his cable saying he would sail from Bombay on Nov. 28th but hearing he would return via Capetown, we reckoned he couldn't be here till the end of Jan. He really came via Suez, calling at Aden, Cairo – he went to the Pyramids – Salonika, Malta and Gibraltar. Apart from a cold caught in bathing in very cold water at Gib., he's grandly well and we had a very lively Sunday evening. Nominally, he's home on a month's leave – surely the war office won't send him back *now*! ... Godwin stayed with us till 3 o'clock to-day enjoying everything, even his food! Perhaps he's thinner, but still a Hercules, with abounding energy and life.

We learn then from the diary that Godwin is posted to Cambridge, 'where he has a hospital post on the Eastern Command, just the berth he wanted and applied for. He hopes to coach the first boat.' While he was working in Cambridge, his name appeared almost daily in *The Times* as he was coaching the first Trinity boat in the Bumping Races. Helton comments that 'he is doing pathological work at Cambridge and very glad to be back in the old haunts.'

This is followed by a sad entry, on March 8th, when the news of the break between Godwin and Rosalind reaches him.

> The tragedy came in a letter from Godwin telling us that for a whole year he and Rosalind have been separated not only by

distance, but in home-love and life – that his home-coming in Jan. was terribly sad, and that Ros says her decision is final. It seems the man who first proposed to her saw her while G was at the War, and she listened to him. She has suffered from Godwin's freedom with other girls and finds she cannot give him true real love. The H.G. Wells atmosphere has vitiated their home-life; if it had been based on loyalty and love to Christ; shown in work for others, this might not have happened. Godwin remains true to his wife and entreats us not to say or think anything unkind about her. But, alas! what will they do? I don't believe either has committed any wrong in the eyes of the law, and it will be very hard if G has to support two houses. We can only pray and hope. God knows, and He *loves*. Mary is bearing this blow so bravely.

It seems that Helton was also 'bearing the blow bravely' at a time when divorce was almost unheard of and would certainly, if Godwin had been seen to be the one at fault, have led to the end of his medical career.

Helton records in his next entry, on March 14th, that Mary had written to Rosalind 'begging her to "wake up" and see how sinful it would be to cast off Godwin and go to another man.' Rosalind replies that she is unable to give Godwin 'the real love', and that she believes 'the beloved Jesus will approve her conduct.' (Being a pagan, Rosalind's reference to 'the beloved Jesus' is surely for Mary's benefit.) She writes that she is aware she won't be able to marry again but she assures Mary and Helton that Godwin will be able to see the children whenever he wishes. It is a terrible blow to them both, but Helton reflects that Rosalind: 'knew all about G's free and easy ways with both sexes long before she married him, and as Mary wrote "that is all froth", and has not touched his true love for her.'

While Godwin was in Cambridge, Rosalind's acquaintance with D.H. Lawrence and his wife Frieda developed into a warm friendship. Lawrence had been a part, though only latterly, of their London group, and now he and his wife had decided to go to Italy to live. He suggested to Rosalind that she might like to bring the three little girls with their nurse, Ivy, and to make their home outside Florence. The cost of living was considerably cheaper and Rosalind would then be protected from the inevitable and unpleasant publicity of the divorce.

Presumably, negotiations for the divorce were in progress, although all correspondence between Godwin and Rosalind at this time has been destroyed. However, a letter from Lawrence has survived, in which he is hoping to dissuade the couple from going ahead with the divorce. He writes to Godwin:

Why bother about divorce? The publicity is hateful and there isn't much to gain. One has to learn that love is a secondary thing in life. The first thing is to be a free, proud, single being by oneself: to be oneself free, to let the other be free: to force nothing and not to be forced oneself into anything. Liberty, one's own proud liberty, is worth everything else on earth: something proud within oneself. I believe if you would both come off the personal, emotional, insistent place, and would be each of you self-sufficient and to a degree indifferent or reckless, you would keep a lasting relationship. It's an ignominious thing, either exacting or chasing after love. Love isn't all that important: one's own free soul is first.

Excuse this impertinence. A second thing – you are a great admirer of Whitman, R said. So am I. But I find in his *Calamus and Comrades* one of the clues to a real solution – the new adjustment. I believe in what he calls 'manly love', the real implicit reliance of one man on another; as sacred a unison as marriage: only it must be deeper, more ultimate than emotion and personality, cool separateness and yet the ultimate reliance. For the rest of morality, je m'en fiche. One should keep one's own soul proud and integral, that's all.

Excuse the tirade. I felt you were running your nose against the wall, as I am. I speak on account of the stars I have seen, bumping myself against the eternal obstacles. D.H. Lawrence.

On 23rd April of that year, Godwin had left Cambridge, and Helton records that he had begun work 'at the Denmark Hill Neurological Hospital (Military), just the post for which he is well suited.'

In spite of the sadness of his homecoming, Godwin was able to throw himself into this new experience at Denmark Hill where he was treating patients with shell shock. He, like Maurice Nicoll, and most particularly, Dr Rivers at Craiglockhart, became deeply interested in this, as yet, unexplored and unknown area, in relation to the effects of war. Godwin made a study of the syndrome, with its effect of total withdrawal and dissociation. It seemed to be a unique problem of the First War with the experience of the trenches and the intense trauma of living close to death for many weeks at a time.

As a result of this work he wrote his first book on psychology, *A Study of Psychosis*, which was published later that year. Many doctors had refused to recognize that such a condition as shell-shock existed. Those who showed the typical symptoms were branded as cowards and during the war many had been shot as an example to others. At home, civilians were inclined to adopt the same attitude. As a result, many soldiers became withdrawn and sometimes for many years afterwards were unable to speak of their experiences. For some, the horrors of the war were locked away forever, becoming a barrier between themselves and life.

Godwin's work with those suffering from shell-shock led to his accepting a post at the Maudsley Hospital to study psychiatry. It was there that he first met C.G. Jung on one of Jung's early visits to England. There was an immediate rapport between the two men and for Godwin, who at the time was alone and desperately unhappy, it was a timely meeting.

The divorce case was now in progress, Rosalind was preparing to leave for Italy with the three little girls and Godwin was both lost and adrift. However, the business of the divorce was to linger on for another year, until April 27th 1921. There was a great deal of unpleasant publicity, the papers reaping the rewards of a scandal involving the daughter of a famous Royal Academician. The case was reported in *The Times*, the *Daily Express*, the *Daily News*, the *Daily Mirror* and the *Daily Mail*, with front-page headlines and a picture of Godwin leaving the court with his Counsel. The relationship between Rosalind and Godwin seemed to remain remarkably cordial and Rosalind agreed to provide all the evidence that was necessary for Godwin to file for a divorce. Love letters from Kenneth Hooper to Rosalind were read out and Rosalind herself was described as 'A woman of rather advanced views'. Headlines in the *Daily Mirror* spoke of 'Decree Nisi Against R.A.'s Daughter' and 'Feminist Divorced' while the *Daily Mirror* wrote of 'Ardent Letters from a Friend since Child-hood'. The case was uncontested.

Godwin saw his family off to Florence; the poignant farewell is described by Chloë: 'The bags were packed, The Myrtles was closed up and our little troop set off. Godwin sorrowfully saw us off at Reading station. Bridget's last memory of the parting is of Godwin heroically jumping down on to the railway track to retrieve her dropped doll. She even thinks that she may have dropped it deliber-ately.'

Part Two

Zurich and C.G. Jung

Chapter Ten

Zurich and C.G. Jung

Give sorrow words. The grief that does not speak
Whispers the oer-fraught heart and bids it break.
                    Shakespeare, *Macbeth*, Act 3, v. 22

Godwin visits Dr Jung in Zurich, and the impact of this first visit
decides the future course of his life. He leaves England and his
studies at the Maudsley Hospital to work with Jung in the hope
of becoming an analyst. This momentous event in his life is
marked by a change of name from Godwin to Peter.

The breakdown of his marriage marked an important watershed in
Godwin's life. The despair he felt on his return from war, to find his
world had fallen apart, led to the need to review his life and to find a
new orientation for living.

His war experiences had changed him and he had moved away
from the group of artistic young people who had been such a central
part of his world. The circle of friends had dispersed. Some had died
in the war, among them Edward Thomas and Rupert Brooke. Godwin
felt distanced from those who had not fought in the war, particularly
David Garnett and also to some extent, D.H. Lawrence. He had drifted
away from both the friends and the lifestyle they embodied; the life of
romancing and dreaming no longer satisfied him and he was searching for a new raison d'être without knowing at all what this was.

His extreme extraversion and omnivorous appetite for life, driven
by his attempt to escape the spectre of his father's illness, had caused
him to neglect his own inner world. It was as though all his life, up to

this time, he had been metaphorically climbing the tallest trees, as he did in childhood, to prove to himself that he had not inherited his father's fears.

Godwin's sister Ruth writes that the breakdown of the marriage, 'took Godwin completely by surprise. Perhaps the rift between his two worlds had widened too much? When he finally accepted the break he was, I think, ship-wrecked.' Godwin's meeting with Jung, while he was working with patients suffering from shell-shock at the Maudsley, was one of those life-changing events which occurred at the very moment when he was in such great need of a new direction. Such meetings do not feel like chance, but can be seen, perhaps, as an example of Jung's concept of synchronicity, when an inner happening is somehow reflected in outer reality. Jung used the term to describe 'meaningful coincidences that conventional notions of time and causality cannot explain.'[27]

Just at the moment when Godwin was searching for another path, and also searching for some deeper meaning in relation to his life, the meeting with Dr Jung occurred.

Godwin described his first visit to Dr Jung at his home in Küsnacht. He travelled by train to Zurich Bahnhof, and from there he took the tram out to Küsnacht. It was a momentous meeting. After a lovely summer's day, the evening sun and cloudless blue sky were reflected in the mirror-like surface of Lake Zurich. He walked up the long driveway of Jung's house and rang the doorbell beside the impressive doorway. Something in him recognised that this was a moment of supreme importance in his life. A maid answered the door and Godwin was shown into the Jungs' beautiful living room overlooking the lake. Jung came to greet Godwin and led him into the room next to this, the consulting room, which was to become the temenos (or crucible) for the astonishing transformation that was to take place. Godwin had a strong sense of recognition during this meeting, as though somehow, somewhere, he had always known Dr Jung and that this was a meeting that was to change his life forever. Later in describing the meeting he wrote of the times, when in his search for his path in life, he had been hither and thither seeking in the arts and philosophies of the world, until at last he arrived at Jung's door, and discovered what he had been searching for. It was for him the beginning of the search for and the discovery of his own soul. He

[27] Allan Combs and Mark Holland, 1990, p. xii.

remembered how this first meeting had given him 'some inkling of that vision of the human soul which arrested me in my talk with Dr Jung on a summers evening by the lake of Zurich.'

Godwin had plunged into something that he could not refuse to serve. He discovered in that first meeting with Jung a whole other dimension to life which he had not, until that moment, been consciously aware of. It was a profound experience and this he maintains is the only way to know Jung; he must be not just known, but *experienced*. He writes: 'An academic curiosity alone will never give you the key to the understanding of Jung's ideas.' He quotes Omar Khayyam:

> Myself when young did eagerly frequent
> Doctor and Saint, and heard great Argument
> About it and about: but evermore,
> Came out by the same door where in I went.

This was also my experience until one evening, many years ago, I went to call upon Dr Jung in his home by the edge of the lake of Zurich. He did not try to teach, to illuminate, or to impress. In fact he made no effort of any kind. But what he said had for me the character of a rare natural experience, as though for a moment I had stood on the rim of the known world and looked over the edge into the source from which all living forms had sprung. I entered a door that seemed like many similar doors from which I had emerged unscathed. But this one was the last; I could not leave it. I had been gripped by a view which went to the roots of mental life, and this experience changed the course of my life.[28]

This meeting took place in the summer of 1919, soon after Godwin's return from the war. It wasn't until the following February, when the marriage was without question over, that Godwin returned to Zurich to study with Jung to become an analyst.

Ruth had written of Godwin's profound despair on his return from war to find his life in fragments. In a letter to her at that time, he had written to say that he was seriously considering taking up farming. However, that was not to be – it was to another form of cultivation that he turned his attention: that of his own inner and spiritual world. The alteration brought about by his change of attitude towards the

---

[28] HGB, 1950, p. 19.

spiritual dimension of life must have been dramatic in his very first weeks with Jung in Küsnacht. As early as March of that year (1920), just a month after he had left for Switzerland, he was writing to his father about his 'reverence' for Jesus – a far cry from his neo-pagan days before the war. Helton records:

> Lately I have had two deeply religious, self revealing letters from Godwin, following up talks here ... on 3rd Feb. His reverence for Jesus, and estimate of His teaching, impress me greatly, and I can see he is feeling his way back to all he learnt in our home; but his point of view is strange for he argues our only knowledge of God comes from the unconscious Divine principle in everyone, and not from any revelation. I am asking him whence that principle originates, and refer him to Christ's words about God. But his letters show so much longing for truth and goodness that they give me great hope and joy.

The early weeks with Jung in Zurich led to some profound soul-searching. Perhaps the discovery of his own inner world and the deeper truths that he discovered within himself, as a result of this totally new experience of introversion, was, for Godwin, like a religious experience.

The beauty of the Jung's house, number 228 Seestrasse, Küsnacht, will certainly have contributed to this. The house is large, built in the spacious and generous proportions of the last century. It is set back a long way from the road, which nowadays is a busy thoroughfare, and the long driveway leads to an imposing doorway with Jung's inscription above the door: 'vocatus atque non vocatus Deus aderit' ['Bidden or not bidden, God is present'].

Beside his desk, which is still kept as it was during his life-time, are three large stained glass windows and in the top quarter of each window are mandalas which depict scenes from Christ's Passion. The room is small and the atmosphere is one of contemplation and introversion. It has the atmosphere of a church in that the windows allow light to shine through but there is no view from within to the outer world. It is in this room that Godwin began the journey to gain understanding of his own unconscious, where the momentous adventure in relation to his own inner work, and the work that was to absorb him for the rest of his life, began. This is the small room where earth-shaking events have taken place. Jung's own confrontation with the unconscious was centred here and this was to have far-reaching effects upon all those who worked with him as well as on the outer world at large.

The garden leads down to the edge of the lake, which stretches as far as the eye can see in every direction. Jung's study is filled with beautiful things and one thing in particular is especially fine: a Roman vase with young men and women, painted in black, chasing each other round the outside. In this place one feels connected with the here and now as well as with the past and all that pertains to the archetypal aspects of the unconscious. Though the room is small, one has the impression that here one is in touch with life in its widest possible sense.

It was at this time, during his early days of analysis with Jung, that Godwin was particularly concerned about his father's health. It seems he was now attending to his father's illness instead of running in all directions at once to escape it. Helton recorded in his commonplace book, 'Godwin arrived at 7:30 p.m., well and cheerful. He convinced me that, tho' weak and giddy still, I must get up, and fight it, whatever it costs ...' Some days later he wrote that Godwin was to return to Zurich after his brief visit home, as Rosalind was due to arrive to stay with him in Zurich, together with Bridget. (It had been Godwin's fond hope that Rosalind could be influenced by Jung, just as he had been, and that this would save their marriage. However, this did not prove to be possible.) A month later Helton writes: 'A week on Godwin's prescription, and I'm splendidly better, able to walk freely in the garden and only troubled in stooping and climbing stairs.' Could it be that one of Godwin's unconscious motives for becoming a doctor, and finally an analyst, was related to his father's illness? Did he have a sense that his coming into the world had somehow precipitated the breakdown? He could no longer ignore its reality nor its effect on himself. Helton records in May of that year: 'Godwin told me he had never realised till this visit what I had had to suffer since 1882 is *since his birth*. I express surprise that he should be such a giant in strength, as he has been all his life, remembering my health was so bad the whole 9 months before he was born, but he told me the male generative cells never vary – health has no effect on them. I am so impressed by his sympathy that I shall write a round-robin to my children ...'

After Godwin's initial meeting with Jung, he wrote a letter to his parents saying that he had 'learned more in one hour with Jung than in all my life before.' His sister Ruth wrote of this time that 'He had found a new home and he never moved out of it.'

At Jung's suggestion, Godwin became known to the world in Zurich as 'Peter'. The reason for this is one for conjecture. Some people have suggested that it was an allusion to Peter the Rock, and that Jung saw Peter as the one who would, as his assistant, help him to convey his ideas to a wider public and also, to deal with the more extraverted aspects of his work. However it came to be, it is the name he was known by amongst all those who knew him after 1920. From now on, he will become Peter in this biography also.

In the summer of 1920, Jung held his first seminar in England. This took place at Sennen Cove in Cornwall and it had as its subject a book with the title *Peter Blobb's Dreams*. There was a small attendance of twelve people which Jung enjoyed as he was always happiest in small groups. This seminar was probably arranged by Dr Constance Long (whose association with Jung began as early as 1916, when she translated Jung's *Collected Papers on Analytical Psychology*). We learn from Barbara Hannah[29] that she was assisted in the arrangements for the seminar by 'Peter Baynes', so it would seem that already, after a period of only four or five months, Peter had become a pivotal person in the Jungian world. During this seminar (of which, alas, no written record has survived), everyone stayed together in the same boarding house at Sennen Cove and Jung gave analytical hours as well as his seminar. This became a pattern in Jung's later seminars, where analytical hours combined with seminars and free social contact existed together and the informal contact between Jung's patients became almost as helpful to their development as the analysis they received from him. Such freedom would hardly be possible, or even permitted, to-day.

Another person who attended this first seminar at Sennen Cove was Dr Eleanor Bertine. She was at that time receiving analysis in London with Dr Constance Long. Directly after the seminar she went to Zurich for a year or so to study with Jung, and while Jung was away on holiday, he suggested to his two latest recruits, Peter and Eleanor, that they get together during this period to analyse one another's dreams. A close professional association developed between Peter and Eleanor during this summer.

[29] *Jung, His Life and Work.*

Zurich Fastnacht
(from left to right:) unknown, Mary Bancroft,
Jung, Toni Wolff, Eleanor Bertine, Peter

It must have been at about this time that a photo was taken during
the Zurich Fastnacht, which shows a lighter aspect in relation to the
world of Jungian Psychology. The Zurich Fastnacht is a time when
the Swiss let their hair down, and all their strict Swiss formalities can
be relaxed for a few days. The Jungian group would join together at
this time – analysts and patients all took part – and each dressed up
as a person who was as different from themselves as it was possible
to be, getting a feel for what it would be like to be in that person's
shoes. The group in the photograph are clearly having a wonderful
time: Jung is in the centre, wearing a city gentleman's homburg hat
and on his knees he has both Toni Wolff and Mary Bancroft (another
of his students); he has his arms around them both. The two women
are dressed as femmes fatales in long flowing robes while Heinrich
Fierz sitting to the left of the picture is wearing a suit, and has his
right arm across both of them. To the right is Peter, dressed as a
Persian sultan. He has a string of pearls around his neck and a turban
on his head. On his knee is Eleanor Bertine, a young woman in her
thirties. Peter has his right arm around her and his left arm stretches

across Eleanor and Toni as he grasps the hands of Jung and the other man.

It was during her second visit to Zurich in 1922, that Eleanor met Doctor Esther Harding. This was the English woman with whom she later founded the first Jungian group in New York, together with an old friend of Eleanor's, Kristine Mann. To achieve this was not an easy task as the Freudians were deeply entrenched in New York at that time. It is important to remember how unpopular psychology was, among the general public, at this period and how deeply it was mistrusted. The prejudice in England was possibly even more deeply rooted than it was in America. To become the pioneer in a new and unheard of school of psychology was a risky and also a courageous undertaking.[30] One risked being ostracized both socially and by the medical profession. Few people had heard of Jung, and to admit that one might need psycho-analytic help was deeply shaming. To overcome these difficulties must have required a very remarkable motivation in these early pioneers, all of whom could have followed a far more financially rewarding and generally acceptable form of medical practice.

Peter's sister, Ruth, who was an intensely shy and retiring young woman, was persuaded by him to come to Zurich. She left Victoria on July 30th 1920 and was due to arrive in Zurich the following day. Godwin was supposed to meet her at Zurich Haupt Bahnhof but had apparently been confused about the date of her arrival. He was camping in the mountains with Dr Jung, and Ruth had to make her own way to her hotel in Küsnacht, which she managed without difficulty. Her friend, Olive Hockin, one of Godwin's earlier admirers, was waiting for her there and together they went off walking and painting together.

Soon after her arrival, Helton received a letter from Peter suggesting that Ruth stay a further three or four months so that she could be analysed by Jung. On August 19th Helton writes in his journal:

---

[30] By 1921, Freudian psycho-analysts were already well established in London. The Tavistock Clinic, which was the stronghold of the Freudian analysts at that time, was founded in 1920. Since the split between Freud and Jung in 1912, Jung's path had diverged from Freud's and Jungian psychology was still virtually unknown in London except to a very few people. For this reason, it was a risky business to adopt Jungian psychology as a means of earning ones living.

On 16th long letters from Godwin and Ruth ... suggested she stay 2 or 3 months longer and be analysed by Dr Jung, the extra expense being £80. This is a bombshell, and reading between the lines, we're not sure she really wishes it. Of course, I expected G. would talk to R. about his pet study, but nothing further. I at once posted the letters to Arnold, asking him to send them to Jack that we might be fortified with their opinions. Today A. replies in strong terms, the verdict being 'dead against it': and that is our view. Mary has written very frankly to G and R using these arguments: (1) I always try to fall in with R's wishes, but doubt whether she has not been over-persuaded about this. (2) We remember she is 28, and a woman. (3) For one so healthy and sane as she, is analysis unnecessary and unwise? (4) The system is in its infancy but if later on, she still wishes it, why not consult one of her own sex, e.g. Dr Constance Long? (5) It's serious to lose a term at the Design School, just as she is so successful. (6) And it would upset Enid's plans even if they could let the flat.

Jack wired to say; 'Mistrust whole business, but she old enough to judge best ... writing.' Ruth wrote by return and Helton records:

Ruth writes in a beautiful spirit about our opinions, but says she thinks psychoanalysis may help her, so she has decided to stay, but if she finds she is mistaken she will break away, and come home at once. Of course Dr Jung's discovery may be as epoch-making as Darwin's 'Origin of Species' but it is in its infancy and has to be proved. We can only bow to Ruth's judgement.

So in spite of considerable adverse family pressure, Ruth did indeed stay, and was, like Peter, profoundly affected by Jung's ideas and by her work with him. For her also this was to be a turning point.

Chapter Eleven

Analysis with Jung

No one can free himself from his childhood
Without first generously occupying himself with it.
Jung, *Integration of the Personality*, p. 111

Peter begins his analysis with Jung with the intention of training
to be a Jungian Analyst.

Peter's analysis began in earnest in March 1920. For the first time in his life, he became introspective and totally absorbed by his own inner world and with the wisdom that came to him through his dreams. With Jung's encouragement, he began to keep a daily record of his dreams followed by long and detailed analyses. The dreams together with his own analyses, which were full of self-revelation and also self-castigation, he would show to Jung. To many of them Peter later attached Jung's analysis as an addendum to his own thoughts.

It was during these early days of his analysis with Jung that Peter began to see both his father and his mother in a more compassionate light. He was also beginning to see himself with remarkable honesty, no longer accepting the evaluation of others in terms of his 'devastating popularity'.[31] Very early in their work together Jung appears in Peter's dream and it is clear that a powerful transference has already begun.

He describes a dream in which he finds himself in a battlemented town:

[31] Quote from Eleanor Farjeon, *'Edward Thomas, The Last Four Years.*

A fortuitous stranger in provincial attire appeared. He reminded one of a clothier's advertisement. He had, I fancy, a straw hat and a greenish lounge coat. I asked him where we were and although the place did seem strangely familiar and I knew I had been there before, there was a slight accent of surprise when he said Dymchurch.

The 'fortuitous stranger' leads the way to an inn and from there they find themselves in a cave beyond which, and far below them, is a 'deep crystal green sea. The FS is teaching some young animals to dive and jump into the water.' These animals, a cross between a dog and a bear, are astonishingly graceful, beautiful and clever. In his analysis of his own dream Peter makes the following observation:

> It is now very clear that Jung is the F.S. He is always in the background, felt rather than seen. This is an extraordinarily clever symbol for Jung as an influence rather than a person. He is never inquisitive. He rarely asks any questions of one and seems to be hardly concerned with the actual nexus and incident of one's life. He is essentially a guide. He shows one the way but the actual business of analysis and self-evaluation he has left almost entirely to my own efforts.
>
> Actually, he knows very little about me and seems to care very little and yet his is the influence which directs and probes and allows no vestige of dishonesty, concealment or self-deception to shield one from the most bitter and bleak self-revelation.
>
> Just now he has gone away to Tunis for a three weeks' holiday (he has been gone nearly a week now) leaving one, without specific direction or instructions, to one's own devices and yet I am as deeply under his directing influence as ever. My analysis has certainly improved while he has been gone and it is done as it were under Jung's eye. His eye is, as it were, the Eye of God and every analysis is made provisionally for his inspections, approval or criticism. Therefore this unseen influence of the FS in the dream is really a brilliant symbol of Jung's personality.
>
> The Sea is of course the Universal Unconscious, which under Jung's guidance and inspiration, I am beginning to explore.

A further interesting association which Peter had to this dream was a weekend spent at Dymchurch, a small village in the Kentish Marshes, where he met H.G. Wells for the first time, as well as the man who was to become Peter's great friend and fellow doctor, Maitland Radford. He writes: 'I was so immensely taken or drunk with this new and eager intellectual milieu that I actually refused to go to my brother's wife's funeral [this was the first wife of Peter's brother, Jack], because I wanted to stay.'

There was also a further important association with Dymchurch for Peter. It was the place where Rosalind stayed for a time with the children, while he was in the RAMC in France, and was associated for him with her infidelity. It was as a result of Rosalind's letter to him while he was in Bombay, telling him that she was pregnant by another lover that he had decided to volunteer to go to Persia. He speaks about this as a time when he had lost his 'home anchorage ... This news made me reckless and restless and acted as a centrifugal force.' The fortress wall of his dream reminded him of the old fortress 'with its high buttressed brick walls at Hamadan.' It was as though the devastating news of the loss of his wife and home base had blown him, like the chance wind of destiny, to strange and exotic lands, which he associates with the 'fortuitous landing' in his dream. Of course, it was because he had in reality lost his anchorage and his way in life, and was in effect 'shipwrecked' that 'destiny' had blown him to Jung, the 'fortuitous stranger'.

This must have been an important dream in the early part of Peter's analysis, at a time when Jung had become for him like 'the eye of God' and there is a sense also of his feeling of loss and abandonment while Jung was away for his three week holiday.

The divorce proceedings were now at their height and Peter was still experiencing his loss and hurt in relation to Rosalind but was also full of self-recrimination and regrets. This is expressed in a dream he had on March 16th 1920. It is interesting at this early stage of the work, while he is analysing with Jung, to see how he approaches a dream. The journal in which he recorded and analysed his dreams is closely written in a fine legible hand, with pen and ink. It is lined and A4 size, but having been through the fire that occurred in 1937 which razed his house to the ground, it is badly singed round the edges and parts are not legible.

I am in a downstairs room of my new house. Jack [Peter's brother] is showing me a little book with a sort of chocolate brown cover. He thinks I have a sister volume somewhere that belongs to him. There are all sorts of odd things missing that I cannot find, fishing rods and all sorts of trifles. I go to find R [Rosalind] to worry her about them. I cannot find her and suppose she is in the W.C. Then I go to her bedroom where there are two separate single beds standing apart (not a large double one as we always had), and there of course I find her suckling the infant (that is not mine). I have a rebellious sense of shame and do not embrace her or greet her but start at once asking her where all these things are that I am missing. I go over towards the window where she is sitting on the sofa and I am vexed to find the floor all wet and soiled from splashings where she has bathed the children. I cannot find a place to sit down so go across and sit on the bed – away from the window – which I take to be mine.

In his analysis of this dream Peter writes that this

deals with my present relationship to R. R's untidiness and rather sluttish, unorganized house keeping. Things are always untidy and I never know where to find my things. Jack has always condemned R since the rupture. He takes the obvious conventional point of view and cannot understand my own feeling of tenderness to R and my own sense of responsibility for the disaster. He advocates harsh measures, stopping supplies etc. etc.

When I look for R I protect myself from my own sense of guilt by accusing her of untidiness and sluttish mess. I do not greet her or show her any love or tenderness. I am selfish, harassed and brutal. She is entirely occupied with her maternal duties and is silent but sorrowful. She is a tragic figure in the dream. This represents my real feeling about her. The two single beds are symbolic of separation. She permits a certain friendship and intimacy but she will no longer be my lover and wife. I have forfeited that privilege forever. Through my wild riding after erotic conquests I have fatally bruised [?] the eternal mother ideal of pure love and she can never accept me again as her lover. She is the fruitful creative energy that demands loyalty, service and loving comradeship. This is the fine human ideal of love sanctioned by the race and I went off on my erotic charger [this refers to a previous dream], and broke this faith and trust and so I forfeit my place by her side and leave her alone to cope with all the cares and responsibilities of motherhood.

This is the tragedy I must live with all my life. It is my burden of guilt.

All the other conscious reasons that I can produce to charge her with; her untidiness, my losses, her own faults, sink to nothing in comparison with my deep spiritual failure as a faithless husband who wildly sacrificed and betrayed the golden gift of love for mere erotic sensations.

The tragedy is not completed for her shame as well as mine must be trumpeted to the world in this loathsome divorce case. Her shame is mine but she will have to bear the brunt of it before society. This shame that she consents to bear is the final sacrifice of the love that she so passionately gave to me.

Thus the first dream [about the erotic charger which runs away with him] gains a new significance for it is now clear that my success in my new life, my ideal of fruitfulness, can only come to pass by this leaping over the dangerous cliff of divorce and bruising and hurting the maternal ideal love which R stands for.

The erotic courser first destroys my marriage and kills the wonderful ideal love that R gave me and then finally must itself be destroyed before the ideal mother image can be reborn from the wreckage. This new ideal image must be bruised and injured by the terrible injury to R and the tragedy of her love of which I am guilty.

A soul can never free itself or forget the sorrow it has brought to Woman.

The dream of the erotic charger occurred early in his analysis and it concerns the central problem which continued to beset him throughout his life. In this dream he is riding a spirited horse. He is sitting much further back on the horse than is normal and the reins are unusually long. They seem to be driving rather than riding reins. Something startles the horse and as the horse springs forward the reins are pulled out of Peter's hands. By standing up in the stirrups he manages to catch the reins and regain control of the horse. 'I had nearly got him under control when we came to the most treacherous bit of country I have ever seen. At the bottom of the incline we were heading down was a chasm or rift and in this chasm there appeared to be a gigantic pipe, either drains or water supply. It was a frightful place to jump. I pulled him off that and went through what seemed a perilous and broken traverse to the left over the stream.' Peter manages to pull the horse to a halt but he was still wild and nervy and too anxious to be able to jump the stony ford with its slippery stones. 'While I realized the predicament he went madly ahead and crashed over a narrow ledge on to the rocks below. I got up unhurt but I could see the horse was done for. He was just a mass of shapeless broken limbs.' At this point, the horse is magically transformed into the maternal figure of an Eve-like woman to whom he is both solicitous and tender as he asks if she is hurt.

The horse reminds him of the war, when he had ridden a great deal. He sees himself in this dream riding 'loosely and carelessly' and too far back to have total mastery of the animal. 'Before I can regain control we are among all sorts of dangers, chasms, rocks, slippery declivities and precipitous rocky ledges.

> The horse is the erotic symbol. One rides a horse and a man rides a woman. I have often used the metaphor ... This wild and eager erotic instinct is my unbroken stallion. I see a tempting women and before I know what has happened I am wondering if she is looking for a lover and I follow her. It is this uncontrolled complex which suddenly takes the bit between its teeth and careers away with the ego who is quite incapable of resistance, that lands me into so many false and dangerous situations ...

> Finally, after negotiating many perilous and break-neck obstacles my erotic uncontrollable mount dashes over a precipitous ledge and is smashed hopelessly. But I (that is my true ego) am hardly injured at all, only frightened. Then behold out of the ruin of my horse arises the original primaeval Eve, the archaic mother-image. The symbol of fruitfulness.

> My attitude to this divine creature is at once tender and solicitous. She leans on me and I am eager to cherish her. There is no lust or eroticism ... She is a venerated spiritual being, a comrade, not a sensual instrument. This is the fore-shadowing of Victory. The rule of the erotic sensual instinct is finished. Out of the ashes of this fire shall arise the phoenix bird of the real spiritual vision of woman, the divine mother of the race, the comrade of man. This image links up to the M [mother] complex. I recently said to her [i.e. Peter's mother] in a letter, 'Only that man has a respect and reverence for Woman who sees in the woman he loves not an erotic mistress but the mother of his children.' He sees the huge pipe that lay at the bottom of the gorge as 'a symbol of the Continuity of Life by sexual fruitfulness, which is a real vital deterrent to eroticism.' He saw this as an important dream which

was showing the way towards a 'new orientation away from erotic conquests to a true creative ideal.'

It was a dream he continued to refer to as his analysis progressed.

Very much later in his analysis, Peter dreamed another dream which this time refers directly to Jung, who then changes from Jung into his father. One wonders whether the FS of the previous dream could refer to the Father Symbol as well as to the Fortuitous Stranger. Jung had become the father Peter had longed for, strong, wise and supporting, the person his own father could never be.

The following dream, which he had after his journey with Jung to Africa shows clearly how Jung and Father had become interchangeable in Peter's unconscious mind.

> There was a large meeting and Jung was lecturing and there was a sympathetic atmosphere. I was quite near the platform to the left of Jung. There had previously been some sort of discussion about a place we had visited together in Africa and someone suggested Cherry Common. I turned this down as incorrect. Eventually agreeing that the place was Loughborough. In his lecture Jung made an allusion (possibly about agriculture). In any case I contributed so that he would hear it as the word Lough, [i.e. Love] which I knew was a sort of witty allusion, a parable of association which he would see but nobody else. He, in his lecture picked up the allusion, smiled somewhat self-consciously and said 'yes Loughborough, quite.' I felt embarrassed at causing this interruption in a rather formal occasion.

> Then Jung became my father and he was still lecturing. Suddenly he lost the thread of what he was saying and looking ill and distressed he came over to the side where I was. I thought 'he has got one of his agoraphobic attacks in this big hall' and wondered at his courage in taking on such a big thing.

> I told him to lay his head down on my knee and pulled him down in order to get the blood back into his head. He was sweating profusely. I felt as I helped him down that he was quite wet under the armpits.

> I think after a bit he pulled himself together and went on. The audience remained quiet and sympathetic. I felt extremely tender and warm to my father.

In his analysis of this dream, Peter writes:

I am a man with two fathers. As Jung's son I have some meaning and importance, but as the son of my father I am given a problem. There are certain times when I simply have to fly to get away from a situation ... It is almost a state of panic. When I have lectured there are times when I have been so panic-stricken that I thought I might break down. I sweat all over and my head sings with fear. Clearly the dream tells me this is my particular version of my father's phobia. Loughborough is linked to P's apprenticeship, [Pat Erskine, who was an engineering student in Loughborough]. I have now served two spells of apprenticeship and I am still hanging on to my father as my father could never leave go of his mother. My sympathy with my father comes from the fact that we both suffer from the same curse. The dream tells me that the inner necessity of my dependence on Jung comes from the fact that I associate my powerful weakness with my father and therefore I worship Jung's strength. He is the father who can support the son and heal the father weakness with his strength. I can lose sight of the stigma of my own inheritance by identifying myself with Jung's strength.

Now I take him on my knee and can realise the fight he put up from within. This is the real reconciliation. I have never understood him until now.

So, a new understanding had begun for the father he could now feel compassion towards, rather than the 'father weakness' he must escape from.

The dreams he had in the early part of his analysis also suggest the possibility of a new understanding in relation to his mother. He experienced his mother as a passionate, forceful and also a somewhat overpowering person. In discussing another dream, in which his mother appears, he makes the following comments. His mother, in the dream, has drawn a figure, and Peter writes:

This question of woman's suffering through man's unconscious Eros is the theme of the dream of my mother. Even in the dream I recognized the phallus which she drew. It means that because she lacked a full and passionate sex-relation with my father, her passionateness went to us children which we of course could not return. She yearned silently for the love that was denied and this created the mother-complex in Jack and me which has dominated our lives. This lets a window into the past. My mother's erotic nature must always have been starved as regards the personal relationship. She was made by the absolute nature of marriage to forego the full love experience. Thus her love life was forced always into the impersonal or racial side – thus to the Father-God on the one side and to her sons on the other.

Perhaps Mrs Bax, who had been such a central person in enabling Peter to follow his destiny, had a similar personality to his mother, but his criticisms of her are much more severe. He comments that 'she got her talons into the souls of her sons and feeds upon them like a vulture. She drains the cup of self-glory to the full.' This sounds like astonishing ingratitude, but he reaches a more benevolent view of her later on. While he was receiving his analysis with Jung, he wrote in his journal:

> I wrote a letter to Mrs Bax yesterday under the compelling desire to express my gratitude and to show her what fruit her benevolent influence was beginning to bear. I even used the phrase 'spiritual foster-mother'. So that is another complex indicator in the slender dream fabric. Her interest in me was as far as I know entirely maternal but this was probably a cover for an unconscious erotic attachment.

Did some of Peter's 'mother complex' become transferred onto Mrs Bax when she adopted a maternal role towards him? Perhaps it was less risky to express negative sentiments in relation to her rather than towards his own powerful mother? He makes further comments about Mrs Bax at this time.

> When my father refused to go on with my Cambridge education after my first year's extravagance, my friendship with Arnold Bax won me an entrée into the lavish maternal heart of Mrs Bax. She has been ever since my spiritual foster-mother. The youngish wife (about 40 at the time, but still young and good looking) of a rich old man, she opened the purse-strings of her husband and financed the whole of my education until I was qualified. This is of course the pedestal of my whole career. Without her help I should have returned to the slime of business life from which she helped me to emerge or I might even have gone on the stage.

The question of money arises again in relation to a dream, during the period that Jung is away on holiday in Tunis. One might wonder how Peter was supporting himself during this period of study with Jung and what his financial responsibilities were in relation to his family, who were now living in Florence. It appears that the date being March 1920, just over a year since his return from the war, he would still be drawing pay from the Ministry of Pensions. While working with shell-shocked patients at the Maudsley, he had asked for leave from the Ministry of Pensions to go to Zurich to work with Jung and had received their consent.

In his analysis of his own dreams, at this period, he is unremittingly hard on himself, as well as on others. He sees himself and his motives in the worst possible light. He compares himself to dream figures who are shamelessly exploiting their own gifts and the women who love them, to achieve their own ambitious and erotic ends. In contrast to this worldly and immoral aspect the figure of Edward Thomas is recalled by a dream image. Thomas had died tragically in the war, and the poems he wrote during the war gained him a place as one of Britain's leading poets. Peter recalls him as:

> The delicate poet who was killed in the war. He was my friend. In my early, eager innocence I tried amateurishly to cure his Neurasthenia by suggestion. I often reproached myself for taking a fee for my childish effort for of course I did not cure him.
>
> He was a generous, witty comrade and in his soul he was saintly. He saw deeply into the hearts and souls of men for he too had known the clutch of the erotic complex and this was the source of his neurosis.
>
> His face was Christ-like and it is his link with Christ the Lover of Man that brings his sorrowful, pitiful soul into his eyes [this also refers to the dream image].

This association with the delicate and tragic poet links Peter to his own innocence and the happiness he experienced in childhood, in the following reflections. He remembers his home, Briar Lea, their horse, Pat, quietly munching hay in the stable and "the peaceful air of home and silent woods, fragrant hay and the rich comfortable countryside as contrast to the fever and rush and stupidity of life.' In these nostalgic reflections he writes of Rosalind, with whom he is still totally in love, and suffering terrible regrets over the loss of her. The happy memories 'linked and associated with Rosalind who I taught to ride on old Pat. Pictures of her straddling Pat, skirt about her knees, bumping exquisitely along Nib-nib-nib on the quiet Berkshire roads;

fragrant, pastoral, a bed for day-dreams and happy songs; hay-making, love-making. Sweet-smelling food ...' and so on. These reflections, arising out of a dream of a cow, quietly chewing the cud in the stable at Briar Lea, feel like a return to the time that was 'innocent, happy, spiritually free'. He speaks of 'a return to the golden-age of innocence' but continues, 'for the innocence of maturity and old age rests upon deep spiritual insight.' These seem like astonishingly mature reflections in a young man who was still only thirty-seven years old.

Although during this time of intense self-analysis Peter blamed himself for the breakdown of his marriage to Rosalind, his behaviour can also be seen as a product of the zeitgeist of that period. The artistic circles and intelligentsia that were linked to The Fabian Society and the women's movement led by Mrs Pankhurst, were a reaction to the strict morality and oppression of women which prevailed in Victorian England. As always, the pendulum swung too far in the other direction and there was a new morality which believed in free love. This gave those who were within these circles permission to cut across the conventions of the time. This spirit was also alive in Zurich, where the prevailing moral code was even more rigid than that in England. The old moral values were being questioned in the circle surrounding Jung, where individuation and self-fulfilment were more important than following the conventions.

This new morality had been the world to which both Peter and Rosalind had belonged and which Peter was now questioning. He recognised that there was a side to him that looked for and valued loyalty and family stability more than unbridled freedom. Peter also recognised with devastating clarity that Rosalind's infidelity was the result of his own erotic incontinence: 'The ghastly truth has to be faced and recorded that it was this dawning recognition of my erotic worthlessness and spiritual rottenness, in Rosalind's soul, that made her idol also turn to powder and she refused further allegiance to a male parasite and she accepted and invited the first attractive and convenient lover that came to hand.'

His hard attitude towards himself is symbolised for him also by his relationship with his father-in-law, Sir Hamo Thornycroft, who as a dream figure stood for the epitome of worldly success, being one of the foremost sculptors in England. He comments that their relationship had been warm and friendly until the 'rupture' and that he had not heard from him since. He felt that he was being blamed by Sir Hamo for Rosalind's unhappiness.

These self-blaming and profoundly self-critical reflections were written in the absence of Jung, but as it were, with the 'Eye of God' over-seeing what he wrote. It is a stark contrast to the young man who, before the War, had known only popularity and success. The 'passive hostility' he was experiencing from his father-in-law reflected his own profoundly self-critical attitude at this time, and his experience, possibly for the first time in his life, of real rejection. Jung's affirmation and acceptance seems, therefore, to have been crucially important at this time of soul-searching.

Perhaps the aspect of this relationship to Jung which he experienced as disinterested and unpossessive (even, he felt, on a personal level 'uninterested'), but also entirely accepting, allowed him, at this period of intense self-analysis, to look at himself with a remarkable and almost terrifying honesty. How much had he been prostituting his gifts and using women, in order to gain popularity and worldly success, he asks himself. One very difficult psychological truth which came to him, through the analysis of a dream concerning Rosalind, was his difficulty in desiring her as a lover once she had become a mother. He recognised an infantile aspect of himself, which was still caught up in the mother complex, and was therefore needing Rosalind to mother him. The 'mother' cannot also be the lover. While he was unconscious of this problem, his erotic interest went elsewhere and caused havoc.

Much had happened during the war that was now, possibly, giving rise to this soul-searching. In a dream which has associations with India, he recalls his time there between 1917 and 1918. 'It was in Bombay that I learnt of R's infidelity by letter and it was this that made me reckless and heedless and here it was that my erotic proclivities had such a time of it.' He writes of the life of an officer in the heat of India, where betting, horse-racing and polo playing, large quantities of alcohol together with the pursuit of beautiful women, formed the pattern for what he refers to as his 'reckless and heedless' life-style. He writes; 'the effect of military life in India upon a young fellow is notorious. Amorous affairs and eroticism generally is the frankly acknowledged aim of life. English people are quickly changed into indolent sensualists and the whole object in life is to have a good time.'

He associated these erotic adventures with contemporary events: he was much taken up at that time with a young woman whose name was Daphne (Seagrave). She had extremely influential social connections and through her Peter had, during the previous year in London, mixed with the wealthy and aristocratic circle with whom she was associated. He describes her as 'an elegant, idle, pleasure-seeking beauty who is only suited to a rich aristocrat who can devote his life to horses, clubs, polo and fine women.' Perhaps she was still a part of the 'reckless and heedless' excesses into which he was thrown after Rosalind's rejection of him. He goes on to say that: 'The D complex links up to this as another variant of the sáme theme. The aftermath as it were of the Indian tropical injection.' He depicts 'D' as a superficial, social butterfly who is in no way either an intellectual or spiritual companion, and yet to whom, erotically, he is hopelessly and slavishly attracted, to the extent that he does, at one point (perhaps because there could have been a possibility of pregnancy), write to her a proposal of marriage.

He is locked in conflict at this time between his instinctive drives and his quest for a more conscious standpoint in relation to his life. After much soul searching and self-analysis, he comes to the conclusion that a marriage to Daphne would prove to be disastrous: 'One can only infer that inherent qualities in me that made marriage impossible with the intellectually and spiritually and physically ideal mate, Rosalind, how much more certainly will wreck an alliance with the indolent, primitive-minded infant, Daphne.'

His relationship to Daphne and her family went back to his time at Cambridge. Daphne's father had been the tutor and professor of Zoology from Peter's Cambridge days: 'the gateway to knowledge' he had so deeply respected. At the time that Peter had been a frequent visitor to their home Daphne was still a little girl. It was during her coming out season in London in 1919 that Peter came across her again and was at once strongly attracted by her beauty. This relationship was violently opposed by Daphne's mother who had schemes for a brilliant match for her daughter, and who also was jealous of Peter's attraction to her daughter: 'I was probably a strong contributory cause in this awakening of primitive female jealousy in the mother against the daughter because I was one of her favourite courtiers in a very *comme il faut*[32] sense in the Cambridge days.'

---

[32] Acceptable, literally, 'as it should be'.

Jung's influence on Peter was all-embracing and as he came to understand more about his own psychology, and what had led to his tendency towards what he saw as 'erotic incontinence', so he also came to regard Jung as the guide, and the model for complete inner integrity that he wanted to emulate. His comments about Jung give an indication of how powerfully the transference to Jung was affecting him during these first months of their work together. He discusses a dream in which Bernard Shaw figures. Shaw was a man he admired; whom he had both heard speak and read thoroughly, though he had never actually met him. He dreams that he was 'sitting just behind Bernard Shaw who is holding a large lute-like instrument between his knees like a 'cello. It had a very massive complicated neck with several manuals (as it were). Clearly an instrument of great range.

> Shaw had come there to give a lecture on something and I thought it odd that here he was deliberately tuning his lute. I suppose this is a new stunt, a sort of lecture recitative. As he tunes his lute I notice the tone is very rich (very clear).

> Later, I am sitting on the left of Shaw at a round table (eventually I am facing him). I am at first embarrassed and do not speak clearly, then I say something witty which tickles Shaw immensely. He laughs immoderately and I am very gratified. Then I go on to give him a really sound and clever description of Jung's introvert and extravert types. At once Shaw is restless. He jumps up and fetches something from his coat hanging on a peg and politely pretends to listen but all the time is doing something else. I want to prove to him that he is a moral extravert.

In discussing the dream, he compares Shaw's extraversion to Jung's introversion:

> Jung dives in while Shaw leaps out. Moral order is the dynamic source of both energies but with Shaw the intimate linking of the moral constellation with his own ego-complex results in the insistent extrovert demand to proclaim and publish his ego which to him is identical with the compelling moral purpose. While with Jung, the subjective moral principle is an absolute moral factor and although it is also linked up to his own ego this is expressed in a much more limited sense in the regulation of his own personal life. His moral purpose is his almost mystical absorption in

Science, his passionate determination to establish scientific truth in psychology, which is the most intimately revealing and subjective department of knowledge. His main, mastering purpose is to add to human knowledge by probing the abysmal depths of the human soul. His desire for personal recognition is quite secondary to his eager longing for the recognition of his work, i.e. of its absolute value as an undying structure of knowledge, an aspect of absolute Truth ...

In earlier times Shaw would have been a crusader or an uncompromising Prince of the Church. Perhaps even an inquisitor. While Jung would have been a mystical recluse either canonized as a Saint or crucified as a martyr to truth.

In this first period of analysis with Jung and also his own self-analysis, there was a sense of his profound regret at what had gone wrong in his life. As well as severe self-chastisement, there was a courageous attempt to understand himself. The process of introspection was absorbing him totally. As a result, he saw himself becoming ponderous, heavy and a bore to his friends, as is so often the case with a new 'convert': 'In my recent self-analytical and moral pre-occupation, I have burdened my poor friends with long and probably dull descriptions of psychological material just as I bored Shaw in my dream. My letters were as a rule witty and sparkling and lively; now they are dull and morally pre-occupied. This is the hobble-dehoy stage of the new orientation the ego has recently adopted.'

Peter was altogether absorbed with his desire, at this stage, to emulate Jung. He writes: 'Jung stands for the parting of the ways at this rebirth of my soul.' He dreams of a young man named Coleman, the model of industry and propriety, who worked alongside him as clerk at the Baynes family business during Peter's adolescence. Coleman 'is therefore associated in time with my first wayward attempts at independence. Adolescent manhood was in my blood. I was straining at the familial leash. It was the opening phase of independent development. The first tentative excursion away from the strict moral and religious atmosphere that suffocated me at home.'

Coleman's industry and painstaking conscientiousness was something Peter admired but did not want to emulate. It was Coleman, on the other hand, who was the 'slavish' admirer of the seventeen-year-old Godwin. He asks himself: why, at this moment in his analysis, does Coleman appear in his dream? He makes a point by point comparison between himself and the young man, which is a revealing account of how he saw himself.

> Coleman was industrious, I was idle. Coleman's work was thorough, mine was amateurish and inaccurate. His writing was excellent, mine was not. (N.B. we were both clerks.) He was punctual, I was dilatory. He was ugly, unprepossessing and oddly clothed. I was rather smart and good-looking. He was morally a rock, I was shifting sand. He kept his position in the office by hardwork and efficiency. I was the privileged son of the 'boss'. He was of a poor hard-working family. I was the son of a well-to-do merchant.

Peter ends this comparison by speaking of the contrast between 'the good hard-working boy, the pride and mainstay of his family, and the over-prodigal son'.

In the dream he is discussing, it is the 'good' industrious hardworking boy who is attracting the attention and confirmation of Jung while Peter is alone and neglected in the next room. He sees a double significance in this. He expresses the belief that on the one hand, only by his undivided, conscientious application to the objective analysis of himself can he attain Jung's affirmation, but also change from the impulsive, intuitive, extravert personality that has ruled until now, with sometimes disastrous consequences. On the other hand, he also associates himself with the almost slavish admiration that Coleman had for Godwin. He recognises the significance of this relationship after having analysed his dream in a depth that covers many pages, assisted by Jung himself. He likens himself, in his attitude to Jung, to 'Coleman's quite spontaneous attachment and subservience to me. He always wished to serve me and do things for me although I gave nothing in return. There was a sort of dog-like faithfulness and attachment, a dumb craving for my love. This note of parasitism I was quite blind to when I first analysed this dream. I only saw my view of him without reading the vital thing which was his attitude to me.'

His final comment about his analysis of this dream is also revealing:

> When I start I certainly have no conscious notion of what direction the analysis will take.

As in recording dreams and the after impressions of talking with Jung, it is as if there were an unrolling of meaning and significance. The very act of writing seems to be the stimulus that calls up the required associations and gathers the meaning of the dream as it gains in mobility and impetus. This is the extravert method of utterances and expressions.

As his analysis progresses with Jung, his sense of his own worthlessness becomes increasingly pronounced along with regret in relation to the situation his own impulsiveness has landed him in. Jung is, for him, his conscience and his ultimate judge. It feels to him as though he is experiencing a real Faustian inner conflict with the devil himself.

He has a dream in which his face is being explored in all its details and contours by the hands of a blind man. Peter's analysis of this dream further illuminates his relationship with Jung.

The blind are no longer deceived by the masks that men assume to hide their true selves. Their perceptions are subtler, more intuitive than are those that rely on visual appearances. Their fingers acquire a sensitiveness and a quickness of apprehension which is on quite a finer nerve (?) than the tactile sensations of a person whose main avenue of perception is vision. There is something uncanny and almost abnormal in this revealing touch of a blind man's fingers. There is a strong analogy between these quick sensitive appraising fingers and the informing penetrating eye of the psycho-analyst (Epicutic) [?].

Indeed in this dream the two are identical. Nothing can be hidden from those searching fingers. Every tell-tale line and pouch and fleshy protuberance will carry its message of my true inner nature. This is the fear of the analyst. Can I show Jung all the intimate, revealing and terrible contents of my soul? Must he read this very book that I am writing in now? Must the soul stand utterly naked, stripped off every vestige of honour and decency and fair-seeming?

I know well the outlines and changes in my own face. I can see the alteration in it when the sensual instincts are uppermost. I have seen the ape in my own eyes. Fire blazing in my cheek.

The blind man's fingers will see all that my soul contains. D used to say my face was the face of an innocent boy but my nose was sophisticated and really wicked. This is the sensual link which flies back to me when I feel the fingers going over my nose again. I am frightened because now I know that he knows and I shall not be permitted to pass (viz, that Jung will abandon the analysis because he realizes I am worthless material and can never be fitted to be an analyst).'

Later he adds: 'The nose is the perceptive organ, e.g. the dog. I am the irrational perceptor. My nose is my psychological weak spot.' Peter continues that the dream deals 'with a deeper plane of the spiritual conflict. Only the aftermath of the erotic battle is in evidence and the battle is rather between the primal forces of good and evil.'

It is important to remember that at the time Peter was having these dreams and was engaged in this self-analysis, each of which seemed to afford him fresh revelations, he had been in analysis with Jung for only one month. He first went to work with Jung in February 1920, and these dreams seemed to be coming every night throughout March. The depth of his own understanding and also his grasp of the significance of symbols, after such a short time, are truly astonishing.

By 1921, Peter was already working alongside Jung, as an analyst. He was one of three assistant analysts working together with Jung. The other two were Jung's wife, Emma, and the woman who had such a profound influence on Jung's life and who had helped him through his 'confrontation with the unconscious' between 1912 and 1914, Toni Wolff.

Ruth gives a description of Peter's life in Küsnacht at the time she was having her own analysis with Jung.

> Godwin's days were full. Seeing patients in the mornings and working on his translation of Jung's Psychological Types in the afternoons. In the evenings he went to Jung's house to discuss questions connected with his patients, also to check his translation to make sure that he had grasped the full meaning.
>
> This translation was a stiff bit of work. It is a long time ago, but I think I remember Godwin telling me that Psychological Types was written in a difficult and learned German, and that Jung said it was necessary to use this language for a scientific book, in Germany anyhow.
>
> Some evenings we would go and swim in the lake from the Jungs' boathouse. Godwin would make them nervous when he dived off the boathouse roof into rather shallow water, but he was an expert diver. Other evenings we went up to the hills behind to

throw a boomerang. Godwin always found time, every day, to stand at the open window and sing a few scales at the top of his voice. And a Swiss gentleman, down the road spent an hour every day, practising on some large wind instrument, but they chose different times!

One evening we went into Zurich for a marvellous performance of *Die Meistersinger* in the Zurich Opera House. We had to book well ahead to get two of the very few seats into which Godwin could pack his long legs.

It was at this period that Peter was to become Jung's chief assistant and by now a warm relationship had developed between them. It was as though Jung recognised in Peter a man of stature who was, in terms of his personality type, his exact opposite. As a complement to one another, they each had qualities that were needed and admired by the other. Jung in his extreme introversion needed Peter's extraversion to create a Jungian community. Jung's typology, as an introverted, intuitive, thinking type, was almost diametrically opposite to Peter's, which was an extravert, feeling, intuitive. Jung introduced Peter to the possibility of a rich inner life. He enabled him to find a powerful source of experience from within himself instead of relying on other people and outer life to give him his sense of himself.

Peter was learning to trust and respect this inner life and his very strong intuitive capacity. The 'nose' that he speaks of disparagingly in his dream of the blind man, as the indicator of his sensuality, in fact represents a valuable intuitive possibility for sensing what is not visible or apparent to the immediate senses. It is a guide for 'knowing' what is not yet consciously known or visible, but is just around the corner. Just as a dog with its acute sense of smell can get a 'scent' of what is to come, and can follow the scent to discover what he is after, Peter was learning at this time to trust his own, considerable, intuitive capacities as well as to value his own unconscious processes. He writes about his method of recording his dreams:

> While I am dressing and breakfasting I do not give a thought to the dreams but when I come to write them down they are unfolded quite faithfully from beginning to end.
>
> The same process holds good for the records of Jung's talks. I just listen then go away without any further concentration; when I write my impressions they unfold like a cinema film. In both cases I rely on a faithful subconscious record.

Jung, with his profound introversion, relied on Peter to deal with the extraverted aspect of his work; that of bringing people together, of providing a base and a welcome for the English-speaking people who came to Zurich to study with Jung, and executing the practical arrangements for the Jungian congresses and seminars. Later, he relied on Godwin to see to the practical details of organising the expedition which they made together to East Africa.

Barbara Hannah, in her book, *Jung, His life and Work*, speaks of the relationship between Jung and Peter:

> One of the first English doctors to come to Jung in Zurich was Godwin Baynes (always called Peter), who soon realised the value of Jungian psychology and, in spite of a rather chequered career, devoted his whole life to it, until his death during World War 2. He was a tall man, even a few inches taller than Jung, a university 'rowing blue', and outstanding in sport and games. He came to Jung originally because his first marriage had run on the rocks while he was in service abroad. One of the first tasks he undertook was the translation of *Psychological Types* into English, so that it was able to appear in 1923, soon after the first German publication, in 1920. Since Peter Baynes did not, at that time, know German very well, his translation of this volume has the advantage of being the only translation of any of Jung's books into any language that Jung himself went through word for word.
>
> Peter Baynes was an extravert and an extremely friendly person; he very soon made himself at home in Zurich. Emma Jung and Toni Wolff were particularly fond of him, and before long he began his first term as Jung's assistant. In many ways he was the best assistant Jung ever had, for he was singularly free of a certain jealousy and a sense of inferiority that working with an outstanding man like Jung unfortunately seems to breed in other men, even those considerably younger. Baynes was a medical doctor but free of the usual medical prejudices and limitations. He never for a moment wanted to go 'beyond Jung', a phrase one hears too often nowadays, though almost always from young men who are still far from beginning to understand where Jung stood or who he was. This period as assistant was the first of several during all of which Peter Baynes was able to be of great aid to Jung in his overburdened practice.

Peter Baynes once told me that beyond doubt his true vocation was to be Jung's assistant, but his extraverted, open nature constantly involved him in other plans. As a result, he was always torn between England and Switzerland, and even spent some time in America. His spells as Jung's assistant were therefore never of very long duration.[33]

Peter's daughter Bridget was suffering from severe bouts of bronchitis and it was considered that the pure air of Switzerland would help her, so during the school holidays in the summer of 1924, when Bridget was eight years old, she stayed with Peter at his house, which was on the other side of the Zurichsee from the Jungs, and while she was there she also stayed with the Jungs in Küsnacht. She describes her memories of the Jung household:

> When I was eight years old I used to call him Papa Jung. He liked children and was always with his own 5 taking part in family outings and presiding at mealtimes.
>
> The house was striking, like a castle, or so it appeared to me, because it was dominated by a central pointed tower. A flower bordered path led to the front door. There was an arched gate where Lili Jung and I boarded a tramcar for a nearby school every day. I remember most the lovely dolls Lili had and their beautiful Swiss clothes. As a girl an imitation liberty bodice which had real button holes and suspenders was treasured by me for many years, and I don't really know whether it was originally lost and found and wickedly not returned by me to Lili. The lawns were shaded by trees where we played; best of all the southern side of the house faced the lake and we could walk down to the water's edge where there was a real harbour for the two boats which were housed in their own boathouse. This afforded us great bathing facilities and the older Jung children were tremendous swimmers. Beyond this the reeds extended out into the lake and unaccountably, a narrow footpath among them led to a round or many-sided hut hung with strange oriental objects. Many of these resembled hanging plates because their colourful patterns all revolved around a central point. These were Mandalas which possessed some 'healing' power; to me ... they were obviously magic. It was like a magician's hideout and I was sure the patients who were directed there would

---

[33] *Jung, His Life and Work*, pp. 140-141.

be given magic cures. Sometimes there would be a period when Papa Jung would retire into a still more solitary retreat among still thicker and taller reeds on an island in the upper stretches of the Zurichsee [Bollingen]. This was accessible to him with his boat and there was some sort of building to house him while he was there. We never went in but we did play a marvellous game of hide and seek among the tunnels formed by the reeds which I will always remember. So I must have visited this island.

Mrs Jung was the perfection of a motherly, loving, quiet, beautiful woman who was also the perfect Swiss housewife. I see also a round table of children, there was joking in Swiss and some cream cheese which Papa Jung sprinkled generously with sugar and gave me a spoon to eat it with. He was a fatherly figure, powerfully built and very tall – as tall as my father who was 6ft 4ins and he carried me on his back to my bedroom high up in the tower, so I should know. He did not then look so hawk-like and gaunt as he did later and he was a heavy man. When I played him at tenniquoit (when I was 15 and living at Kilchberg), the game was memorable because he refused to obey the rules of the game. He liked throwing and catching the ring in both hands. So I told him he could play by himself!

These were rich memories for Bridget. Although Peter was busy with his schedule of seeing patients and translating, the little time they had together was valuable and special for her. She felt at home in the Jung household, under the all-embracing motherly wing of Emma Jung, and they accepted her as an integral part of their large and lively family. She remembers how, at breakfast time, all the children would recount their dreams to Jung and Emma and a general discussion of these dreams would ensue.

It was in 1921, during Peter's early months of working with Jung as his assistant, that he met the girl who was to become his second wife; a young woman who had come from Edinburgh to see Jung because she was suffering from severe bouts of depression. There was a hope that Jung would be able to cure her, for at the time she was quite unable to lead a normal life.

Chapter Twelve

Marriage to Hilda

When sorrows come, they come not single spies,
But in battalions.

Shakespeare, *Hamlet*, iv. v

Peter meets Hilda Davidson, a fine pianist and a patient of Jung's. They have a Quaker wedding and settle in Campden Hill Square. Peter becomes the first Jungian analyst to set up a practice in London. Hilda gives birth to a son, Christopher, but Hilda's depressions become chronic and when the baby is a year old, she takes her life.

Hilda Davidson came to Zurich to work with Jung in the summer of 1921. Ruth described her as 'a lovely woman with long golden hair, literally long enough to sit on. She was naturally a gay, happy person, even brilliant, but she was one of Jung's patients because she had bouts of deep depression which no one could account for.' Hilda and Peter got to know one another while Hilda was staying in Zurich and he was attracted by her musical talent, attractive personality and by her beauty. At that time patients, Jung's students and the analysts working in Zurich met freely together, attended seminars and also dined and socialised together, so there was nothing unusual in a friendship between Peter, who was by now Jung's assistant, and Hilda, who was there as one of Jung's patients and was at the same time receiving help from Peter.

Ruth writes:

One evening Hilda invited Godwin and me to her flat for coffee and music. She was a fine pianist. It was lovely there and we drank our coffee on the balcony overlooking the lake. Then we went inside and Hilda played one of the Chopin Sonatas. She started to play another, then suddenly stopped. One of her bad bouts had come, her 'bogeys' she called them. Godwin knew that she wanted to be alone when this happened, so we came away. That was her life. It was as though a light was turned out.

During that summer Godwin and Hilda became engaged. It was a love marriage, and I think he also hoped it might cure her. Soon after their engagement we three took a trip into the mountains. We walked over the St. Gotthard Pass, then went by train to Lugano for two nights. But Hilda spent her days in Lugano in a darkened bedroom.

Hilda very much wanted a wedding in Church, but they could not find anyone who was allowed to marry a man whose earlier marriage had ended in divorce. At last they asked the Quakers, who readily agreed, and the wedding took place at Jordan's Meeting House. A Quaker wedding is quite an ordeal, as having no clergy or minister, the couple face the audience and conduct most of the ceremony themselves.

The divorce between Peter and Rosalind took place in May 1921 and on November 18th of that year there was an announcement in *The Times*: 'The engagement is announced, the marriage to take place in January, between Dr H.G. Baynes, third son of Mr and Mrs H.A. Baynes, of Mortimer, and Hilda Mary, younger daughter of the late Mr E.A. and Mrs Davidson, of 10 Belgrave Crescent, Edinburgh.' Helton comments: 'We regret this notice following so swiftly. I don't think G. is responsible, and remembering all that has happened, he and all of us should lie low ...'

Soon after this, Peter brought his bride to be to meet his parents. On December 24th Helton records: 'Godwin and Hilda arrived. Bringing her into our home I caught her under the mistletoe, and won the first kiss. All our first impressions are favourable and G. looks supremely happy. He soon introduced Hilda to the woods ...' Later he writes, on December 25th: 'We're keeping the festival tomorrow, but enjoyed the dear old Carols to-day – many were new to Hilda. She is quite at home with us all and it was good that Ruthie knew her so well. She is fair with a bright, refined, thoughtful face, hair inclined to auburn, calm dignified demeanour, and slight graceful figure. I should imagine the archbishop's family circle are excellent folk. What does Hilda think of us? ...' The next day they celebrated Christmas together with Jack and his second wife, Dorothy, and 'After supper, bridge and wonderful piano pieces by Hilda and songs by Godwin.' The couple left the following day to meet Hilda's uncle, who was at that time the Archbishop of Canterbury.

Their wedding took place on 14th January 1922. They were married at Jordans in Buckinghamshire. Helton writes of the wedding: 'The Friends were doubtful if they ought to open Jordans for the marriage of a divorced man and only two days ago they finally settled it at Devonshire House, by creating a precedent, so G. sent wires to family guests, and all is happy now.'

It was a fine January day, sharp and clear. Family and friends had gathered for the wedding and strolled about on the lawn outside Jordans, enjoying the scenery and also the historical associations of the place, for the hour before the ceremony began. Hilda's mother had come down from Edinburgh (her father had died some time previously), and a select group of her relations were also there including two uncles: Fred Pitman, Hilda's mother's brother (an old Cambridge rowing blue) and her Father's brother, the present Archbishop of Canterbury, Randall Davidson (who had the longest spell as Archbishop of any other during the 20th century. His ministry lasted from 1903 until 1928). He was there together with his sister, Miss Davidson. The two families intermingled, and one can imagine the two very different worlds that these families represented. Hilda's family were of aristocratic lineage and had, in the 18th century, made a vast fortune in the West Indies. They lived in grand style in a fine Georgian house in Belgrave Crescent in Edinburgh, with a staff of cook, nurse, butler, chauffeur and gardeners to minister to them. This was very different from the low church, modest respectability of the Baynes family. Would there perhaps have been a slight concern in the Davidson family about a divorced man, without significant means and with no aristocratic lineage, marrying their beautiful and gifted daughter?

Peter arrived at the Meeting House in morning dress with a red carnation in his buttonhole. Hilda looked fresh and lovely in a close-fitting cream-coloured lace gown, setting off her slender, graceful figure. She had her fair hair done up into a bun with a crown of white roses giving her an almost ethereal appearance. Her pale face and deep blue eyes, her thoughtful look and gentle grace, gave the impression of a Greek Goddess. She seemed a little anxious and looked repeatedly at Peter for reassurance. They walked together into the Meeting House and sat side by side in the two seats set apart for them, facing the congregation. The Meeting House was full with friends and family and also some of the regular attenders of the Meeting House.

One of the Elders, Mr Warwick, rose to his feet and gave a short address explaining the way a Quaker wedding is conducted. A woman reminded the congregation that they were all in the presence of God and invited those present to make their own contributions to the service. Peter and Hilda faced one another and repeated their vows after the elder, promising to stay true to each other 'until death do us part'. Then the pair made their individual vows and the congregation was invited to say their own prayers and petitions for the couple. There were long periods of silence followed by moving expressions of love and prayers for their happiness from Mrs Bax, from the Archbishop (at some length) and from Mrs Davidson. Once or twice Hilda seemed close to tears and Peter placed his large hand on top of her small delicate one. It was a poignant demonstration of their love for one another and of the love that seemed to surround them that day. Both fervently believed that this day would bring the possibility of change into their lives. Peter hoped that he could ward off the terrible fears that had plagued Hilda for most of her life. Another hope was that now he had 'plighted his troth' to this lovely creature, his erotic wanderings would cease and he could find peace at last. Alas, how seldom it is that the dreams of happiness on the day of marriage can ever be fulfilled.

After the ceremony there was the signing of the register. Mary signed after Hilda and she was the first person to receive a kiss from the bride. There was already a warm relationship between Hilda and her future mother-in-law. Mary felt tenderness and compassion for this vulnerable young woman and Hilda warmed to Mary's vital and all-embracing personality, a welcome change from the austerity of her Edinburgh upbringing. The wedding party walked up the slope leading from the Meeting House to the Hostel where light refreshments were served and once again the guests enjoyed mingling with one another.

It was 5 p.m. when Mary and Muriel arrived home. Mary seemed elated and quite fresh and related in detail all the happy events to

Helton, who had longed to go but dared not face the long day. This marriage, in which they had been included, was more welcome to Peter's parents than his marriage to Rosalind. They had found Rosalind's progressive ways too different from their own to ever feel quite at ease with her.

The Times announced the wedding the following day and Helton wondered: 'What does Rosalind think and feel? Godwin is treating her liberally.'[34] A few days later Helton records in his Commonplace Book that 'Snowdrops peeping round the acacia tree in the front ... are harbingers of spring and we rejoice in them.' Perhaps Peter shared this sense of new hope in the air after the dark days since his separation from Rosalind.

How very different this somewhat sober ceremony was from Godwin's wildly romantic Irish wedding to Rosalind. After they were married the couple settled in London, where they bought a small house in Campden Hill Square. Peter was attempting to make the difficult transition from general practice to the virtually unknown field of analytical psychology. Ruth remembered the very day when he sold his medical instruments, as though this symbolised his complete separation from the world of conventional medicine. He must have felt considerable qualms as he did so. At the beginning, there was a tiny trickle of patients and he must have wondered how they would make ends meet. However, the practice soon began to grow and Peter's days became filled with his patients and with the founding of the Jungian Analytical Psychology Club (the APC) in London. At this time there were about twelve members, all of whom had received an analysis with Jung, or with Peter.

The early days of their marriage were full and happy. For a time Hilda seemed better and her bouts of depression were fewer and further apart. She was kept busy in her role as Peter's wife and became increasingly involved with entertaining friends and with outside engagements. Peter's busy social London life was once more in full swing. They sometimes entertained members of the APC at their home for musical evenings: Hilda would play Peter's accompaniments, Schumann and Brahms, and on one occasion she played

---

[34] As Rosalind had accepted the legal responsibility for being the guilty party, Peter was not, at that time, obliged by law to give financial support to his family. The considerable support he gave to them was seen by his parents, therefore, as being unusually 'liberal'.

them Grieg's piano concerto. Her old nursery upright piano was sent down from Edinburgh so that Ruth, who was also a fine pianist, could play the orchestral part to accompany Hilda, who played on her beautiful concert-sized Bechstein grand.

Peter began a new journal during his marriage to Hilda. This is in a fine leather-bound book with gilt edges which somehow escaped being damaged by the fire of 1938, when his home was burned to the ground. On the title page, written in script and in pencil, he has written the words: 'The Book that Groweth'. On the following page is the Latin quotation that is above the Jung's door: 'Vocatus atque non vocatus Deus aderit' (Bidden or not bidden, God is present). Under this is written a single verse:

> Jung waren wir
> Jung heissen wir
> Der ewigen Jugend
> Gehoren wir.

> [Young we were, young we are called.
> Eternal youth belongs to us.]

Then under this verse he writes:

> 'Freuet euch, denn euch ist heute ein Heiland geboren.'
> ['Rejoice for to-day a Savour is born.']

On the following page he has written in ink:

> This book shall be the story of a man who has learnt to despise himself and who by virtue of this scorn and bitter hatred goes out to command and if possible, to love himself.
>
> It is begun on Sunday January the eighteenth, nineteen hundred and twenty five. It is finished: – [no date is given, but this book is not finished until May 28th 1942.]

Hilda and Peter had now been married for three years and things had begun to go radically wrong. He opens the book on a sad note:

> Four days ago, to wit, Wednesday the 14th January, the third anniversary of our wedding-day came and went unremembered both by my wife and myself. An ominous red light burns at the heart of that forgetting. Our marriage is as yet no more than a pious hope. The nature of its reality is easier to forget than to remember.

Three years have we spent in a penitentiary. Three years of the straight waistcoat have made plain to us our sins.

Now! by heaven! I will to live again. There is that in me which turns an eye of loathing on the chains which long enough have chafed my hands and feet.

Much of this book is a dialogue within himself, which results in a some-what stilted and ponderous style of writing. The dialogue is with the 'She' of the unconscious, the inner feminine to whom Jung has given the name anima. Having caused the break-up of his first marriage, she is still tempting Peter and trying to lead him astray during his marriage to Hilda. Hilda is a woman who has lived almost entirely on the spiritual plane and has denied her own physical nature, so Peter is living the life of a celibate. The bright hopes for this new marriage are already in tatters. Now, in his unhappiness he turns to prayer:

It seemed that I began once more to have faith in the value of prayer. I saw that to pray with simple faith is still possible if only one can lay aside the self-sufficient, purposeful attitude of the self which is blind. My father was a praying man. I have the same malady as he. I cannot pray to the god that he prays to. For me that god is sick and dying. I cannot pray to the sun because I cannot reach that fiery star with my small human cry.

To cry to the void in the hope that some god would hearken seems only the folly of childhood. To what god can a stricken man appeal for light? O Father Philemon then, who speakest to the heart of my friend, wilt thou also be my guide? I cannot live in darkness and with hatred against my wife ... Understanding I must win or my life will lose every vestige of meaning and reality. I would wrestle with thee as Jacob wrestled with the angel and I will not let thee go till thou hast blessed me. I know there is in me a terrible lack and therefore a terrible fear. I think my great love for my great friend is the measure of my need of thee O Father Philemon.

At the time he was writing this, Hilda's bouts of depression had not improved, and Peter was carrying not only a profound sense of failure in respect of another unsuccessful marriage, but also a sense of his failure as a doctor who had been unable to cure his sick wife, as they had both ardently hoped he would at the outset of marriage.

The journal now paints a bleak picture of their life together and Jung appears repeatedly as 'The Friend' whom Peter longs to emulate, and at this stage in his life, even to be. There is an almost religious intensity in his references to Jung in the diary.

His entry of 1st March 1925 is the cry of a lost soul in the wilderness:

> I am being driven irresistibly to face some experience which fills me with nameless dread. I know it is impossible to escape this experience and I believe God is in it. To live without the presence and knowledge of God in the soul is for me emptiness and mockery. Therefore whatever may come of it and whatever it may mean I write now, without reserve I AM WILLING. And may the NEW GOD have mercy on my soul.

> The dream on Feb 17th in which I had to ascend to heaven with my father and his fear, has for me this meaning. My father feared the God of the future and for this reason he clung with rigid fingers to the dead God of the past. He is my father and bequeaths to me his fear.

> Therefore this idea of the father has to arise and be transfigured that he may exchange the lineaments of mortal limitations for infinite love of the wise Father Philemon.

For Peter, the transference to Jung is as powerful as ever and perhaps Jung *is* Father Philemon. Philemon was one of the figures whom Jung encountered in his journey into the unconscious in 1912. He was Jung's inner protector and guide and represented for Jung the archetype of The Old Wise Man. It is to this Old Wise Man within himself that Peter is appealing now. He has an appearance very much like that of Dr Jung who is still, at this time, the 'Eye of God' and the centre of Peter's universe. He, who in his youth was hero-worshipped by so many, has now found a man to whom, unlike his sick father, he can give his whole-hearted allegiance and admiration. Who can become for him the role model he has always lacked, as even his two older brothers did not fulfil this for him.

There is almost a religious attitude of the Imitatio Christi[35], as he speaks of Jung – My Friend – almost in the same breath as he speaks of discarding the old God in favour of the new. Although Peter's formal analysis was now over, the process of individuation continued

---

[35] Imitation of Christ.

and Jung stood for the inner possibility of wholeness. 'In Christian symbolism the totality is Christ, and the healing process consists of the imitatio Christi.'[36] Perhaps Peter was also experiencing Jung in a powerful transformative sense as Father. Jung writes of the importance of the Father Imago, in relation to Miss Miller, in *Symbols of Transformation:* '... the idea of the masculine creative deity is a derivation, analytically and historically psychlologic of the 'Father-Imago',[37] and aims, above all, to replace the discarded infantile father transference in such a way that for the individual the passing from the narrow circle of the family into the wider circle of human society may be simpler or made easier.'[38]

In other words, the inner experience of 'father', for Peter associated with his own neurosis, and with Helton his outer father, needed to be replaced by a more positive 'father imago' which could enable him to grow to his full potential; this is associated with both Jung and ultimately with God.

It is interesting that nowhere in his journals does Peter use the word transference in his relationship to Jung. Perhaps this was still not a concept that was commonly referred to in the therapy relationship at that time. It was not until much later, in the early 1930's, that Peter was able to discover his own true identity and the ability to value his own very different personality type and his own natural way of working which was, as a feeling extravert, so very different to that of Jung' s.

Perhaps it was through the love, respect and reverence Peter felt towards Jung, that his relationship to a father figure (and also to God) could now be transformed and this new, strong, internalised father could give him a profound sense of his own essential worth and inner integrity. Up till this time he had relied on others' admiration, especially the love of women, in order to feel positively about himself. The consequence of his love for Jung is encapsulated in the opening statement to this book, that 'a man who has learnt to despise himself', *can* learn 'to love himself'. Also, of course, *The Book That Groweth* is about his own potential for growth as the process of transformation is enacted. The suffering he experienced during his marriage to Hilda

---

[36] Jung, CW 7, p. 138.

[37] Image of father as experienced subjectively, based on unconscious fantasies rather than on outer reality.

[38] Jung, *Psychology of the Unconscious*, Routledge, London, 1991, p. 48.

was like his dark night of the soul and was, perhaps, an essential part of this process. It may be that profound change can only come about as a result of intense suffering.

In contrast to Peter's forebodings about his marriage, Helton's remarks about Hilda are positive. One year after their marriage he records, after a visit from Peter and Hilda: 'Hilda happy with us and a dear girl, but many things in Godwin I would like to see different. To speak would, I fear, do more harm than good; prayer is my resource, and God will answer. These meetings may be few, yet in the 3 days there was no earnest talk and G's great desire seemed to be funny and provoke a general titter; no effort to enable me to hear and join in at meal-times.' (Helton was at this time becoming increasingly deaf, a problem that was later inherited by both Jack and Ruth.)

On June 24th of that year Helton and Mary paid a visit to Peter and Hilda's London house, a momentous event for Helton. The journey there is described by him in minutest detail. On the way they passed the house in Adelaide Terrace, near Westbourne Grove, where Helton was born. This was close to Horbury Chapel where there is a tablet commemorating Helton's father, John Ash Baynes. He gives us a good description of Peter and Hilda's home:

> No 24 Campden Hill Square is quiet, on high ground, commanding fine views from the upper windows, in front Ladbroke Grove and St John's church, to the left White City and right Hampstead and Highgate. Godwin had a patient till 1 o'clock, then we carefully inspected the garden, which proves Godwin's hard work and industry. Lunch (ie dinner) very recherché and special (Hilda only has the French cook) ending with 'intemperate fruit salad', viz sherry, but everything was A1. Strong coffee in the drawing-room, where G and H entertained us, he with lute and songs, she with piano pieces on her Bechstein grand. We went all over the house, and I noticed many unusual things. Soon after 3, we walked in the Square in front, and said goodbye to the happy couple at 3:30.

So outwardly, all seemed very well: a lovely house; Peter working from home and the practice growing; his keen interest in gardening beginning now to provide an important antidote to his work; a garden that reflected his labours; a fine French cook to supply them with A1 meals; and music-making together.

Another visit to Mortimer by Peter and Hilda marked a red-letter day for his parents in February 1924, when Hilda was five months pregnant. They had a happy time going for walks, playing bridge and reading and listening to the wireless. The 'happiness' expressed by Helton in relation to the visits, however infrequent, of Peter and Hilda are in marked contrast to Peter's expressions of profound unhappiness, which is perhaps known only to his journal, and possibly, by this time, also to Jung.

On June 17th 1924 Hilda gave birth to a son, Christopher. Helton recorded, on June 26th, 1924, 'Godwin 42 to-day: a little son came to him and Hilda on 17th. She is in a nursing home and doesn't like it. Both doing well.'

Hilda was in her 30's, which was considered old at that time for having a first baby. It was thought that a baby would help relieve her depression and make her less self-absorbed. However, after the birth, her bouts of depression became chronic. Peter and Hilda's great hopes of happiness together had melted away. Peter's feelings about Hilda are encapsulated in his reflection, prior to their marriage that: 'Only that man has respect and reverence for woman who sees in the woman he loves, not an erotic mistress, but the mother of his children.' But one wonders whether, in marrying Hilda he had separated these two aspects of woman. Hilda was indeed the mother of his son, the woman he held in deep reverence, but she could only satisfy Peter's spiritual needs. She had so little relationship or contact with the physical aspects of life, and this, alas was also true of her relationship to her baby. She was so absorbed by her own problems, it was as though she had nothing left to give to her child.

Christopher Carl Randall (he was christened Carl after Jung and Randall after his great uncle) was an outstandingly beautiful baby. With his birth came the ardent hope that things would improve for Hilda and for the marriage. It was as though nature had provided her with a child who looked like an angel, as an attempt to enlist her for this life and to connect her to her physical and maternal potential. But sadly there was no sign of bonding to the baby with his cherubic face and head of golden curls. She was really too sick and even feared that if she came close to her baby she might do him harm. The poor infant was relegated to a nursemaid and Hilda scarcely attended to him.

On 6th June 1925 Peter writes despairingly about Hilda's tragic inability to bond with or to care for her beautiful child, or to be there in any real, or temporal sense, for her husband:

> For it is often just that woman who is too helpless, stupid and incapable of performing any simple objective task, even the care of her own children, who proves to be a transparent window of celestial meanings. Such a one is my wife. Not even the simplest and easiest of objective tasks lies within her competence to perform.
>
> She is untrustworthy in everything she has ever undertaken with voluntary purpose. But a man is forced to serve her and render her the homage of his instinct, because she is as clearly transparent to the invisible powers of the Spirit as she is opaque to all the practical considerations and necessities of life. This must be said in her capture of me for her husband and in the bearing of Christopher our son. She showed no suspicion of the incompetence which marks the rest of her worldly activities.
>
> Living with such a woman is to gain a rather terrible impression that her love and solicitude are tendered only relatively to the self one is and knows about. Her real concern is for the fruits which still lie hidden from one's knowledge. She will even plague and torment one past all endurance in her dire solicitude for that future harvest, or beyond-self, which she seems to discern. Nothing that lies within one's present capacities, no effective performance in the world of to-day is able to prompt more than a perfunctory appreciation. Her entire will and effort, her very hope of life, is set upon something which is invisible to present-day mortality. She is driven by the past and lives only for the future. This is her perpetual crucifixion. But because she is unable to redeem herself from this cross, she looks helplessly to me to accomplish that task, by which she can attain the merit of spiritual parentage.
>
> She has to germinate in my soul a living fruit by virtue of which her Magnificat may resound through heaven.
>
> She seems to want me but she really wants my fruit. To live day by day with embodied reproach is intolerable to mortal flesh.

This is a cry of despair. Was he at this moment on the very edge of endurance and perhaps confused between the suffering and the emotional demands of his lovely young wife and the sufferings of his own soul. Peter's need for woman was all consuming yet it seemed to be impossible for him to find a woman who possessed the spiritual qualities he yearned for and who was at the same time connected to the physical world and to her own physical being. He had felt with Rosalind the impossibility of desiring the woman whom he experienced, after Bridget's birth, as a mother. Now with Hilda he seems to have made a separation between the spiritual woman, who in spite of motherhood remained in her essential being a virgin, from the woman who is sexual, earthy and fecund. He must either worship woman as a spiritual being who is placed outside the physical world, or enjoy her erotically but without commitment. One is reminded again of his comment, before he married Hilda: 'Only that man has a respect and reverence for woman who sees in the woman he loves not an erotic mistress but the mother of his children.'

He has found the woman he can revere in Hilda but Eros has no place there.

> It is almost impossible, without doing violence to this basic instinct to accept the image of my wife as the receiver of [my] erotic libido. It is not merely a question of the emaciated body but much more her virginal state.
>
> Toni [Wolff] is almost equally handicapped physically, but there is no difficulty at all in conceiving her as the vessel for Eros. It is not just because she [Hilda] is my wife, for even before we were engaged I could never so conceive her. My civilized side that is strongly orientated by the idea of duty holds her as a necessary object of service and devotion, but my savage African, dark side, remains obstinately divorced from her ...
>
> Either I have to live a life of monastic chastity with an invalid ... wife who is without any of the cunning and knowledge of the sensual woman, or I must concede to myself the 'natural right' of a man to full sensual experience and take a mistress who can respond to that need.

This conflict preoccupies him throughout his marriage to Hilda. He dreams of his brother Arnold, who is struggling with the same conflict, identifying himself with the dream-image of his brother. In the dream Arnold is dying:

> My brother Arnold is important as a symbol and I had a magic sense of his early death when I saw his thin, almost emaciated face

in the photograph. The skeleton begins to show through the living tissue, as in Hilda's case too. He abandoned the call of his natural instincts. He was too much at the mercy of his wild anima and in order to preserve himself from destruction he made his wife his moral keeper and became entirely enslaved by her.

He escapes the call of instinct by the twin expedients of working himself to death and secretly hating his wife, just as I have tried to do. Thus he chose death instead of life.

And so, in his comments about Arnold, he was of course talking about himself. He too had chosen a wife who would be his moral keeper and he too was working himself to death.

Helton is unaware of these difficulties when he speaks of a visit from Peter and Hilda in November 1924: '… G as lively as usual, but I hear next to nothing – he left early on Mon. but Hilda and Co stayed till Thurs, to our great joy as we got to know and admire her more and the baby is a charming cherub – beautiful features and temper in spite of a sore vaccination arm.'

The following year Ruth moved into Campden Hill Square for a time in order to help Hilda. There was a warm friendship between the two young women and she could reassure Hilda when Peter was pre-occupied with work. Helton comments that Ruth 'seems able to help Hilda, who suffers from delusions and bad dreams – query, is psycho-analysis responsible?' And then a plaintive note added at the end: 'They don't confide in Mary and me, so we don't know.'

Soon after this, in March 1925, Ruth decided to return to Zurich to analyse with Jung. She returned to join Peter at an important Jungian conference in Swanage during August. Ruth was Peter's confidante in his unhappiness, but she was also the soul of discretion, and none of Peter's confidences were reported back to their parents.

Peter's subjective experience was that he found himself caught in a trap from which there was no escape; enmeshed in the web of Hilda's neurosis and the victim of her neurotic demands on him. At the same time, in his heroic effort to heal and to meet her need, he was himself starving for the want of any real human or reciprocal love. In reflecting on the situation he has got himself into he reproaches himself: 'I am arrogant. I could set no being above myself and so I married a woman who seemed to be so much weaker than I. But now I begin to see the baffling strength of her spirit.' He perceives the relationship as an almost life and death struggle: 'Thus all my positive qualities are threatened with extinction by a woman like Hilda. If I fell into the Yin-pools[39] which her eyes implore me to do, I should be swallowed up completely as Arnold has been. It means the death of the Self. Self-extinction. Is this what the soul demands?' (Arnold was suffering at the time in a hopelessly unhappy marriage from which he felt unable to extricate himself.)

Peter's relationship to woman was clearly a troubled one. Toni Wolff commented to him that he seemed more able, at this time, to trust himself in a relationship with a man than with a woman. In view of what had happened in his close relationships with women, this may not seem surprising. However, the comment that he made later in life, that 'a man marries the woman he deserves' is perhaps more revealing. He would have seen his relationship to Hilda as a reflection of the relationship he had to his own inner feminine nature, his anima. His inner dialogue with her, which forms the major part of his self-revealing book, 'The Book that Groweth', is full of anger, disapproval and blame, being levelled at him from his own anima. She lashes him with her tongue and questions his motives in every aspect of his life, including his reasons for marrying Hilda:

> You think it was an heroic act, a noble gesture to marry a sick woman, but it was not. There was a slavish lack of choice. There was avarice, there was a supine compliance and an inability to take any other course. The best thing you have is your wish to be worthy of your great friend. That is genuine. But to women you only give the semblance of love. If you really had faith in love you would cut your old dusty worked out, jumble shop of stale ideas out of your heart and mind and learn afresh as Christopher, your boy is learning. Look into the eyes of your wife. Keep looking there and you will see what love demands of you.

Then, a little later, he is blaming himself, but also seeing himself through the eyes of the anima. He speaks of Hilda and the fact that she has never really surrendered to him: 'Rosalind could not accept me and neither can Hilda. To both of them I seem to promise much but give little. I go through the correct movements of the adult male, but the intensity that goes with them is but the flickering flame of a

---

[39] Yin/Yang is the Chinese circular symbol of two fishes, one black and one white, representing the feminine/masculine principles.

child. No woman could be content with the meagre substitute of love I have offered my two wives.'

So as Hilda's emotional and psychological demands on Peter became more overwhelming he appears to have become aware of his inability to deal with them. She was pathetically dependent on him and found it difficult to be left in the house without him. It became increasingly problematic to leave her in order to fulfil the demands of his work. In the spring of 1925, Peter was taken up with the practical aspects of preparing the East African expedition which Jung was planning in order to study a remote tribe, the Elgonyi, who lived on Mount Elgon in Kenya. In the 1920's, this tribe had had no contact at all with the outside world and Jung wanted to make a psychological study of the inhabitants before they became affected by Western influence. Jung had left all the organisation of this expedition to Peter. There was a lot to think about in collecting the correct gear for a six-month journey, much of which was to be spent on safari to the remote regions of Mount Elgon. The sea voyage had to be planned and the expedition members consulted.

Hilda was unhappy about the prospect of Peter's long absence. She had deep misgivings about her ability to manage without his support. He had become the lover, doctor and devoted friend who came between her and her 'bogies'. These episodes which completely crippled her, were thought to be connected to the death of her father, with whom she had had a particularly close relationship. The 'name-less dread'[40] of her affliction became overpowering and Peter seri-ously considered bowing out of the expedition. But with his extraver-sion and organising ability, he was the lynch pin of the project, and it would have been difficult for Jung to undertake it without him. Peter wrote to Jung in confusion, feeling that he had come to the end of his tether. On 1st July he records: 'On this day I wrote my last despairing letter to C.G. about the terrible hardness of life with Hilda. There was a profound protest against my fate in this. Then Rosalind came and told me she was going to marry Hugh Popham. So even that door is closed. I have to stick it out. There is no escape.' Jung's reply to Peter's cry for help was to admonish him and to say that on no account must he give in to her emotional blackmail (i.e., her threats of what she might do if he insisted on going to Africa with Jung). He said if Peter succumbed to these threats now he would become increasingly

[40] See p. 157.

imprisoned by Hilda's neurotic demands on him. With heavy heart Peter continued to make the preparations for Africa. The plan was that they should leave in October.

In August of that year Peter was also involved in the preparations for the Swanage conference, which marked Jung's second important teaching conference in England, in which he spoke of dream analysis and the great god Eros, god of relatedness and also of Logos, the god of form. It was well attended – about one hundred people were present – and during the conference, which lasted from July 25th to August 7th, Jung gave twelve lectures. Already he had begun to be regarded as something of a celebrity in England. This was a very different event from the Sennen Cove seminar in 1920 where there had been just twelve participants.

Peter's difficulties were beginning to take their toll on him. There is an entry in his journal in which he comments on the different ways he and Hilda are marked by their respective suffering:

> I have sometimes wondered why it is that Hilda, who has spent her life suffering, has a face that shows no trace of it, while I, who have lived and worked and seem to have repressed suffering from consciousness have grey hair and lined face and sorrowful eyes. Is it true, then, that the thing that is repressed finds its expression in the body? Hilda's bodily fatigue and emaciation suggest a life of arduous work and strife. Is this her counterpart of my grey hairs? Clearly I have suffered but my inherent optimism would never allow the full realization of suffering in my experience. I always wanted to turn it at once into an asset and thus to minimize it.
>
> Now with Hilda I have suffering to live with which cannot be minimized or explained away but simply endured. I have to learn how to bear it.

Things went from bad to worse for this little family and most tragically, Hilda's suffering was at last more than she could endure. On October 21st she jumped from the roof of their tall Campden Hill Square house and killed herself. This was an appalling shock for Peter, and he blamed himself, once again. The Baynes parents were told that Hilda had died of heart failure in Hampstead Nursing Home as a result of injections given to induce sleep. Helton writes that finally 'the stuff reached her heart and poisoned it.' He continues: 'Godwin promised Dr Jung months ago to sail with him to E. Africa on the 15th, but of course he did not; and when Hilda died today we wondered what he would do. Hilda was a sweet girl, a true lady, admired by everybody. Ruth has known her well and loved her: she felt at home with us and we with her. Poor Godwin!'

On October 24th, Hilda was cremated at 9:00 a.m. and the funeral service was at the Hampstead Cemetery Chapel at 11:00 a.m. Only close family members attended. This included the Archbishop's wife, Mrs Davidson; Hilda' s older sister, Mrs Ellison; and her husband, who gave a beautiful address. Others who attended were Jack, Peter, Ruth and Ruth's friend Enid. Muriel had set off early but arrived at the crematorium too late. However, she was there later that day with Ruth and Enid to see Peter off from Victoria Station where he caught the train to Genoa to join Jung who had already left by boat for Africa.

In her will Hilda left everything to Peter. He had no time to consider the practical implications nor to come to terms with her death. No time even to consider the effect of this tragedy on his poor little abandoned son. Ruth was left at no 24, together with Enid, to care for baby Christopher until Peter's return and to manage the household, together with Christopher's nanny and the French cook.

One can only imagine Peter's state of mind as he set off on this expedition, on the very day that he buried his wife. How did he manage in those few days between Hilda' s death and his departure? He had to prepare for her funeral, to take leave of his rapidly expanding practice and his busy household, as well as seeing to the final details of an expedition that was to take them far into the hinterland of Africa. Communications from there would be difficult and the expedition was to keep him away from home for six months. Somehow he managed it, with the help of his faithful sister Ruth. She was, as always, a tower of strength, as she comforted him, helped him in his departure and in her sweet and gentle way made sure that Godwin's household and above all, his son (now just over a year old), would be well cared for in his absence.

Chapter Thirteen

Africa

We carry within us the wonders we seek without us:
There is all Africa and her prodigies in us.
                    Sir Thomas Browne, *Religio Medici*, pt. i, par. 3

Peter accompanies Jung on his 'Bugishu Psychological Expedi-
tion' to study the Elgonyi tribe who live on Mount Elgon in
Kenya. This is one of the last tribes to remain unaffected by West-
ern civilization. The expedition includes an American, George
Beckwith and a young English woman, Ruth Bailey. The expedi-
tion is away for six months.

The 'Bugishu Psychological Expedition', which was to be such a
momentous experience for Jung, was undertaken with the sanction of
the Foreign Office in London. The expedition was to travel through
Kenya and Uganda, both of them British Colonies, in November and
December. They were to trek in the bush into the land of the
Kavirondo and from there march for five days together with forty-
eight bearers, until they reached the foot of an extinct volcano called
Mount Elgon. In January they planned to take a boat down the Nile
to Khartoum, and from there to Egypt before returning home.

While Jung was in London in the summer of 1925 for the Swanage
seminar, he had visited the Wembley Exhibition in London and wrote
that he 'was deeply impressed by the excellent survey of the tribes
under British rule and resolved to take a trip to tropical Africa in the
near future.'[41] This was to be a difficult and demanding venture.

---

[41] MDR, pp. 282.

Barbara Hannah writes: 'This was a much more complicated journey, involving a great deal more preparation than any he had as yet undertaken ... a trip to a remote tribe in tropical Africa, arranged with two Americans and one Englishman none of whom were acquainted with the area, required a great deal of planning and carefully chosen equipment.'[42]

With Peter's help (he was put in charge of all the practical arrangements for the expedition), permits were obtained from the British government. The necessary camping equipment and articles for survival in the bush, as well as the weapons and provisions, had to be researched and then bought. Most of these were obtained from the Army and Navy Stores in London.

Peter was also the expedition's photographer and had brought with him a cine camera, a rare thing for a private individual in 1925. So we have a visual record of the party of four, Jung, Peter, a young American, George Beckwith, and a young English woman, Ruth Bailey, who joined them later. The film shows the party on safari in the bush with a long line of bearers; it shows them camping and talking with the Africans. There are shots of Jung talking to some shy African children, giving one a friendly pat on the head before the child runs away to hide in a cave. We see them watching a snake charmer at work and taking part in a tribal meal round a great fire while they watch the tribesmen dance before finally joining in themselves.

The fourth member of the party was to have been an American called Fowler McCormick. He was at the last moment unable to join the expedition, so it was a trio who first arrived together in Mombasa. Peter, because of the tragedy of Hilda's death, was unable to start the voyage with Jung and George Beckwith.

It was actually while he was packing to go that Hilda had taken her life. She had threatened to do this if he left her and now the threat had been carried out. Peter had decided that he could not let Jung down. He was also influenced by Jung who had made it clear that Peter must not give way to his wife's increasing emotional blackmail. He could see no other course of action, yet his sense of guilt and the 'if onlys' must have obliterated all other impressions at the outset of this venture.

In order to catch up with the expedition, Peter had to travel overland to Genoa to join his companions on the Woerman liner. The

[42] Hannah, 1976, p. 165.

voyage took about six weeks and it was a welcome interlude. It was for Peter a necessary time for reflection. For Jung, it was an opportunity to study Swahili, so that he could communicate with the African tribesmen.

This was not an easy time for Peter. Barbara Hannah writes: 'His wife's death made the African journey difficult for him, although it also meant a great deal to him, especially in retrospect. Peter once told me – with the endearing self-criticism of which he was capable – that he had been a terrible wet blanket on the trip.'[43]

While on the voyage to East Africa, Jung and his party had become acquainted with Ruth Bailey. She was part of the young set on board who referred to Jung and his companions as 'the three Obadiahs.' During their stop-over in Nairobi, the party had got to know Ruth better and they all enjoyed her 'sporting attitude' and sense of humour.

From Nairobi, the expedition travelled by the Uganda railway, which was still in the process of being built, to its terminus at Station Sigistifour (sixty four). From there they had a bumpy drive in two cars containing Jung and his two companions and their 'quantities of equipment.'[44] They arrived at Kapsabet, which was the government station for Tandi District in Kenya. It marked the end of the road and what lay beyond was no more than a neglected earth track.

The Assistant District Commissioner at the time was a man named Francis Daniel Hislop, a retired British foreign officer. He remembers the unexpected appearance of the travellers as they arrived in 'a large safari box-body car'.

> They had got out of the car and were looking at me speculatively as I approached.
>
> I said, 'Good afternoon. Can I help you in any way? I'm the ADC here.'
>
> The tallest of the three, a reddish-faced man, replied, 'We're trying to get to Mount Elgon and would like to know the best road to take.' I told them there was no direct road to Elgon from Kapsabet and they could not possibly get there in daylight. I went on to explain that Elgon, where I had recently spent several weeks on a boundary job, was a sprawling land mass with extensive

[43] Hannah, 1976, p. 166.
[44] MDR.

foothills, and it would be about seventy miles on earth roads, either by Kakamega or Eldoret, to get to there. Then it would be over twenty miles to the summit.

'We aren't interested in the summit', said the spokesman. 'We just want to get to the foothills.'

From where we were standing we could see the blue-grey shape of Elgon away to the north-west receding into the usual mist ...

Then the tall man said: 'I am Dr X' (the name escaped me and I have never discovered who he was) [this of course was Peter] 'This is Dr Jung.' He indicated a burly man, middle-aged. with a reddish-brown country face. 'And this is Mr Douglas, our secretary, an American.' Douglas [Beckwith] was a young man, about twenty five, athletic looking and darkly handsome. He appeared bored by the proceedings and I do not recollect that he ever uttered a single word – perhaps the perfect secretary. On the other hand I noticed that they had no African servants with them and it occurred to me later that perhaps this explained young Douglas's gloom.

I led the way to my bungalow, and over tea Dr X again took up the batting.

'It may seem odd to you', he said, 'but we are in fact psychologists intending to do some field work.'

I started mentally. 'Did you say Dr Jung?'

The burly man smiled and said. 'Yes, I am Dr Jung.'

'Of Zurich?'

'Yes, of Zurich.' He looked surprised and pleased.

'I cannot help wondering', I said, 'what kind of field work you will find to do on Elgon.'

Dr X explained. 'Dr Jung', he said, 'is interested in dreams and their interpretation, and as a change from studying them among the highly civilized people of Europe, he wants to get further back and see if he can learn anything from a fairly primitive people. After considering the possibilities everywhere we decided that the tribes on Mount Elgon would suit us best for this purpose. And so', he concluded, 'we are devoting our summer vacation to this work.'

Hislop goes on to say how difficult such a mission would be because of the language barrier. Peter reassures him that 'Dr Jung has learned Swahili for the purpose.' Hislop continues that these remote tribes have a language of their own and do not understand Swahili, even though this is the lingua franca. He offers to arrange an interpreter for them, adding that even a good interpreter might have difficulty as the more primitive the tribe, the more purely materialistic the language, which is therefore a poor medium for expressing abstract ideas or emotions. At this point Peter intervened saying that 'they had their own methods of getting results.' (History doesn't relate what these methods were!). He continues that the discussion then moved to camping conditions on Elgon and the subject of the Elgon caves was also raised. Jung asked if Hislop had ever been inside them:

> 'I have been inside one', I replied.
> 'What did you find inside?'
> 'Fleas', I answered.
> Dr Jung gave a great bellow of laughter, and Dr X joined in a little more moderately, but young Douglas only gave me a sort of sour smile as if I had taken an undue liberty with the great man.'[45]

Hislop went on to explain that the caves had been used by tribesmen as cattle shelters and the floors were covered with deep layers of dung. He recognized their interest in relation to primitive cave paintings and said that as far as he knew, none had ever been found. After this, he set them on their way to Eldoret.

As they approached Kakamega at twilight they were hit by a tropical storm and they arrived at the District Commissioner's house soaked from head to foot, half an hour before midnight. The DC welcomed them with a blazing fire and a glass of whisky in his impeccably English drawing-room. For a day after this, Jung was incapacitated with a fever and laryngitis.

On the day following, they set off together with their column of bearers, supplemented with three Askaris as military escort, a corporal and two privates, on the trek to Mount Elgon, in Uganda. Jung gives a description of the route through dry savannah country, which was covered with umbrella acacias. There were numerous small tumuli between six and ten feet high; these they discovered were old termite colonies. Along the route there were grass-roofed huts which were rest houses for travellers.

Jung describes an unpleasant encounter with a pack of hungry hyenas who were attracted by the savoury smells of their roasting lamb. One hyena had gone into the hut belonging to their cook and had nearly killed him. The three travellers had seized their weapons,

---

[45] *C.G. Jung Speaking* 1931, p. 50-53.

a 9 mm. Mannlicher rifle and a shotgun, and fired several rounds at the glowing green lights of the hyenas' eyes till the pack dispersed. This event was re-enacted over and over again the following morning as one of the boys played the sleeping cook and another the creeping hyena. This scenario and the shouts of laughter accompanying it Peter has managed to capture on film.

Already, friendly relations had developed between the bearers and the three white men. The 'boys' had given them each a nick-name. Peter was known as 'red-neck', Beckwith as 'bwana maredadi' – the dapper gentleman, and Jung was 'msee' – the old man, because of his grey hair (although he was only 50 at the time).

The expedition passed through the Nandi Forest and though we see this on film, it is only black and white so the wonderful colours of the Nandi flame trees with their splendid red blossom have to be imagined. Along the route they saw great beetles and magnificent, brilliantly coloured tropical butterflies. Peter would stop and with his butterfly net, which was always with him, catch as many of the African species as he was able and these became a part of his vast butterfly collection. His passionate interest in natural history was always with him.

They finally reached the foot of Mount Elgon, which had been towering ever more impressively above their heads, and stopped at the rest house there. They began to climb along a steep narrow path. Here they met the local chief who, unusually, was mounted on a pony. They learned from him that his tribe belonged to the Masai but lived here in the isolation of Mount Elgon.

At the foot of the mountain a letter awaited them from the Governor of Uganda requesting them to take a young English woman under their protection. She was on the way back to Egypt via the Sudan, and as they were following the same route, it seemed sensible for her to join Jung's party. This was Ruth Bailey and she made a welcome fourth to this triad of men. She was an unusually intrepid young woman for that time, and somehow she managed to make her own way, under considerable difficulties, to meet her companions at the foot of Mount Elgon.

As the expedition trekked deeper into the wilderness, they encountered a rich variety of wildlife and would often hear the calls of leopards and lions as well as hyenas and they encountered several enormous snakes. They climbed up to 2900 metres, where the bamboo forests were full of black buffalo and rhino, which represented a considerable danger and made it necessary to sleep with their guns ready.

Along the route Peter remembers the little ghost mud houses that were built by the Elgonyi along the side of a path that led to a house or village. These houses contained two or more rooms and inside was placed a spread of food consisting of milk, corn and other offerings. These were designed to attract the ghosts and spirits and waylay them, to prevent them from going to the house or village to make the inhabitants sick. It was particularly the ghosts of dead relatives and ancestors who were held responsible for sickness.

The shaman's most responsible task among these remote tribes in East Africa was considered to be the cure of souls. He was the one to dispel the negative effect of unquiet spirits and keep the community free from sickness. The cure of sickness itself was considered to be a relatively elementary aspect of the shaman's art.

While they were in Uganda, the party was allowed to see one of the houses to which the ghosts, or the souls of the dead, are led. Peter writes: 'They are really churches. Often a considerable amount of art and devotion has been given to these ghost houses where the spirits of the ancestors are housed. The churches of our English shires, standing in consecrated ground among the graves of the dead, are really ghost houses.'[46]

The expedition set up their camp near to the kraal[47] which the Elgonyis inhabited. It was in a clearing near to a waterfall and underneath a grove of umbrella acacias which provided shade in the heat of the day. Here, each day, Jung and Peter would conduct their daily palavers with the Elgonyis in a combination of Swahili and sign language. It was now that the real business of this expedition began as Jung and Peter began to converse and interact and to join in the lives of these wonderfully natural, dignified and beautiful people.

Jung describes how a young man, known as Gibroat, invites him to meet his family. The young woman, his sister, and her family are introduced to him when they visit her home. She is 'middle-aged' (i.e. about thirty!), and strikingly lovely, wearing only a cowrie belt, arm bands and ankle rings with copper ornaments hanging from her greatly extended earlobes. Her four children are shut in the hut and

[46] HGB, *Mythology of the Soul*, p. 468.
[47] African village containing round mud huts with thatched roofs, with sur-rounding protective fence.

at Jung's request she lets them out, but it is a while before they have the courage to emerge. There is an enchanting scene in the film where Jung approaches one of the little boys, touching him gently on the face. The little boy retreats rapidly, only to emerge again a second later, curiosity getting the better of him. Once again Jung touches him in greeting and the child gives him a shy smile.

About the mother, Jung writes: 'I had the feeling that the confidence and self-assurance of her manner were founded to a great extent upon her identity with her own wholeness, her private world made up of children, house, small livestock, *shamba* (field of bananas, sweet potatoes, kaffir and maize) and – last but not least – her not unattractive physique.'

Jung goes on to comment that women in the West have lost this sense of their own natural wholeness and he wonders 'whether the growing masculinisation of the white woman is not connected with the loss of her natural wholeness (shamba, children, livestock, house of her own, hearth, fire) and whether the feminising of the white man is not a further consequence.' He adds: 'My companions and I had the good fortune to taste the world of Africa, with its incredible beauty and its equally incredible suffering, before the end came. Our camp life proved to be one of the loveliest interludes in my life. I enjoyed the "divine peace" of a still primaeval country.'

During the palavers Jung, sitting on a small stool, would converse, with the help of a dictionary, in Swahili, and contrary to Hislop's prediction, most of the natives spoke enough pidgin Swahili for simple conversations to take place. At first he was not able to persuade any of them, even with the offer of rewards, to tell him their dreams. On one occasion a palaver with the richly arrayed medicine man revealed the reason why his tribesmen no longer had dreams. He said, with tears in his eyes: 'In old days the *laibons* (medicine men) had dreams, and knew whether there is war or sickness or whether rain comes and where the herds should be driven.' However, since white men had arrived the dreams had ceased: 'Dreams were no longer needed because now the English knew everything!'[48]

After this blissful time with the Elgonyi, the expedition struck camp and continued to trek along the southern slope of Mt Elgon where they encountered higher mountains, denser jungle and blacker natives who lacked the grace of the Masai. This was the territory of

[48] MDR, p. 295.

the Bugishu. Here they stayed for a while in the rest house of Bunambale with its vantage point high above the Nile valley.

They continued their journey to Mbala where they were met by two Ford trucks which took them on to Jinja, on Lake Victoria. A paddle-wheel steamer took them on to Masindi Port on the Nile, and from there they travelled by truck to Masindi town, between Lake Kioga and Albert Nyanza.

They were making a journey on foot, from Lake Albert to Rejaf (in the Sudan), walking in the early morning from 5:30 a.m. until 9:30 a.m., after which the heat made walking impossible. However, on the third day, because their progress was so slow, they comman-deered a truck to take them the rest of the way to Rejaf. It was during this exhausting walk that they had an exciting adventure, colourfully described in Jung's memoir.

They found themselves being entertained by a tribe of the blackest Africans he had ever encountered. The chief proposed a dance for the evening to which the party of four and their bearers were invited. In spite of the heat, a huge fire was built, drums and horns sounded and about sixty men appeared with lances swords and clubs, while the women and children remained at a distance. There was an uneasy feeling about this group which made Jung and his companions nervous, while the boys and the government soldiers had simply disappeared. The women formed a large circle around the fire and the men made an outer protective circle, surrounding the women. As the dancing and singing rose to a crescendo of excitement, Jung and Peter rose to their feet and joined in the dance. Jung described the scene in his memoir:

> It was a wild and stirring scene, bathed in the glow of the fire and magical moonlight. My English friend [Peter Baynes] and I sprang to our feet and mingled with the dancers. I swung my rhinoceros whip, the only weapon I had, and danced with them. By their beaming faces I could see they approved of our taking part. Their zeal redoubled; the whole company stamped, sang, shouted, sweating profusely. Gradually the rhythm of the dance and the drumming accelerated.
>
> In dances such as these, accompanied by such music, the natives easily fall into a virtual state of possession. That was the case now. As eleven o'clock approached, their excitement began to get out of bounds, and suddenly the whole affair took on a highly

[text continues p. 193]

Hilda Davidson (ca. 1924)

Hilda's son, Christopher (1930)

Peter, Ruth Bailey and Jung, in Uganda (1925)

George Beckwith, Ruth Bailey and Jung, in native dress

Jung and Peter at the District Commissioner's house in Uganda (1925)
(Jung is second from the left, and Peter is third from the left.)

*Jung, Ruth Bailey and Peter, at their camp
on Mount Elgon, in Uganda (1925)*

Skiing holiday in Gstaad (1929)
Peter and Cary sledging

Cary on horseback

Peter in Africa (1925)

Peter
He was an expert with the boomerang.

Cary Baynes at Marlowes House (ca. 1927)

From bottom upwards:
Bridget Baynes, unknown, Lille Jung, unknown, Franz Jung
on a wall near the Jung's home in Küsnacht (1921)

*Bridget Baynes and Franz Jung
by the Jungs' home in Küsnacht*

188

Lille, Bridget, Marianne, Franz on the Jungs' sailing dinghi (1921)

Franz, Bridget, Lille, Marianne

Henri Zinno (Cary's sister), Peter, Cary and Joseph Henderson
in Gstaad (1929)

HGB in 1921, at the time of his analysis with Jung

HGB and Jung (man in the middle unknown)
at an International Conference in Copenhagen

curious aspect. The dancers were being transformed into a wild horde, and I became worried about how it would end. I signed to the chief that it was time to stop, and that he and his people ought to go to sleep. But he kept wanting just another one.

Finally, Jung took the matter into his own hands, seemed literally to grow in stature as he ordered the dancers to cease, swung his rhinoceros whip semi-threateningly and swore at the tribesmen in Swiss German, then distributed cigarettes to the assembled company. The possession died down and the dancers scattered into the night. A very tense moment had been averted.

It was soon after this incident, when the companions had arrived once more at the District ommissioner's, that the DC expressed horror when he heard of their experience. He said their party had had a lucky escape as two men had been killed by this tribe only a short time before.

At Rajif on the Nile, the trek came to an end and on the 15th January 1926, the four travellers took the paddle steamer, together with all their gear, to Khartoum. They floated down the Nile for six weeks, on their way to see the pyramids in Egypt. The remainder of the journey was peaceful, as they explored the Sudan and Egypt. They were approaching Egypt from Africa, as Jung had always wished to do, coming from the darkness of the primaeval experience into the light of an ancient civilization, and flowing with the ancient life-force symbolized by the great River Nile.

Jung made his notes and considered the powerful effect Africa had had on him; an adventure, epitomised by the wild African dancers, that had taken him completely by storm. It was a time for reflection and for digesting the profound experience the African expedition had been for them all. He now recognized how much this journey had been to satisfy, and come to terms with, something within himself, as though it was a meeting face to face with, and an acknowledgement of his own primaeval self; a direct experience of the collective unconscious. The research they had done in relation to the primitive psychology had become a secondary factor. He also recognized his powerful need to escape from Europe where the atmosphere in 1925, so soon after the Great War, was difficult and uncomfortable.

On their way home, the four visited Aswan and Luxor and the Valley of Kings. To reach the Valley they had to travel by camel and Peter's previous experience of these wilful animals, during his time with the Red Crescent Mission, gave him a certain advantage. While they were in Cairo, they visited the mosques, museums and the pyramids before sailing for home from Port Said.

The African adventure was a powerful experience for Peter, but he was like a man haunted by the ghostly presence of his dead wife. This made him a difficult and moody companion and though Jung understood his unhappiness and made allowance for it, George Beckwith found Peter intolerable. In a conversation with Katey Cabot (who spent many years in Zurich analysing with Jung), Jung told her the story of an incident when he was together with George Beckwith in their tent, on Mount Elgon. A shot was heard from the forest nearby and Beckwith commented, somewhat sourly to Jung, 'I hope that is Baynes blowing his brains out.' So one can imagine that there may have been times of considerable tension among the four of them.

Peter spent a few days in Zurich before returning to his home in Campden Hill Square and his little son, Christopher, who was now nearly two years old. The return to his home and to the aftermath of the life he and Hilda had lived together was a poignant and difficult one for Peter; there was still unfinished business and he had much grieving still to do.

What was the enduring effect of this momentous journey on Peter? The only reference to it in 'The Book that Groweth' is a single sentence: 'More than a year has passed since I last wrote in this book. During that year the fate that pursued my loved wife overtook her and she died, leaving me broken and for a time quite impotent. The manner of her death made a gulf between her spirit and mine which the awfulness of Africa helped finally to bridge.'

Chapter Fourteen

A new Marriage: Cary de Angulo

For the joy of love is too short, and the sorrow thereof, and what cometh thereof, dureth over long.

Sir Thomas Malory, Le Morte D'Arthur

Jung's two colleagues, Peter and Cary de Angulo, both involved in the translation of Jung's books into English, and both left with the care of a young child, make a 'sensible' marriage. They live together for a time near London then take a year's sabbatical in San Francisco. They return to Zurich where Peter works once more as Jung's assistant.

Peter's return from Africa brought him face to face with the terrible tragedy of his wife's death. He speaks of being haunted by her spirit. The power of her spirit is all the greater because her physical grasp on life was so uncertain:

> She could not free her soul from the clutching fingers, which caught her out of the chaos of the past, by means of life. Therefore she was forced to free herself by death. Freedom she must have at all costs and I was merely part of the cost. Life had proved too much for her and she had to give it up. Her last word to me was her undying belief in Love …
>
> Yesterday I stood beside her grave and wondered if her spirit was in the breeze that rustled the autumn leaves.
>
> Throughout the year her spirit had been with me. By negation of the body and its functions she went over almost completely to the life of the spirit so that the shedding of the body became an

inevitable need for her cramped and tormented soul. Thus she became a spirit of great power and constantly she affects me.

Whether this relation exists in the world or solely in my soul I cannot say, but for me her spirit lingers. She is my guide, because her main preoccupation was religion. Religion seized her and broke her ... only from the angle of religion does her life appear meaningful and intelligible. Her religious instinct was her only paramount guide by which she held her precarious course.

Therefore like Pallas Athena, Hilda often assumes the guise of Mentor and stands beside me holding me to that same quest and striving in that same warfare.

But her spirit has gone through a transformation. She has relinquished her personal and limited notions of truth ... she has become an influence that is in a way personal in effect but celestial in intention. Very like the influence which Pallas Athena exercised upon Ulysses.

It was during the Jungian conference in Swanage in the fateful year of 1925, that Peter had first come into close contact with Cary de Angulo. Cary was American, a woman of Peter's age and in a similar situation: her first marriage had come to an end in 1924, although she remained on friendly terms with her ex-husband Xaime De Angulo. He was an anthropologist and a Spanish aristocrat but he had become an American citizen by the time he married Cary. They had one daughter together, a child a little older than Christopher, called Ximena.

Cary had come to live in Zurich in 1921 with her sister Henri Zinno, and they had a house together on the far side of the lake from Küsnacht. They were a lively and highly intelligent pair and created a welcome refuge and meeting place for all the American and English-speaking students who came to work with Jung, as well as teaching them a great deal about Jungian psychology.

On his return from Africa Peter spent a few days in Zurich before returning home and there he received a warm welcome from the two sisters. During this time he renewed his friendship with Cary, finding in her a ready and empathic ear: although she was not herself an analyst, she was able to listen with understanding as he spoke to her of his anguish over Hilda's death. It was this friendship with Cary that enabled Peter to recover from the trauma and guilt which he suffered in relation to Hilda's death and soon the friendship blossomed into love.

They had much in common: together they were involved with the translation of Jung's books and they were both working closely with Jung. Both had suffered marriage difficulties and had a young child to care for; both were fine swimmers and regarded themselves as intellectuals. On the face of it, it seemed like an ideal union.

It seemed to both that a marriage between them would also please Jung. However, Jung did in reality have grave misgivings about this union. They were far out on the Zurich See, swimming together, when Peter proposed to Cary, and Jung saw this as an indication that they were too much in the unconscious with regard to their relationship. But his main concern was that Cary, although she was a fine looking woman, was essentially not Peter's anima-type. She was a big, strong-minded, independent woman of forty years old, and Peter was still dreaming of his inspiritrice, a young, slender girl of exquisite feminine beauty. He describes her thus, in an image that arose from a waking dream:

> There, standing up in her virgin dawn of bright beauty, was a maid slim in body, and her hair shone. She was looking down into the water. Then it seemed to me that she looked up and saw me with eager and innocent love. She flew to me and immediately embraced me with all her youthful heat and she had no shame and no shrinking and I wondered what fair being should be born of such a mating under the Sun.

He relates earlier loves to this image of lustrous beauty. First, his love from Cambridge days, Isabel 'and the golden age of love, before I had tasted the keen flavours of the strong evil in me.' Then, 'Rosalind also tasted that dream of the golden age, but … evil came and sowed weeds in our garden.' Then there was Daphne. She and I tasted the exquisite magic of that dream and we bathed naked in the river in her virgin beauty. But it is a dream not meant for the real world.'

There follows a time of soul-searching and spiritual confusion. All his reason tells him that Cary is the ideal mate, but his heart and instinct do not concur. He longs for a mate and for the stability of marriage, so that he can also become clear in his mind about the book that he is hoping to write. He sets out a list of pros and cons in relation to Cary. Her age and want of erotic arts and beauty; her lack of feminine grace as well as an absence of all adornment, weigh

against her. She also has a somewhat 'forbidding' manner both with
children and with Peter, which feels like criticism, 'and this is very
dampening to an enthusiastic soul.' However, he recognizes his
fondness and admiration for her and his appreciation for her gentleness and constancy; above all for her loyalty, the quality that Peter
valued most of all, because loyalty had been for him such a great
problem. He sees her as truthful and uncompromisingly honest,
spiritually superior to him and an 'aristocrat' in her thought and
tastes. He writes of her as a 'a good woman', and 'above all I believe
she really loves me and will stick to me through thick and thin.'

But he is tormented by indecision:

> On the one hand is a firm partnership making for duration and
> lasting values.
>
> On the other hand is the power and glory and delight of the
> body, the pursuit of pleasures and adventures and temporal sub-
> stance.
>
> Which is it going to be, the known and real and incorruptible
> Cary or the unknown deity of all delights? ... When I have made
> this choice my work will also be clear.
>
> Now choose and stick to your choice.

Finally, they came to a decision together and Cary and Peter were
married on Saturday March 19th, 1927 at Marylebone Town Hall.
The only witnesses to this marriage were his dear, loyal sister Ruth
and her friend, Bertha. After all the indecision he comments: 'I say I
chose but in fact no other course was really possible for me. Cary and
I have been mated ever since Swanage and the logic of this fact was
undeniable.' Before being able to take this step he speaks of having to,
'endure the most persistent and almost overpowering resistance from
the side of the anima.'

Peter speaks of having 'to realize the terrific power of the past. I
was merely filled by vague unseizable longings.' But having at last
made his choice, he writes that: 'There is now a profound sense of
relief and I am happier than I have been for many years.' However, he
adds, the power of the unconscious still awaits and it is necessary for
him 'to make the descent ... Therefore I must persistently bore
through the conscious resistance and let myself go as Jung had to do.'

It seems that Hilda was still Peter's anima figure, 'the blue-eyed
goddess'. Even though Cary's generous understanding allowed him to
reveal so much of his deepest feelings to her in relation to his tragic

Peter and Cary's home, Marlowes House, in Hemel Hempstead

love for Hilda, he writes of an aspect of his relationship to Hilda which it is impossible to discuss with her:

> 'It is as though there existed a taboo so that an understanding with her about the nature of the religious attitude was for the time forbidden. Last night it happened again when Cary asked me to tell her the meaning of the dream in which Hilda came to life again. I spoke of the talk I had had with Jung and at once my spirit was closed to her and hers to me. What is the meaning of this?'

On his return from Africa, Peter sold the house in Campden Hill Square and bought a large and attractive Victorian house on the edge of Hemel Hempstead, called Marlowes House. This is where he and Cary began their married life and all Peter's family could now be included in their home. Bridget, Chloë and Nan could come and visit. Christopher lived with them together with his nanny, and Cary's daughter, Ximena. So now at last, after Peter's wanderings, there was a sense of a settled home life.

The house was near to a golf course so it was possible for Peter to develop his interest in golf, which was to occupy him, as a passion, for the rest of his life. Marlowes House had a lovely big garden and

Peter continued to devote an increasing amount of his spare time to gardening. He found the plants, which grew and developed without the need for speech, a welcome antidote to his patients. Chloë describes the house and her memories of her visits there.

> The house, which was long and low and had a canopied veranda leading out to a sloping lawn, was set in four acres of garden. A small stream ran through the grounds and there was a tennis court, a rose garden and a fine vegetable garden. The house was run by a married couple from Ireland. Keating, who was the cook, boasted that he knew 365 ways of cooking potatoes, one for each day of the year. His wife Bertha saw to the house and, with a nurse, helped to look after the little boy Christopher. There were also two gardeners, which made it quite an establishment even for those times. One of the attractions of the place for Godwin was that it was conveniently near a beautiful golf course at Berkhampstead. He took up golf partly as a relaxation from arduous analysis sessions, partly for the exercise, and he became a very good player. I remember when we children went to stay with him for part of our school holidays, Godwin would take us round the course with him. We were supposed to look for the ball when it went into rough grass and on one occasion after we had hunted for it everywhere, it was discovered in the hole itself. Godwin had made it in one.

The family also occupied much of Peter and Cary's time and all her step-children found Cary an affectionate and sympathetic 'mother' who shared her warmth and her attentions equally. Bridget, especially, began to feel increasingly a part of this family home and began, perhaps for the first time, to feel that she was a real part of Peter's life. For Chloë, who had never had a chance to really know her father, he remained a distant and somewhat inaccessible figure. He was, as always, too occupied with work to see as much of his children as he would have liked. A letter written to Bridget in July 1927 gives an impression of their life at this time.

> My darling Bridget, Your enthusiastic letter delighted me, and it was awfully nice to have your birthday wishes.
> Cary and I motored up to North Wales to try and see the eclipse, but we got wet through instead.
> About your birthday, I hate to disappoint you, but I am afraid I shan't be able to come. I get so done in with my work that I simply

have to rest during the week-ends. So please forgive me, and please tell me what you would really like for your birthday: I want to give you something nice.

When you come home next you will find a very nice little Shetland pony wanting to play with you.

My very best love, Your loving Daddy.

So, Marlowes House, complete with pony, became a child's paradise, but a Daddy who was creating a niche for Jungian Psychology in the somewhat antagonistic professional world of London had no time to join in the celebrations of his daughter's thirteenth birthday. Another letter from Bridget in November prompted Peter to make a visit to her and Chloë at their boarding school, Frensham Heights, in Surrey.

It was in the spring of 1927 that Peter experienced a severe personal loss with the death of his mother, Mary, to whom he was particularly close.[49] She had been the dynamic force in his life and it was from her that he inherited his vitality and warmth and his astonishing gift for human relationships. He wrote a letter to Bridget edged with black, asking her to think of her grandmother on the day of her funeral.

In the spring of 1928, Peter and Cary took a sabbatical and went together to live in her house in Carmel, California. Soon after they arrived in New York, in May 1928, Peter experienced a pain in his left eye and for two months he was unable to use his eye for reading or writing. The doctors eventually diagnosed optic neuritis and there was a danger of losing the sight in that eye. He had a total overhaul in the John Hopkins Clinic in Baltimore and the septic focus was finally discovered in his tonsils, an upper molar tooth and the ethmoid sinus at the back of the nose. To remove the sites of infection required three operations and left Peter feeling weak and exhausted. He found that he had lost 17 lbs in one week.

It took a while before he was able to use that eye again and he was then faced with the correction of the proofs of the two books he was translating for Jung, and a backlog of work. When the eye was out of danger, Peter and Cary continued to California to spend the rest of that year in Carmel. They remained until the summer of 1929.

---

[49] Helton Baynes survived his wife by two years. He died on 20 February 1929.

Both Cary and Peter were occupied with the translation of Jung's books and papers into English. Cary also undertook a translation of the *I Ching* (*The Book of Changes*), into English, from the German translation of Wilhelm, and this is still the standard English version of that great Chinese book of wisdom.

Peter describes his first impressions of California in a letter to Bridget:

> It is surely a lovely country and the Sierra Nevadas are simply grand ... we were up there among the giant Sequoias and the little brown bears. It is as grand as anything I ever saw ...
>
> We have amazing hospitality wherever we have been and the doctors especially have been extraordinarily kind. But you know I can't tell you about America in a letter. It is simply terrific. New York and Chicago simply stagger you. They are beautiful and enormously luxurious but somehow they are terrifying and wrong. The human personality is just overwhelmed by the vast machinery of social life.
>
> As soon as we left Chicago I began to feel better towards America and out here it really feels human and friendly, and you can take it in without being swept away.
>
> We made a detour up into the country of the Pueblo Indians where I made friends with a fine Indian whose name is Mountain Lake. I will show you his photograph when I get back.
>
> This little ring is for your birthday with a great kiss and my fond love. It was made for you by a Navaho Indian. The stones are turquoise.

Peter goes on to say that now Bridget has reached her teens, he would like an opportunity to know her better; he adds:

'Often when I think of writing to you I find myself slightly embarrassed because I don't really know what your mind is seeking or where you stand.' He suggests that when he and Cary return to England, it would be good to go on holiday with Bridget.

One can only imagine what a powerful effect such a comment would have on a little girl who's Daddy has always adored her, but who, for most of her life, has always been somewhere else.

He adds a PS to this letter about Cary who also sends her love and who is 'very happy to be living in her own shack again by the sea.'

Another letter, written in July 1928 to both Bridget and Chloë, speaks of his decision to remain another six months in California, until the following spring. This must have been a blow to both little girls, and especially to Bridget who had been promised a special holiday on her own with her 'splendid Daddy'. The reasons he gives are that he is doing much important work in California.

Another reason for prolonging their stay was on account of Cary's daughter, Ximena, who had been infected with tuberculosis and had been under the care of a Swiss doctor. The doctor had recommended that she should not be allowed to spend the winter in England, so Cary had arranged for a friend, who was returning from Europe, to bring Ximena and Christopher (then four years old) with his nanny, Eva, to New York by sea, and from there, by train, to California. They were to arrive in California on July 22nd.

Perhaps Peter recognized Bridget and Chloë's misgivings about whether their Daddy would ever come home again, for he adds: 'But you need not be afraid of our settling over here. It is wonderful for a spell and the sun shines all the year round, but I could never leave England for good. I feel I could not really belong here. ...

It is a grand place to work, because after I have been seeing patients all day, I can run down to the beach and wash it all away and come back absolutely fresh again. So that I can do my writing work all the evening.'

Again he promises that they can take a holiday together when he is back home and he speaks of his own dilemma in being pulled in different directions:

> One simply has to decide which way one ought to go as best one may. I can't help feeling that my work has to come first, because the things I teach people and the psychological investigations I am doing are really more important than my own personal desires.
>
> I hope one day you will understand why this is so. As soon as I can explain my work to you I think you will sympathize with my enthusiasm for it.
>
> I find the people out here tremendously entertaining and lively and very eager to learn new points of view.

Maybe Bridget and Chloë, however much they might love their exciting Daddy, felt that he had always had something 'more important' to do, than spend time with his two little daughters. He was a father who was greatly loved and much admired, but who was essentially elusive.

It was at this time that Peter and Cary first met Joseph Henderson. Joe was working as a journalist and was in analysis with a student of Jung's called Elizabeth Whitney. He had become fascinated by Jungian psychology and was asking Elizabeth questions that she was unable to answer. Cary and Peter had just arrived in California and their house in Carmel was near to where Elizabeth Whitney was spending the summer, so she arranged a meeting between them. This meeting was to change the course of Joe's life. He writes:

> I met Godwin (Peter) Baynes first when he and his third wife, Cary, were staying in her house in Carmel, a seaside resort on the Monterey Peninsular in California, in 1927-28. They had taken a sabbatical year off from their work in Zurich for C.G. Jung where they had been translators of Jung's books and where Peter had acted as an assistant analyst. I was in analysis with Dr. Elizabeth Whitney in San Francisco, a recent student of Jung. I had gone to her after my graduation from Princeton University and I was looking for my vocation. Jung's psychology had been recommended to me and I was eager to learn more about it separate from my work with Dr. Whitney. She was seeing me in Carmel where she was spending the summer, and she advised me to talk with Dr. Baynes.
>
> He was full of enthusiasm for Jung and his work and conveyed this to me in his dynamic and inimitable style. No one could have provided a more effective demonstration of Jung's archetypes of the collective unconscious and I was duly impressed. Among other things, he became what my friend, Maud Oakes, called an opener-of-the-way. Certain people come into one's life, she said, at significant times to enable one to take steps in development that could never happen without them.
>
> Peter opened the way for me to continue my analysis with Jung two years later and after that he opened the way for me to go to medical school at his old hospital, St. Bartholomew, in London, where I spent the nineteen-thirties and my real life in the world began.[50]

When Peter in his typically optimistic way told Joe he must study with Jung in Zurich, Joe was only aware of the impossibility of this. He could foresee no way of finding the necessary money. Peter had

---

[50] Reminiscences of H.G. Baynes, by Joseph Henderson (MD), April, 1998.

said to him: 'You should be in Europe, studying with Jung, why are you out here on the West Coast? If you want to do it you will find a way.' Joe comments 'that was a very good approach in that he left it up to me, rather than telling me how to do it. He was being a good analyst, a good psychologist, knowing that I should be thrown back onto myself to find the answer to my problem.' For, he observes, 'I was tightly in my little introverted world.' Sure enough, Joe did find a way.

During one of their first meetings, Peter showed Joe one of Jung's paintings of a Gnostic mandala. Joe was fascinated by Gnostic philosophy, which held the belief that those who professed Gnosticism had a special knowledge and understanding of the profound spiritual mysteries. These mysteries were expressed in the form of a mandala, a circular shape with four subdivisions which Jung interpreted as representing the psyche and especially the Self. Mandalas can at times symbolize both individual and also cosmic wholeness and are often used as religious symbols. There was a lively interest at the time, in the University of California's English and philosophy departments, in Jungian Psychology and all related subjects. There were no Freudians in California at the time, so there was no conflict. Joe felt himself to be a 'natural Jungian'.

The Gnostic philosophy is described in Jung's book, *Seven Sermons of the Dead*, which he wrote while he was experiencing his confrontation with the unconscious, in 1912.[51] It was from this profound inner experience that all Jungian psychology has evolved. When Elizabeth Whitney heard that Peter had introduced Joe to this book, she was shocked. She exclaimed: 'He gave you the *Seven Sermons of the Dead*? But you're only 25! ... This book belongs to the second half of life.' The mandala is a visual impression of everything that is contained in the book. When Joe saw the mandala he said that he then *knew* that he had to work with Jung.

After meeting Peter, Joe gave up his job as a journalist working for two magazines; his heart wasn't in it. He then returned to his old school, Lawrenceville, in New Jersey, a school based on the model of an English public school. The headmaster offered him the job of assistant housemaster and teacher of French, Latin and English to second and third form boys. During the year he was there he 'lived like a monk' and managed to save almost his entire salary. He then

---

[51] In this context, see the painting on p. 278.

wrote to Jung to ask if he could work with him as a patient. He was accepted, and began his analysis with Jung in the autumn of 1929. Almost immediately the Great Depression began and he realized that if he hadn't arrived at that time it would have been doubtful whether he could have gone at all because of the appalling financial situation. Many years later, when his training as an analyst was complete, he was to become the pioneer for Jungian analysis on the American West Coast. At the age of 98, he is still in practice there.

In the late autumn of 1929, Peter and Cary were again in Switzerland. Bridget was to go with them to inspect a possible school where she could go in order to benefit from the pure air, as she was suffering from bronchitis. By this time she had left Frensham Heights and her parents were trying to decide where she should go next. In October Peter wrote to Bridget to say: 'I have found the school for you. It is at Felton in lower Engadine and to my eyes it is what the Americans call "swell".' He sent the details of the school to Rosalind and wrote to Bridget that many girls in the school had been sent there because of their asthma and bronchitis and have been cured. He continues:

> It has I think the most glorious view I have ever seen and it is particularly favourable for the training of the body; skiing and tobogganing in winter and tennis, mountaineering and swimming in the summer. There are some English and American girls but they are mostly Swiss and German. I advise you to have a German girl as your room-mate so as to learn to speak German easily and naturally. The girls range from 14 to 21 and there are between 70 and 80 girls. It is a modern post war school with a very fine building. Music and painting are both good.
>
> You will have to leave Weybridge on the 27th or 28th and start with me and Christopher on the 29th. (December).
>
> I want you to stay on there during the Christmas holidays in order to give your lungs a clear winter. The air is pure and clear all through the winter there, [its] about 5600 feet above the sea.

Peter suggests that they might drive all the way in the Sunbeam as he also intends to spend the winter in Switzerland and it would be handy to have the car with them.

During the autumn and winter of that year, Peter and Cary were living together in the suburbs of Zurich, in a village called Kilchberg. Here they created another family home with Ximena and Christopher and Christopher's nanny. This home also became the centre for all the

English-speaking students of Jung and among their frequent visitors at this time was Joe Henderson.

> In Zurich Peter and Cary befriended me and I was frequently at their charming house and I saw them regularly at Jung's Wednesday morning English seminar during the academic year 1929-30.

In a recent interview, Joe has stated that there was no formal training at that time in Zurich and the Jung Institute was not founded until after the Second World War; so nothing was happening of a professional nature except the Wednesday morning seminars. They were referred to as dream seminars and all Jung's patients were able to attend. These seminars began in 1929 and they provided a welcome meeting ground for patients who had 'nothing to do except wait for their next analytic hour.' Joe speaks of those who were working alongside Jung in Zurich at the time. They were; 'Toni [Wolff], Cary (who never worked as an analyst) Peter, Emma Jung and "C.G.".'[52]

Peter attended the seminars regularly. They went on all that year. Peter and Cary were very helpful to me, and I was also some help to them as they were having difficulties with the children.' On being asked what these difficulties were, he replies: 'Ximena was impossible. Very pretty and intelligent, but spoilt. I remember Peter saying, 'she's the best goat-catcher I know.'

Joe refers to Peter's unhappiness after Hilda's death. Peter was very troubled and didn't know how he would bring himself together: 'Jung told me he [Peter] was quite difficult in Africa – he didn't seem to understand that Peter did need to mourn, and to take time to recover.' Of Peter and Cary's relationship, Joe says that it seemed fine on the surface, 'but not underneath. They never felt married to me, as though they were playing at being married rather than really being married. Jung said they felt they should marry to please him, but that wasn't true. This was the big mistake: although they outwardly played the happy family, inside there was no true love.'

During the early days of Joe's analysis with Jung, he was having three sessions a week. After that, during the following year, he had two sessions a week with Jung and one with Peter. He referred to Peter as 'my part-time analyst'. Jung felt that it was important for Joe to work with someone who was different in every respect so these

---

[52] C.G. was the nickname given to Jung by his Anglo Saxon friends; Barbara Hannah notes: 'I think the custom originated with Peter Baynes.'

sessions with Peter were especially valuable for whereas Jung was the same personality type as Joe, an introverted thinking-intuitive type, which meant that they could understand each other perfectly, Peter was the exact opposite: an extravert feeling intuitive. Joe describes Jung's approach as 'deeper' and Peter's as 'broader', the two together, 'encompassing the whole dimension of the cross, with both the vertical and the horizontal characteristics.'

Peter spent the Christmas holiday in 1929 with his family at the ski resort in Gstaad. He wrote to Bridget that he would pick her and Ximena up from their school on December 21st and that she would stay with them until the middle of January. He tells her: 'We are all going to Gstaad for Christmas where we can feast as a reunited family.' He adds that Henri Zinno, Cary's younger sister, will also be with them. He speaks of her as 'a grand woman, she is a born artist. I was looking at the paintings she did in Mexico, at Papa Jung's last Sunday, and it is simply unmistakable. A toreador tense on tiptoe conveying the courage of a barbarous folk before a descending black bull. It has the power of a blow between the eyes.' Henri was a highly gifted and intelligent woman, but she had times of severe instability and her talents were never fully realised. She suffered from schizophrenia and when she returned to Cary after a trip to Mexico in a disturbed state, she destroyed all the beautiful paintings she had made.

Rosalind, Bridget, Chloë and Nan joined Peter, Cary and their children, Ximena and Christopher, in Gstaad, so the children of all Peter's three wives were together on this holiday. They all stayed in a pension and Joe Henderson, who was also invited, stayed in a hotel nearby with a girl he was seeing at that time. This was the first year of the Great Depression and many people were staying in Gstaad who would otherwise have been in a more luxurious place.

Joe describes the times he had together with this large and strangely assorted family party. They had taken over the entire pension and he and his girlfriend spent a great deal of time with them there: 'I thought this was the ideal family gathering, free, open, and unjudgemental. I had no idea there was anything wrong. Peter was in his element, so good at that. He was everywhere – knowing everyone, interested in everybody, making everything come out right, making everyone happy. There he was with Cary and his first wife and he managed to make them all accept the situation and not feel conflict...'

'We would go for picnics up on the hills and he was the perfect host. They seemed perfectly happy [Peter and Cary], as though their troubles were over. I thought they were going to make it. However, when Peter returned to Zurich, that was the end of the marriage.'

So in spite of the impression of family harmony, things at this stage were not going well for Peter. It was as though, with his robust extraversion and warmth, he could create an impression of gaiety and harmony while the difficulties were buried out of sight. The house in Kilchberg that Cary and Peter were renting for the winter gave a sense of warmth and welcome to all who came there, but for Peter the relationship was already under great strain. They were sleeping apart and Peter had realized by now that he had made a terrible mistake.

He had written a sad entry in his journal, before their trip to the States, recognizing already that the marriage was a disaster:

> A beautiful day in a blue-eyed garden under a halcyon sky. Brilliant, life-giving wonder of a summer's day.
>
> But a cloud lies over my heart, for I am not at peace with Cary. Ever since that shadow of the moon swept across the land [This was the eclipse that Peter and Cary had seen during their holiday in North Wales] and I felt for a moment the darkness and vertigo of the abyss, I have felt that the heart of life was cut out. My holiday had no holiness and no real joy.
>
> We came home a day sooner than we had planned as on both the other occasions when I had tried to seize some respite from the ceaseless tension that consumes me. We found that the faithful Hans, [their Welsh terrier], the symbol of our relationship, had been poisoned while we were away. He lay on his straw bed emaciated, trembling and utterly pitiful. I injected morphia to give him sleep and in the night he died. Possibly the morphia killed him. Who knows?
>
> Cary was broken with grief and Ximena sobbed hysterically. I dug his grave near the spot where I buried Dougall [Peter's previous Welsh terrier] and there they both lie. Fate continues to aim the cold wind of death at every attempt I make to organize and remake my love-life.
>
> Ever since this new blow fell a shadow lies between Cary and me. Her courage is ebbing away. Yesterday she seriously suggested that she leaves me. She feels that our attempt has failed and we ought to go our separate ways. Her indifference and lack of energy lies on my spirit like lead. How am I to infuse life and enthusiasm and courage into the deepest habitation of dread.

She wants to come along and face life with courage, but always she stands aloof. What life she has only appears when others are here. I only see her doubts, her timorousness, her tired voice and crushing apathy. When she sees me reaching out to youth and beauty and new life she only falls the deeper into her pit of self-deprecation.

Is there something in me which destroys life and makes every effort vain and every goal fruitless?

This was a time of deep dejection for Peter: once again his high hopes of happiness had ebbed away and he found himself trapped in a loveless situation. This is indeed an irony for someone who needed so much love and who apparently had so much warmth to give. It is as though the different needs of his gigantic personality were in continual conflict.

On the one hand, he needed a companion who could satisfy his intellectual and creative aspirations and whom he could respect for her integrity, insight and spiritual maturity; someone, perhaps, who was of equal calibre to the women who were part of the Jungian circle in Zurich, and in this, Cary was indeed the ideal partner. But he was also in need of a woman who could inspire and delight him and who would to some extent reflect his anima, and with her sensible clothes, her fine intellect and her poor relationship to her womanly warmth and physical being, this was something Cary could never fulfil.

Jung was aware of this and could see from the beginning that the liaison between two of his closest colleagues would end in tears. Joe Henderson comments that Peter 'tended to think that the marriage was what Jung would want him and Cary to do and Jung said himself to me once that he had no such idea at all. It was as though Peter had sold himself on the idea that Jung did want him and Cary to marry. Now it *was* a good *idea* but it didn't work.'

Joe thought that Peter had treated Cary badly and he felt sorry for her. He remarks: 'I remember her saying, "I always said I would never be the rejected woman." That in itself tells us something about Cary too, that she was so sure that nothing like this would happen to her; but it did. It was a blow but she weathered it and I saw her some time later and she was not seriously wounded by it.' To Peter's sister Ruth, who was also fond of Cary and was for a time her confidante, she once said: 'Men always want to marry me but they never like it when they do.'

Peter writes of Cary:

> She has the honesty and integrity of a man in not indulging this dark side of her. She consumes her own smoke as well as she can. But she is very hard to live with.

With characteristic honesty, he adds:

> But so am I ... My life is complicated by the fruits of much desiring. She, if anything, has desired too little. She seems to have very few needs and wants, whereas I hang out of the window, always wanting something out of my grasp ...

He continues with reflections on Jung's similar struggle with his 'desiring':

> C.G. has the same problem. His libido is still strong and possessive. He is never content. He built his tower as a tribute to the dream of life he would have liked to realize and never could. [This was Bollingen]. He had to compromise because his nature is essentially complex. He wants simplicity because he is not simple. He has always tried to foist upon Emma the tangible burdens of his complex strivings. He accumulates and then cannot maintain. Thus he is also surrounded by the decaying heaps of things and people from which his libido has receded and which are left to Emma to deal with. She expresses this remorseless continuity, this Abraxoid[52] character to his desiring vitality.
>
> Always she reminds him of the debt intuitiveness piles up in the world of real things. He hates sensation because it is unexpressive, inarticulate and quite remorseless and indifferent to the flutters and strivings of intuition which is for ever trying to escape from the real and the actual.
>
> New desires that add more and more to the heap of tangible liabilities must be renounced if this essential simplification is to be attained. Things cannot create happiness. They only make Egypt more lascivious and terrible in its effect. They only make you forget, like alcohol and infatuation. This is terrible Abraxas which makes life and death with the same breath and in the same act. The

---

[52] Abraxas was a god created by the Gnostics consisting of a lions head and a snakes body. It represented a philosophical idea, embracing all that enters into the sphere of reality. It was beyond good and evil.

right way for me is toward an increasing simplification of life in the midst of a world which goes ever towards an increasing specialization and complexity.

As the relationship with Cary was nearing its end, Peter wrote:

> She simply wants to separate ... Beckwith [The third travelling companion in Africa] said she would not stand me six months. She says she brought me all the passion of her heart and I have never been more than luke-warm. All of this is from her angle perfectly true. I can see it too like that. The body is against it.
>
> All her adornment of her personality is in her intellectualism. There is no pride of the body in her. There she is abased and timorous. She is turned upside down. She tries to base herself on her distinctiveness or her differences from the common clay. But man's instinct goes to the deep general womanhood, not to the monument to the ideal of individuality.

Peter goes on to write of his great fear of opening himself to a woman after his experience with Hilda and he sees this as an irrevocable barrier standing between him and Cary. He experiences in the neediness of 'woman' a 'vampirizing' effect and at some level he feels that Hilda still holds his soul and that he is not yet free to truly love another woman.

After seeing the play *Dracula*, he speaks of the deep psychological significance of this play. He sees the victim of the vampire who by 'sanctioning' this victimization, takes on the characteristics of the vampire and becomes a vampire herself, as representing a universal psychological truth.

> Thus stripped of its concretism it is the theme of possession by an overmastering unconscious complex. It is the picture of just such a case of animus possession as Hilda's.
>
> Why it hit me was the implication that since I allowed myself to become involved in her deep psychology I am also infected and that is why I fear to come too close to Cary or anyone else. I dare not say 'I want you.' I can say I want or I need in general but I cannot designate the actual person. I can see in the life of C.G. how in every case where he said 'I want you' to a woman, he opened his breast to a vampire. The relationship with Hilda stamped deep into my soul the fear of the specific needing of the specific person in this vampirizing way. I cannot and will not lose my soul again in

an intoxication with a specific woman. I will not blot out the general beauties and delights of free Nature in this convulsive concentration on the particular personality of the woman trying always to draw my homage to her own erotic personality.

The vampire in Hilda was perhaps the sense of her total dependence on Peter for her very survival. He had become drawn into this and saw himself as her saviour, the one person who could save this beautiful and talented young woman from her own self-destruction. But of course, this is an impossible task. None of us can become wholly responsible for another's life and Peter had become increasingly deeply drawn into Hilda's neurosis. The more he attempted to save her the more her dependence on him sucked at his vital energy and held him totally captive. This was why Jung had insisted that Hilda's dependence should not prevent Peter from joining the African expedition. The 'vampirizing' could end by destroying them both. However, something of this 'possession' from which Hilda suffered continued to haunt Peter long after her death, so, as he confesses to himself, he was not at that time available to the love of a woman.

It was soon after his marriage to Cary that Peter was already having fantasies about a beautiful young woman called Agnes Leay (who had some years previously been a patient of his). In his active imagination, he allows the anima to lead him on his inner journey. He writes on Good Friday, April 15th 1927, just one month after his marriage to Cary: 'Therefore I must persistently bore through the conscious resistance and let myself go as Jung had to do.' Now he writes of this downward journey, which has the title, 'I go down.'

He is at first digging a hole where water rises up from a defective drain. He digs down through sodden earth, then through stones and gravel and the roots of a tree, using a pick and a spade. He hacks his way down through a massive layer of masonry, which is like an ancient floor. With the point of his pick he loosens four large stones to reveal a vault underground. It is deep and there is water at the bottom like a well. He lets himself drop down into the black water like a stone, and is totally submerged. The well is without a bottom and he swims in the direction of a river. There is a vaulted passage low over his head which leads him to the left. He sees stone steps leading up to an old metal door in the wall of the vault. Using the heavy and rusty latch and key he manages with difficulty to open the door. This leads him to a steep spiral staircase worn by feet through the ages. In the faint light coming from above he makes his descent, very cautiously, down to a great depth. It is cold, his teeth chatter and bats fly past him.

> I seem to see the face of Agnes Leay ahead of me, suspended in the air, flying ahead luminous like the moon.
>
> This is the source of light but very pale. The spiral goes deeper and deeper. Now it leads onto a paved way. I put out my hand to feel something. I catch a filmy garment, which is snatched away at once. I must challenge. "Who goes there in this dungeon?" No reply. "If it be a spirit come near." A deep voice: "What doest thou here in the halls of the dead?" "I am seeking my soul." "If thy heart be pure go in peace." The moon face of the desired girl glows brightly in the distance. "If thou would'st find thy soul put these other thoughts away. There are seductions enough." The moon-goddess smiles amorously and beckons me ... She is the only light in this nether world.

This is the personification of Peter's anima who has bewitched him before in many forms. She haunted him in the form of Hilda, and 'called to me all through Africa.' And since then the anima has taken the form of others: Enid and Olive (both friends of Ruth's) and Dorothy (another of Ruth's friends): 'and finally I lit upon the girl Agnes and imbued her with beauty and desire ... For all these women called to you because of their distress. Their insanity, their loneliness, their fear of ghosts.' The dialogue continues between this young woman and Peter and also includes the figure of an old man he calls 'Father'.

Finally, the Moon Goddess stands before him in her human form. She has been bound naked, a captive in this dark and fearful dungeon, by a huge and revolting hairy monster called The Sloth. Peter, as Orpheus rescued Eurydice from the underworld, manages with heroic effort, and with the help of a gleaming sword, to obtain her release. When she is at last free she says to him:

> Sit down here at my side and tell me how you find me now that at last you behold me face to face.

He replies:

> When I first looked upon you as you stood bound before the Sloth I was astonished at your divine beauty. You seemed to be all that

my heart had ever desired of womanly loveliness. Now that I see you in the clear light and can watch you more narrowly a sense of hunger and of foreboding seizes me which is like fear clutching at my very heart. If peace could rest in your eyes instead of that fathomless longing then all the meaning of life would be held in the compass of your surpassing beauty and grace. Tell me lady, how can that hunger be satisfied? I place my brain, the centres of motion, my hand and every executive function at your command, Oh Soul.

Her reply:

Know then that this is my estate. I am the purpose, the meaning, the beauty of your life, but I am unreal, a shade, imponderable and invisible. I am the dream that harks back to the far past and points on to the future. But I have no blood, no warmth, no tangible reality.

In this fantasy Peter has had a direct encounter with his anima guide and also with the person who was to personify his anima and who later was to become his wife. It was as though, with such a powerful image surfacing from Peter's unconscious, the marriage with Cary was doomed from the beginning.

Joe had become a confidante of both Peter and Cary and he was probably one of the first people to know that their marriage was on the rocks. He had both an analysand's devotion and admiration of Peter as well as seeing him through the eyes of a young man who was devoted to Cary, but his loyalty during the break up of the marriage was to her. She had given him a home from home and had been something of a mother to him in this strange country, especially during the long breaks in his analysis when Jung was away. He writes of Peter with both admiration and censure:

Everything about Peter seemed geared for action ... Wherever he went, Peter was a centre of attention. Later on this image of the genial patriarch broke down when he divorced Cary, his life in Zurich ended, and he returned to England for good ... Just as Peter returned to his roots in England, Cary ultimately returned to her country and settled in Connecticut where she became an important figure in the formation of the Bollingen Foundation which published Jung's Collected Works and other things of cultural importance for Analytical Psychology.

Cary did not long suffer the pain of a rejected wife, but while she was still in it, I was temporarily disenchanted with Peter, not for divorcing Cary, but for not seeming to recognise her sense of loss.

However, before he could finally make the decision to separate from Cary, Peter was to be plagued by indecision and doubts.

Part Three

A Separate Path

Chapter Fifteen

Indecision

Belief consists in accepting the affirmations of the soul;
unbelief in denying them.

Ralph Waldo Emerson: *Representative Men;*

Uses of Great Men; Goethe.

Peter is torn between his love for Anne and his sense of loyalty to
both Cary and Jung. Marriage to Anne will mean a final separa-
tion from Jung.

Agnes Leay (she preferred to be called Anne), had been to see Peter
for help when she was twenty-one. She was in love with a married
American man who was already well established in life with four
children. They fell in love on board ship when Anne was on her way
to America to stay with friends. She described this man as 'an Apollo,
a veritable sun-god'. She recognized the impossibility of the relationship and yet her whole world had been turned upside down by him
and she felt unable to get on with her life.

An American friend called Laura Wolsey had been receiving help
from Peter, and she recommended him to Anne, who was dismayed
that anyone should suppose she needed that kind of help. In spite of
this, she made an appointment to see him. There had been problems
in her family that were affecting her: her sister had been diagnosed
with schizophrenia and her father suffered from paranoia; she felt
that psychic balance was a precarious thing but was also reluctant to
admit that she might be suffering from any imbalance herself. She

arrived in Peter's consulting room, a radiant looking young woman, slender, self-possessed and stylishly dressed. Her beautiful and gentle face, together with her natural and somewhat ingenuous manner made an immediate impression on Peter. Her opening words were: 'I don't know why I've come.' His reply to this was: 'So you've come out of curiosity I suppose!' Suddenly all her defences fell away and she wept and wept.

Something of the vulnerability and sadness of this beautiful girl had entered Peter's soul and it was soon after his marriage to Cary that he began to dream of her as his anima or soul guide. He was intent at that time on making the marriage with Cary work but he had not taken into account the needs of his own soul nor the power of this search for a soul mate who reflected his anima and who could give him the warmth and support he had been yearning for. Anne was the moon goddess who had, unbidden, entered the scene of Peter's unconscious world and she was there to stay, no matter how much he might make vows that he would 'sacrifice the desires engendered' by her.

Anne was intensely feminine and an ideal person to reflect Peter's anima. Her raison d'être in life was to make a man happy and to bear his children. But something had prevented this. Many men had both loved and wanted to marry her; men who were young, attractive and financially secure, but each time one of her admirers proposed she would burst into tears. She had no idea why this happened, but her fears that she might become psychologically unstable, like other members of her family, had begun to haunt her.

Anne was altogether different from the other women who had been important in Peter's life. Whereas Rosalind was an artist and feminist with very definite ideas of her own, Hilda a talented pianist and Cary a woman of very considerable intellectual gifts, Anne was just herself, and happy to give herself totally to the man she loved. She had no desire and no ambition to be anything other than Peter's wife. She always said about herself, 'I have no desire to be the captain of the ship but I make an excellent mate.' She was above all an enabler. After so many failed relationships, it was her ability to give herself wholly in loving which was like balm to Peter's troubled soul and which brought him the greatest happiness he had known since the early days of his marriage to Rosalind. But the decision to divorce Cary and to marry Anne only came after months of agonizing indecision.

Between Peter and Cary there was a warm mutual friendship and a creative professional collaboration: they were both working closely with Jung. Cary was involved with translating his papers and Peter was sharing the load of Jung's practice and seeing patients for sometimes up to nine hours a day. But from the start, the physical side of their relationship had been absent. Although Peter initially felt one would develop, he wrote after their marriage that Cary had 'explained she did not feel like a wife and would not be a wife in the conventional sense.' He went on to say 'she was after something else and I got a renewed sense of inferiority from just having those expectations which I could not see were to be expurgated from marriage. Well, then I was at sea. Going about together, signs of affection, were not in her programme, so at length I settled down to the acceptance of pure collaboration and that is really the only aspect of our relationship which has borne fruit. It was not until my feeling was absolutely convinced that Cary was not interested in what seemed to me the very core and pith of a love relation, that my libido finally turned away to look for a mate who agreed with the old way of Adam and Eve.'

He continues: 'She felt it a humiliation to accept the woman's role in marriage and wanted to forge some other conception.' Cary was a typical intellectual of her generation and perhaps felt that the physical side of the relationship between man and woman was for the less gifted, 'biological' kind of woman. Among the women of her era who had fought hard to be seen as intellectually equal to men (a movement spear-headed by Virginia Woolf), there were some who were not prepared to give this up to satisfy the physical aspects of womanhood.

Yet something in Cary remained unfulfilled and desperately sad as a result of this betrayal of her own instinctual life. Peter comments on the 'terribly sad look on her face. Whenever I surprise that sad, forlorn woman looking out of her eyes I just want to go off and weep.' Peter had attempted, soon after their marriage, 'to teach her the arts of womanhood' and to meet this longing he could see in her eyes:

> I cannot teach her that woman's role which draws warmth and enthusiasm and desire and I cannot simulate love. And she will not have my compassion even if I were Christ-like enough to develop pity as a basis for a love relationship. She is the most decent woman in every respect and I think the most devoted and conscientious and the cruel thing is that it is her very decency which has

betrayed her. Her decency says to her; 'you have no right at all to keep this man tied to you when his heart is not in the game' and yet if she had been less decent she would have made appeals to my feeling and begun to play the woman's role. And I am sure if she had done this I would have responded. But she is just too proud to make the smallest appeal. And whenever I give her any expression of feeling she distrusts it because she says it does not really belong to her. It is not only me because C.G. found exactly the same thing. He has always been fond of her. Once he said to her 'suppose I were to say here and now that I really love you what would you say?' She replied: 'I simply would not believe it.'

Cary had a generous and noble spirit. She recognized that she was unable to give Peter what he needed and that he was profoundly unhappy. It was she who had originally suggested he should find himself a love partner. However, he struggled with his sense of betrayal. His whole being was now crying out to make a commitment to Anne, and yet he felt his betrayal was not only to Cary but also to Jung. He wrote in a letter to Anne:

> I feel all this world over here has already condemned me because I have chosen the way, the only way, which can release her and me from a life of growing bitterness. Does this feeling of being condemned come from a sense of failure in my own soul or is it reality? That is what I am going to analyse with C.G.
>
> If it comes from a sense of failure and guilt I must get square with it or it will bode ill for our relationship. But if they are actually condemning me for doing a criminal thing I must really under-stand their judgment because it could also one day be my own verdict or even yours.

Jung had been hoping to hand over his practice to Peter during the following winter in order to concentrate on some writing. Peter's threat to leave Cary and marry a much younger woman was a blow to him: he did not feel it would be possible for Peter to continue working in Zurich after his divorce. Marriage to Anne would mean a final break with Jung and would necessitate Peter's return to London. He longed to find happiness with Anne and yet to break with Jung felt like the loss of all he valued most dearly in life.

An ardent exchange of letters took place beginning on 10th July 1930. They started after the talk with Jung when Peter had 'with the help of C.G.' in November 1929, decided 'that Anne is altogether too fragile to stand the squalls and whirlpools of my anima.' As a result of this, he withdrew from her and for a time had a lightning romance with a patient of Jung's whom he refers to as Maggie R.[53] He told Maggie that he was in love with Anne and they had a brief affair with that understanding. However, by July the following year he was writing to Anne again in passionate terms, saying that he would talk with Cary when he had a chance and ending with, 'I wonder what will become of us?' He had left his beautiful Sunbeam sports car in England with Anne so that she could learn to drive, making her feel that he was already making plans for their future together.

Peter had Christopher, now a child of six years, living with him and Cary in Kilchberg. After visiting Anne in London, Peter introduced Christopher to a photo of Anne. Christopher's response on seeing her portrait was, 'She's cute!' When he repeated this three times, it seemed to Peter like an affirmation that Christopher would be prepared to accept Anne as his new mother, and perhaps there was a secret hope in little Christopher that this mother would prove to be more permanent than the mothers he had so far experienced.

Peter returned to Switzerland with the intention of setting things in motion for the divorce. He commented: 'It is rather dreadful here. But I knew it would be. It is an awful fact that every new attempt in life is ushered in or accompanied by a more or less ruthless severance.'

This outer 'severance' was causing an acute 'severance' within Peter himself. His doubts are expressed in a dream he had soon after his visit to Anne in England. He dreamed about a huge Negro who was being lashed unmercifully by another Negro. His interpretation of this dream was: 'I wonder if it means that if I let my desire go in the Othello fashion I shall also suffer the lash of fate. It must be a warning to me that the eagerness of desire must be kept always under the rule of the heart or one is given up to devils.' He continues, with a cry from the heart: 'Oh Anne my beauty, how hard it is to love right. It is the sternest discipline that life sets.'

It was indeed, for Peter, the sternest of all disciplines. His heart and his desire had been in conflict, each one undermining the other. He had chosen two women for wives who had commanded his respect, love, admiration and even worship, but not his desire.

---

[53] A Dutch woman who was a talented artist called Maggie Reichstein.

Peter's chief anxiety was in relation to Jung's judgment of him. It was as if his desire, symbolized by the anima in his internal world, and by Anne in his outer life, was at war with the logos or rational aspect, which is symbolized by the old wise man of his fantasy, and in outer life by Jung. All his feeling and desire was rushing, like a stream in flood, towards Anne. But because his anima had up till now led him such a dance, he was unable to trust these feelings. It was the siren's song leading him once again into deep water, leaving him without will or consciousness. He was dreading the necessity of confronting Jung with the question of his divorce from Cary. He wrote to Anne on July 12th 1930:

> C.G. has been away in France with Emma ever since I got back. I had only a word with him over the telephone before he left so I have been wondering a lot what he will think about my divorce. I know he is counting on me taking the burden of his work from his shoulders next winter because he wants to get to work on a new book on dreams. I have an idea he would like to have a talk with you. As he said to me, he is always on the side of fate, but he also knows that neither you nor I can afford to make a mistake. We both need to go all in with colours flying. I would like you to know and to love the finest human being I have ever found as I want you to know the finest things and the best experiences. I think it is because I love you truly with all my heart that I want to be as certain as we can ever be that you are not making a mistake in choosing me for your mate. It is a very queer thing that love can at the same time give you a vision of things that before were quite dark and also blind you to things you need to see.
>
> There are difficult things I have to tell you and explain to you and I am rather shirking it, because I hate the risk of giving you pain. But I must tell you all the essential things of my life and I know you will understand rightly.

These 'things' Peter needed to write to Anne were preying on his mind. His confession represented for him the possibility of bringing together the diametrically opposed aspects of his nature. His desire on the one hand, which he perceived as a renegade, or a run-away horse; and those areas of his life that he was now feeling were under his conscious control. These were both his thinking capacity (which he had felt to be his inferior function) and his spiritual aspirations. It was as though Hilda had personified his spiritual nature: she appeared to him to be pure 'geistlich' (spiritual) with no relationship to her physical self, whereas Cary was pure intellect and for Peter represented the logos aspect and was only able to relate to a man through her thinking. In each marriage Peter's sexual drive was excluded and had to find release outside the marriages. Perhaps the puritan inheritance on both sides of his family had left him with a profound sense that sexuality was either confined to the restrictions of a joyless marriage bed or otherwise was experienced as sinful. He had made a clear division between the 'good' woman, that is the woman worthy of admiration, and the woman who could be 'enjoyed'. He mistrusted and to some extent despised his own sexual cravings, and they took on a life and tearaway energy of their own. With Anne he hoped at last to bring his love, his worship of woman and his desire, under one roof. However, the next months, as he tried to determine what direction to take in his life, were months of tormenting indecision.

Peter wrote again to Anne about the 'difficult things' that he had by now confessed to her. This confession was in relation to a married Dutch woman, Maggie R. She was an artist, and Peter described her as 'a devotee of Eros'. Peter had spoken to Jung about Maggie and told Jung, 'of the extraordinary impression she had made on me'. He (Jung) said: 'She is the ideal anima-woman. It is her vocation.'

> At that time I was doing my utmost to follow C.G.'s advice, which was not to involve you in my problem. He knew of course I was in love with you, but he was strongly of the view that I must do everything possible to maintain my marriage with Cary. Rationally, I agreed with him and also I never believed it possible that you would love me with your passion. I knew you would always need my love and my support, but I had definitely renounced the hope that you would ever choose me for your lover in the real meaning of the word. But even though she had such a powerful effect on my erotic feeling I was not happy about it. I, of course, told her I was in love with you but I could not tell you about her.
>
> I think this was partly because I was not really happy about my relation with her, but it was also because I had deliberately excluded or rather withheld my sexuality from you. I felt I had to guard you and not bring you my personal need, which as you can imagine was almost intolerable then through sheer privation. I used to see her about once a week. We dined together and

sometimes danced and always when I was with her I felt this vigorous stimulation and pleasure ... I had no actual sex relation with her until Whitsuntide when I went away with her for a few days. When I came back I found Christopher ill and at the same time had a real conflict about you. I had a sense of disloyalty to you in spite of my reason. My anxiety about Christopher was inextricably bound up with this sense of disloyalty and conflict about you.

Whenever I have sensed that quality of fate gripping me irrevocably, I have always done something to test whether this fateful grip can be broken. It is not exactly a resistance or rebellion against fate, as a professional need to be sure that it is fate and not a fantasy that grips me. I tried to break my relation to Jung as soon as I felt that fateful grip on my soul. There may be a neurotic lust for freedom, a wild desire to break bonds that could limit and contain me.

Once he had made this confession Peter was immediately torn by terrible doubts and apprehensions about how this would be received by Anne. He wrote that he had gone on a journey the previous day and found that he had left behind his keys and his money. It felt as though in giving this confession to Anne he had lost some vital part of himself and this was affecting his outer life – that he had somehow given over his sense of being in control of his life. He was now being blown about by the whims of fate and was feeling desperately vulnerable as a result. Peter wrote again to Anne expressing this feeling of intense anxiety:

I have become accustomed to the idea that my own personal love-life was my own affair, since Cary and I could not share it, and now I discover this is not so. It is no longer my own sole concern. Since I find myself vitally and desperately concerned in your understanding and appreciation of the inner necessity which has moved me. Also I wondered why it was that I had no difficulty in telling Cary everything and I had to simply force myself to tell you. I could see that at once. I had to face the risk of losing you and that is just awful.

Peter's letters to Anne were being written every other day. They express the conflict which was in truth the conflict that had divided him throughout his life. He wrote to Anne with great honesty about this inner turmoil in a way that must have been almost intolerable for her, as he veers from the side of intense and passionate feeling to that of rational and sober reason. Many a time she must have felt she was losing him to the Jungians of Zurich. In the same letter he wrote:

> Perhaps Cary and C.G. were right and it was a sort of infatuation which ought to be given up both for your sake and mine. I never believed that, but none the less such thoughts came like crows and settled in the branches and made their raucous clamour. Of course I knew only too well that the sexual tension was abnormal and was obscuring my mind so that I could not reason sensibly about you.
>
> Of course, never having been a man you cannot realise how he detests to have his mind (which he relies upon for regularity and efficiency), dominated by anything of an obsessive character.

Here the rational Peter is ascendant, but then, the reality of his love for Anne prevails, and near the end of the letter he writes this paean of faith in love, which after many more months was eventually to triumph.

> Love is a unity and cannot be divided. Its whole passion is for unity and simplicity. To thread all the complex themes and motives and conditions of one's life upon a single passion, that is the meaning of the riddle. The unity of will and the unity of desire, the unreserved surrender that withholds nothing – this is the body and soul of love as a true mating, and candour is its breathing. When passion is alight your best reality is challenged. Platonic relations can exist on elevated sentiment, but the love of man and wife demands one's utmost reality. So, my darling, you have got to let me reveal myself as I am. We are always deluded when we think that love cannot stand human nature as it really is. If we build our house on rock, it will stand … For the love I have for you has in it the shout of victory as well as a humble prayer. When you wrote: 'Not only does all that is best in me belong to you, but I believe its very existence is dependent upon my love for you too' … I am moved to my very depths and it is a feeling I have never known before. I have loved before and loved bountifully. I have enjoyed women, many and various and in the many ways that the world offers, but this feeling for you which moves in this new way, it is as though I had died and come to life again, as though I had been going through a dark forest where the way was tunnelled through

the thick growth and now I had come out into an open land with the sea gleaming beyond the line of white breakers.

Something earth-shaking and momentous is happening to Peter and at last he is allowing himself to go with life, a feeling that he likens to a river in spate. He is expressing something that he has, perhaps in theory, always known, but has not until now allowed himself to live. His masculine will needed always to be in control. He spoke later of the immense distance between intellectually knowing something and actually realising it. He was experiencing for the first time the fruition of his many years of work with Jung: the coming together of mind, heart, soul and the realization of this also in the physical realm. It was this truth that Jung so passionately stood for and yet ironically it was this very integration in Peter which led to the separation from Jung and which Jung fought so hard to prevent. Peter continued in his letter to Anne to write of the mystery of love in which he could for the first time experience his own sense of wholeness:

> I see another picture of you and me joined in passionate love in absolute surrender, and coming from us and encircling us is a soft and radiant light. Perhaps this means that the faith of the spirit and the realization of the body are two aspects of a single truth and that men who try to find that truth by either way alone can never understand the mystery. I have a curious feeling that you have known this from the beginning and that is why you waited. But I had to discover it through you, so to speak. I could have said that these two things were required theoretically, but never before have I experienced it as a clear and self-evident reality. With you I know that the intensity of erotic passion and intensity of the spiritual faith make a single whole.
>
> This totality is for me like the birth of a new Sun in my world. I know it always has been true and it always will be true, but it has never been true for me before in my whole life. That is why I told you that looking back I seem to have been blind.

The somewhat hothouse atmosphere in Zurich, which prevailed around Jung in the thirties was at times too intense for Peter. Students and patients alike were all in Zurich to analyse with either Jung or with one of his assistants: Emma Jung, Toni Wolff and Peter were the three people who were working most closely with Jung. In between their analytical sessions the students and patients had nothing much to do other than talk to one another and compare notes or go to Jung's weekly seminar groups which Peter and Cary also regularly attended. There was no tradition against meeting with patients outside sessions so patients and analysts met together socially and patients were regularly invited to the Jungs' house on a social basis.

Jung felt that the contact with analysands outside the sessions, during conferences or at social gatherings, was often the most helpful of all. But with so many transferences floating around it created a somewhat incestuous situation, with everyone vying with one another for Jung's attention. Although the concept of transference was acknowledged and worked with in a positive way, the implications of it were understood very differently from the way we understand them today and this informality did at times create an atmosphere of uncomfortable intensity. Peter found some refuge in golf which still absorbed much of his leisure time. He was representing Zurich in matches against Lucerne and Bern and found the physical challenge a welcome relief from the atmosphere in Küsnacht.

However, the question of his divorce from Cary preoccupied Peter to the virtual exclusion of everything else. On July 12th he wrote to Anne:

> I am going to see Jung this afternoon at Bollingen. I feel it is going to be a momentous talk, because we shall decide whether I stay on here in spite of the divorce or come back to England.
>
> I feel more and more inclined to come back to England and start my practice again in London. I promised C.G. that I would not involve him in the disagreeable consequences of my divorce, and I knew he would hate being in any way connected with it. But in any case, whether I decide to stay on here or come home, I think we certainly must be together throughout the winter, Anne … but I must away to Bollingen.

Peter goes on to write of the time they plan to spend together during Peter's vacation in August. He agrees that Anne should leave the Astors, as she had suggested (she was working as Lady Astor's political secretary), and that they should spend some time together; 'and if we simply cannot find a chaperone we shall have to rely on our own discretion because surely we must be together somewhere, even if we have to lie about it to save the face of society.'

The meeting with Jung at Bollingen continued throughout the day. On his return to the house in Kilchberg, Peter wrote to Anne:

Anne my darling,

I am tired out and my heart feels like lead. I cannot tell you yet all the arguments which C.G. used which have caused this war within. He was so tremendously impressive because his humanity spoke to me. He did not say I made you love me on false pretences, but he said that to marry me as he knows me and as Cary knows me would not be a natural choice for a young and gentle woman. He said that I could not possibly raise another family at my age and with my experience because you are at the beginning of the biological phase while I am at the end of it. He believes that I have allowed myself to be misled by my anima and have interpreted your feeling for me, and have even sought to awaken it, on a mistaken basis. His idea is that owing to the collapse of your relation to your father you had no psychological means of realizing yourself as a woman. That you absolutely needed to be fully accepted erotically by an older man whose authority and interest were unimpeachable, in order to discover your true erotic personality.

That the real meaning of your relation to me was this need of becoming aware of yourself as an erotically mature and valued personality in order to choose a husband who would be really able to appreciate your quality. He is confident I was right in getting you to realise your fine quality as a woman, but he maintains I was wrong in wanting to possess you as my mate.

With regard to my greater experience of life and all that that means, he said either you would have to repress this fact or else you would have to create an animus against me in order to defend your less developed personality from being overwhelmed.

He believes if we can hold our love now with the rein of wisdom it will be for both of us a supreme good for all our days, because it is real and fully accepted. But if we marry we shall surely kill Eros again because the psychological reality is too heavy for any real success. The inequality is too great and the sacrifice of other real interests too formidable.

Oh Anne, we talked all day and I tested and retested everything he said. But what weighs most is the fact that he spoke from love. He never attacked me, or blamed me or disapproved. He said here are the things you are blind to because of your desire. These are the things you need to see because of your love. If you really mean to be worthy of her love for you look at all the facts and let her see all the facts. He also said that I was mysticizing [sic] sexuality and that my attitude to sex was hysterical, because I had not sufficiently differentiated spiritual motives from sex motives. He said the mysticizing of sex had surely made a deep emotional appeal to you. And that this would certainly lead to disillusionment and disappointment, with consequent resentment.

The upshot was, wait. Not to fan the flames but to see if wisdom and reflection would not bring the relationship into its own real course.

I am writing all this as though by command. Love had made me weak. It feels almost like cutting out the pith and beauty of life. But my love for you is real. It is greater than my own will.

The old wise man in my heart is not just opinion. It is the fruit of a life long love and study of the human soul.

Anne, it is best that I do not come to England now. I am so weak. I would make you love me compassionately. You must let me fight for the wise way against my own weakness. I think you had better come out here in October and let C.G. carry on the task which I failed in. You need him Anne, to find your real self. I cannot believe it is ever wrong to love, but oh Anne, it is hard to renounce.

Your Peter.

Unfortunately, none of Anne's letters have survived, so one can only guess at how she must have felt on receiving this letter. The visit to England was postponed and Peter suddenly found himself holding the fort in Zurich while Jung was away in Bollingen. He was heavily involved, not only with the care of Margaret Radford (sister to his dear friend Maitland Radford), who had had a psychotic breakdown and had been admitted to the Burghölzli asylum, but more recently, with the breakdown of Cary's sister, Henri Zinno, who had turned up suddenly at the Burghölzli in a state of acute confusion; she was having hallucinations and was hearing voices.

In the mean time, Anne had written a letter to Cary to try to put matters right between them. Anne had already had a warm friendship with Cary from the visits she had made, together with her friend Laura Wolsey, to Peter and Cary's home in Hemel Hempstead, before they went for their sabbatical in California. The two women were genuinely fond of one another. Cary's reply to Anne's letter is dated 22nd July.

> My dear Anne,
> Thanks very much for your letter. I never thought of you as wanting to take Peter away. The problems of his own nature do that.
> It is a difficult situation all around, but if we are honest and keep our heads, we will certainly find the right way. It isn't as though there were any hostility in the air. It is that that makes people do unwise and selfish things in cases like this.
> I don't believe I can get over to England this autumn or winter, but you and I can keep in touch by letters. They are a poor substitute for a personal talk it is true, but better than nothing.
> Sincerely yours,
> Cary F Baynes

This letter was enclosed with one from Peter.

A few days later, Anne arrived unannounced in Zurich. She had travelled out on impulse from London having wired first to Peter. When she spoke of this later she said: 'I was coming out just to have a talk with him and Cary and to get things clear. He was so wavering … so uncertain.' She could feel that Peter was slipping away from her so she took the matter into her own hands. She stayed with Cary and Peter at their home in Kilchberg. She later described this momentous visit. Peter suggested straight away that they should go to Bollingen to talk with Jung. This was on a Sunday and Jung was staying there together with Toni Wolff.

Toni was Jung's first assistant and was also a woman of unusual intuitive flare and rare intelligence. She had been an essential help-meet and guide to Jung during his confrontation with the unconscious and had become his mistress for a time. She was to remain closely associated with him in both a personal and a professional sense, until her death in 1953.

Emma Jung accepted the situation although, inevitably, she found it extremely hurtful. Emma is reputed to have said, later in life, that she was forever indebted to Toni for assisting Jung during his powerful and difficult experience of the unconscious, when he felt at times in danger of losing his way and his very identity. Emma felt she would have been unable to give him the support and understanding he needed. It was as a result of this powerful experience of his own

unconscious depths that Jung was later able to formulate his concept
of the collective unconscious and his understanding of archetypes. It
was this understanding which he gained from his own personal
experience that enabled him to find his own separate direction from
the psychological theories of Freud and finally led to the break
between them.

Anne recalls her first meeting with Professor Jung:

> It was on the 27th July, 1930, the day after his 55th birthday …
> It was a very hot morning and C.G. and I sat on a large log at the
> edge of the lake, looking out over the lake, and talked for two hours
> concerning this whole question of my relationship to Peter – if this
> was to go on or come to an end, because he was deeply concerned.
> He didn't want to lose Peter at all. He asked me many searching
> questions and did his utmost to dissuade me from going on with it,
> because he was anxious that Peter's and Cary's marriage shouldn't
> break up. He felt so very strongly about not losing Peter. He
> depended upon him very much as his assistant and when it was
> suggested that Peter might leave Zurich again – he said to me; 'But
> what am I going to do?'
>
> After this long talk by the lake, I was taken upstairs and shown
> his wonderful paintings. He had a sort of bunk bed; it was the early
> version of Bollingen … and (there were) these marvellous murals
> that he had done, Philemon and a mandala. Then we left. I
> remember there was a tremendous thunderstorm …

Anne acknowledges that this was a powerful and also a very
difficult day. She continues:

> I had never met anyone like him. The first thing I remember was
> that he asked me to take off my hat, as he was interested in the
> contours of a person's head …

Later in their conversation, Jung asked Anne whether she had
experienced any obsessions.

> I knew nothing about psychological ideas, and had never heard of
> obsessions. But I had been very much in love and said, 'yes, I have
> been completely obsessed by the thought of someone I loved.' I had
> no idea what he meant. These were the only kind of obsessions that
> I had.

This meeting had ended with Jung and Anne on friendly terms, but each had made their situation perfectly clear. Jung was naturally concerned that his friend should not enter into another unsatisfactory marriage, and he was also unhappy at the thought of losing Peter. Anne was now more resolved than ever that a marriage between her and Peter was absolutely the right thing for them both. She knew this in a deep instinctive way, although from every reasonable and rational standpoint it certainly seemed most unwise. Jung's final words to Anne had been: 'Well, if it doesn't work out, don't blame me.' Anne laughed and replied: 'Of course, I never will.' Jung said: 'Well, some people have.'

Jung had presented to her all the difficulties and pitfalls he had spoken of with Peter, but with Anne his arguments made no impact at all. Peter commented later that she was able to withstand all Jung's arguments and emerge triumphant. In her passion and her total faith in and defence of their love, she reminded him of a tigress.

At first Peter felt put out by her sudden unannounced arrival in Zurich. He wrote of his 'resistance to your coming over without consulting me first', and that her impetuousness was 'pushing things in Cary's favour.' He continued:

> My talk with Jung aroused the most profound emotional conflict. Because although he neither said it nor even hinted it, yet I began to sense that the choice involved not only my relation to him but also my whole work and position as an analyst.
>
> I realise that at bottom your attitude to C.G. was alien. Or rather you felt him to be a hostile critic, rather than a man counselling from the authority of immense experience.

It now felt to Peter like an ultimatum. If he chose Anne, he would lose the friendship and support of Jung and of all he had worked for. If he followed Jung's advice, he would lose Anne, which felt for him like the loss of the very essence of life itself. He was caught on the horns of an agonizing dilemma, and was reduced to a profound sense of his own impotence and vulnerability.

Anne wrote to Peter on her homeward journey on the train: 'I still believe somewhere that I am more necessary to you than anybody else in the world.' This total certainty was exactly what Peter needed: it echoed something powerful within himself, but it seemed impossible for him to believe in the authenticity of this inner certainty, and to distinguish the voice of his own soul from that of the siren which had so often driven him off course in life. Peter responded with the affirmation:

> That is the simple truth. There is an emotional centre which is constant and which stands apart from the tidal motions of sexuality. It is neither an affirmation nor a plea, but a light that burns steadfastly. [There is] a new steadiness since you gave me your passion … I can see that when fate weaves the tie between us it is not a matter of instinct alone or feeling alone (although both these are woven in the thread) but also a spiritual force which is concerned with generation, creation becoming. This is the overwhelming factor which cannot be gainsaid and if that is present we have to obey or lose the most vital meaning of life.

He is still doubting, however, and writes to warn Anne of her need to make a distinction between the heroic archetype, which she is projecting onto Peter and which has invested her with such determination, steadfastness and inner power, and the real man. He points out that his own reality is particularly un-heroic:

> You would just wake up and rub your eyes and see me as not in the least beautiful or heroic, but as a rather self-important, middle aged gentleman, with considerable gaps in his teeth which art has to supply, and a pronounced tendency to long-winded psychological explanations, lying in bed at the moment with lumbago of all things. The fact that I love you is really true, but then you are essentially lovable, indeed, more so than any other woman I have ever seen or known or heard about. So I have every reason to love you … I want to know that you have taken the whole tale of my 48 years into account with all that that means. You need to look at every wrinkle of an aging horse to see what he is good for.

Peter was with Cary and the children in the Swiss Alps, staying in the Valsana Sporthotel in Arosa. His plan was to go to England, arriving on August 22nd, to spend some time with Anne. However, he was struck with an agonizing attack of lumbago as he was packing to leave. He had lifted the tray of his trunk and was suddenly overcome by excruciating pain in the back and lay groaning on the floor for half an hour, unable to move, before help came. Then four men were needed to lift him onto the bed. (He said he had never before experienced pain like this, except once, as a young boy, when riding his bike. He was coasting down a steep hill which took him across the ford of a stream. He put his legs up as he crossed the stream and was thrown backwards off the bike. He landed on the rear wheel crushing his testicle and causing himself agonizing pain.)

He recognized his present pain, which had postponed yet again the longed for meeting with Anne, as being a psychological barrier. But could it also have been that he had played two games of tennis a day, giving the game everything he had, in an attempt to recapture the physical shape of his youth, so that he would be more acceptable to Anne? The 'psychological barrier', he writes, is about his disbelief that she can really love him:

> I find it terribly hard to believe that you are really mine as though I had something deep and primordial first to overcome in myself before I shall be allowed to possess you. Perhaps I have to burn out the spirit of mere desirousness in my soul before I can achieve the true flaming reality of feeling, which would give me the right to be called your husband.

At the same time, Peter longed to give to Anne the holding and warmth that she craved. She had been badly bruised and disappointed by life.

Her mother suffered from depression and had committed suicide the previous year. Anne had arrived home on April 15th 1929, after staying in Malta, to find her mother had taken an overdose of sleeping tablets. Laura Leay had been separated from her husband, Fred, for seven years. His paranoia and his bizarre accusations against his wife, in relation to infidelity and the embezzlement of his money, had become intolerable and he had finally been committed to an asylum. Anne's sister, Freda, who was four years older than Anne, had gone to an asylum when she was only nineteen with catatonic schizophrenia, from which she never recovered. The problems had become more than Laura could bear. Anne found this poignantly sad little note beside her mother's bed: 'Am so sorry to cause you trouble, am quite helpless. Goodbye darling Agnes, don't grieve. Am happier so. Mother.'

A dream Anne related to Peter gave rise to some reflections on suicide and its after effects. He wrote of the powerful effect the ghost of the suicide has on those who are close to them. This ghost becomes, for the living, the unconscious wish to die and to steal a person away 'from the real purpose of life'. He too had been trying to recover from the after effects of a suicide and had a warm sympathy for Anne's preoccupation with her mother. He wrote to her:

> It is because of the ghosts that we absolutely need to hold on to a warm human hand and replenish the larder of faith by human consideration and understanding. The ghost of your mother seduces you through your pity. You cannot harden your heart against her just as I could not against Hilda and for that reason, Jung says she nearly pulled me over into unconscious suicide when I was in Africa. We must surely find how we can release her [i.e. Anne's mother's] spirit and set her free.

Inevitably, Anne had been left with a sense of guilt as a result of her mother's suicide. While she was enjoying herself as the guest of Admiralty House in Malta, being fêted by the British Navy, her mother had reached the ultimate moment of despair.

At this point in her life Anne felt absolutely alone in the world, without a single member of her family left who could give her love or support. Peter sensed this fragility in her and was moved by it. He wrote to her about his sense of her fundamental solitude, in spite of the warmth of her feeling and her many friends. He said it was as though,

> You had been unable to meet anyone with your whole self, or better still, as though your deepest self had not yet awoken out of timeless slumber. So that when that deep self is touched and warmed into life by a man, you would be wholly given in love and this could only happen when you felt profoundly secure and also profoundly understood.

Her vulnerability touched him and he longed to reach out to her and give her the comfort she yearned for. He found himself moved to his very core:

> There is a depth in me that has never yet been given to a woman, an emotional nucleus of a curious innocence and sensibility that no sophisticated hand could ever release. It is this which you laid your gentle hand over, cupping it in a kind of brooding warmth. I knew that this was what I had always craved from a woman, just that cupping of the hand over that inner nucleus of feeling and the agony I had last winter was that I had actually found the woman I had always longed for but it was too late.

The time in the mountains recovering from his attack of lumbago was a time of healing and of reflection. He had been running an exceptionally demanding practice in Zurich as well as dealing with the problems of Margaret Radford and Henri Zinno, both now discharged from the Burghölzli asylum. In addition he was feeling crucified by indecision over the question of whether or not to marry Anne. This was a time of deep, refreshing sleep when he was being forced to rest, instead of leaping into action.

During this time of convalescence in the mountains Peter was also able to make his peace with Cary. She could express to him her tenderness and warmth and he responded warmly to her. He wrote: 'It seems as though when one is not seeking and clamorous, life opens her arms and showers warmth and riches.'

While enjoying the beauty of the mountain scenery, lying naked in the strong mountain sunlight, he continued writing his fantasy, with Anne as his guiding spirit. On August 29th he wrote a letter to Anne enclosing a *Hymn to the Sun*, which he had written that morning. After his tormenting doubts and soul searching, it is a powerful affirmation of life. It ends with a strong belief that the union between Anne and himself will come about, in spite of all the opposition.

> Let man renew his love in thy pure rays
> He shall fill the womb of his Beloved
> With the joyful seed of his loins in praise and wonder
> For his joy springeth from the foundation of thy power.

During this time of convalescence with his family in Arosa Peter found peace at last. In his letters to Anne the doubts, when they appear, are the last waverings of his indecision. At a much deeper level he had already made his commitment to a marriage and a new life with her. It was for him a vitally important transition and marked his separation from Jung in the sense that he no longer needed to live in Jung's shadow. He felt able at last to move away and to live his truth and find his own centre, independently from Jung. Anne's absolute certainty about the rightness of their relationship and her determination to win him away from the claustrophobic atmosphere of Zurich and the circle surrounding Jung, enabled him to do this.

Peter returned to England, finally, early in September 1931. He enjoyed some glorious days in Devon, together with Anne. Peter later referred to this as the happiest time in his life. It left them both with the absolute conviction and certainty that they must be together, whatever the cost of this decision might be.

That they would marry was now clear to them both and it was decided that Anne should leave her job at the Astors and do the Truby King training in caring for babies, as she had absolutely no experience of a practical kind. Peter wrote that Hilda also had done this training before Christopher was born (though apparently with very little effect). Anne eventually managed to find a place at the St Thomas' Baby Hostel and was able to begin her training later that autumn.

After their holiday together Peter went to join Christopher in Scotland where he was staying with his grandmother Mrs Davidson, and her old nanny Mrs Brown, always known as Brownie. They were at Tillydrine, Kincardine O'Neil, in Aberdeenshire. Peter stayed there with Christopher from September 19th to the 30th.

He found the traditional and aristocratic atmosphere of the Davidson household not at all to his liking. He considered it 'rigid' and 'clannish' and a far cry from the liberal atmosphere of the Jungian circle. To Anne he wrote:

> Every time I hit this kind of place I have to lash out because to me it is a clear denial of beauty. And I hate every system that kills beauty and freedom. And yet it is a superb country and the fair curves of the highlands are as good and rich as honey is sweet.

Peter spent his days there fishing the Dee for salmon with Mrs Davidson's brother Harry; playing golf with Hilda's unmarried sister, Nonie, who played a good game; and playing a hand of bridge in the evenings with Nonie and Mrs Davidson. He spent as much time as possible with Christopher, telling him an endless story,

> That adds a little to its length every day. Today we reached an island due south of Lands End and there is a seal he rides upon and then we started building a little house, because we knew the next time we came you would be with us. So you see, you had to come into that too, Anne … He wants to write you a letter …
>
> Anne, I cannot think how life was tolerable at all before I loved you. I think very few men are able to realise how deeply unhappy they have been until they know what it is to love …
>
> There is no drawing back before the doubts and difficulties, but a deep calm, like the smile of heaven.

The letter from Christopher arrived in a separate envelope on the same day. Peter had written the letter to Christopher's dictation:

> Dear Miss Leay,
>
> Thank you Miss Leay for the tops. Tell her I can't do the peg top, I am too little to do it. Tell her I can do the whipping top and the one that sings. Tell her we made a little house in the wood and Daddy is making it because I can't do it. Tell Miss Leay you are telling me a nice story about living on an island. Thank her very much for the little flowers will you?
>
> I would like to see you again,
>
> Love from Christopher.
>
> Make kisses there at the bottom. xx

Peter expresses great delight in his little son. Once again, as in Switzerland, Christopher is the only male companion in an all female household and Peter has a sense of real enjoyment in his son's company. He loves, especially, the wonderful fast flowing river and writes of it to Anne in the same vein as he writes of Christopher, as something alive and flowing in contrast to the sense of 'deadness' in this Scottish family. He writes to Anne on Sept 19th:

> I run to the river first because, like Christopher, it is alive and has no reservations. He is glorious too, almost riotous in fact. This ménage spends itself in disciplining him and the dogs and when I arrived he looked at me as though asking 'and have I got to behave even with you?' Then he leapt into the middle of me and let himself go. He is quite fat and really looks splendid, but you know these women who only know how to spend their instinct in fuss are a tremendous weight for all his fine horses to pull. Still, he is doing well and on the whole has a pretty good time. Probably the discipline and system is very valuable for him so long as he knows he is free to leap like a salmon when he comes to lively water.

In Scotland, Peter is absorbed with his game of golf and comments that he had played a splendid game at Aboyne and had done the eighteen holes in '77; 39 out and 38 home with 6 bogies, 5 birdies and an eagle.' So, notwithstanding the uncongenial atmosphere chez Davidson, there was plenty to occupy him.

He had by this time written to Cary and had received a reply from her:

Answering one from me in which I said I felt absolutely certain about you and you about me and that I thought on the whole we were well suited to live together whatever the experts said. She wants me to make the separation now and come over just to finish up there and then return to London and settle in on a new basis while she stays over there. I am not sure about this, because of my undertaking to C.G. and my patients, but I do realise that to go on living together after we have definitely decided to separate would be an unreal situation that would be unprofitable as well as unpleasant. Also, I don't think C.G. would want me to work on there in such a camouflaged position.

Before returning to Zurich, Peter and Anne spent another few days together, at the Crown Hotel in Framlingham. This was a time they each remembered with particular poignancy and happiness. Perhaps it was here that the real commitment was made. It is clear that after it, although Anne was still a virgin, her hesitations with regard to the physical side of love and her own instinctual response, had been overcome. It marked another important watershed in their relationship and after this Peter no longer mentions his doubts. The decision was now made, against the advice of Peter's colleagues in Zurich. It was as though Peter could at last trust his own judgment, without needing 'the experts' to guide him in what he should or shouldn't do.

Peter's own attitude to his instinctual life was also undergoing a sea change. What he had regarded as his main problem in his analysis with Jung, his 'erotic complex', was no longer driving him: his 'erotic charger' was at last broken in and was under his command.

He wrote a letter to Anne after their time together in Framlingham about his thoughts on sexuality at that time. They had both recently been reading D.H. Lawrence. Peter's comments about Lawrence's attitude to 'the natural man' was that it was written by someone who was essentially an intellectual and he therefore expresses an over-insistence on the value of sex. He maintained that Lawrence liked to preach and to get excited about the things he felt strongly about:

> He himself had the flame and the austerity of the spirit so his worship of sex conceals the unrecognized spirit, the opposite principle. He wanted to disallow science and intellectual knowledge. He himself was passionately intellectual and yet made a cult of the emotions. All this means that Lawrence certainly had magnificent intuition and ideas, but gave them all the wrong

emphasis and perspective. His words became insistent and you begin to wince at them when you see them coming.

Peter and Anne had been discussing Lady Chatterley together in their letters. Could Peter have known, when he wrote his views on Lawrence, that Rosalind had had an affair with him and was, perhaps, Lawrence's model for Lady Chatterley?

Peter was himself finding a new orientation to his sexuality, which is perhaps why they had both been reading Lawrence. Peter wrote of 'the spirit of desirousness', i.e. lust unattached to feeling, as evil, because it is 'ruthless and cold and pays no reverence to human feeling or the beauty of life.'

> It is not sexuality that is wrong but always it is a man's attitude to it which determines its character. My fight for the last two years [i.e. since falling in love with Anne] has been to build and shape an attitude which accords with love and agrees with Nature. If one thinks always of one's own need one loses consideration and warm feeling for the loved woman. If you think of her too much you can lose touch with the necessities of your own nature and try and live through her as it were. It is a razor edge.

In another letter he writes, in relation to a dream he had, of his inner conflict between the artist and the priest. This dream 'intimated that I have never yet found a way of reconciling artist and priest, the secular and the sacred. The artist opposed to the priest goes to sensuality. The priest excluding the artist is always a forlorn, frustrated creature.' In this sentence, he had expressed in a nutshell the nexus of his life's problem and the conflict that had been raging within him since he was a young man. He was, as his old friend Arnold Bax described him, a most astonishingly all-round man, but he also contained within him extreme opposites which could not easily be reconciled.

He saw Anne as the one person who could effect this reconciliation between artist and priest: 'If they could agree together, life itself would be the moral art work fed by the passion of both.' This was his great dream, which seemed almost to be at the point of realization. At the beginning of his analysis with Jung, he had spoken of this conflict in him, between the doctor-scientist and the singer-artist. Jung's advice to him then was 'to sing his analytic work'. He had been trying to bring all aspects of himself into the same song ever since, but much of it had gone sadly out of tune. In Anne he found the simple faith and wisdom, which, as he said, she had 'always known'. It was she who was now able to teach him the wisdom of his own soul.

On his return to Zurich, Peter's mind was at last made up. He returned with Anne's warmth infusing him but to the inevitable difficulties in Zurich resulting from his decision. In his letter to Anne he remembers her, Venus-like, emerging from the sea, and it is clear that love has triumphed:

> To see that lovely creature rising splendidly out of the sea with all the pearly foam dripping from her shoulders and the warm slumbers of love in her eyes …
>
> I think love is faith and perhaps that is why despair and fear of the future seem to be a treachery. Loving is the measure of our faith in life. It is a host on the march. And your letter, Eve, has more power than a battle song.

This faith in life and faith in love was something they had been able to give to one another as both had had their initial faith in life badly bruised. However, while they could sustain their faith in life together, a disaster which occurred in outer life seemed to convey that a faith in the future can never be trusted altogether. In the same letter Peter writes to Anne of the terrible calamity of the R101 which had occurred on the previous day, October 5th, making a deep impression on him. This British airship was built at Cardington and was used during the First World War. It was filled with inflammable hydrogen and caught fire when a spark of electricity jumped from the mooring mast to the airship as it was docking. It blew up killing more than twenty men on board. This appalling accident marked the end of these airships. Peter wrote, 'it is always the bravest of men against whom Fate sends her thunderbolts.'

Peter returned to Zurich and as Cary had suggested, he moved out of their home in Kilchberg and took his belongings to the Pension Florhof in Zurich. The separation had at last been made.

The night after his return to Zurich Peter attended a semi-formal party at the Jungs' house. Both German and English-speaking people were present and there was an attempt on both sides 'to embrace bilingually'. Peter thought that perhaps there was a certain 'froideur' in Jung's greeting, but on the other hand, he might have imagined it. However, the greeting he received from Cary, Henri and Ximena was exceptionally warm and friendly. Peter commented: 'I really feel Cary is the most devoted friend and I know if I were not married to her my friendship would never be shaken.' All his friends in Zurich commented with surprise on how relaxed and rested and well Peter was looking. Toni Wolff, especially, was tremendously curious to know what had happened to him. Peter wondered whether 'perhaps she reads something in the middle of my forehead, like a seal of victory.'

Peter returned to a busy schedule in Zurich. Jung was taken up with a huge German seminar from 8th October. He was lecturing to an audience of about eighty people for two hours every day, as well as leading discussions and attending other meetings. As a result, it had not been possible for Peter to speak to him alone. Peter found listening to so much German exhausting, and he was also preoccupied with how Jung would react to his decision to leave.

> C.G. is very distant and obviously with intention. He feels that I am going wrong and am cutting myself off. At least, that is what I have gathered from Cary and Maggie ... But Cary has been unusually friendly and human to me, and Emma Jung has been very nice too. Naturally C.G.'s coldness troubles me very much and as soon as he is through with this week's turmoil, I shall ask him for a talk. I shall tell him that if he thinks I am acting under illusion I would like to submit to analysis, for of course nothing lasting and real can be founded on illusion. No, the truth is that I have to be torn in two because two absolutely essential parts of my life, the two most vital aspects of myself, are pulling in opposite directions. But Anne, there is no panic or disorder, because I am certain of the reality of our love. That stands like a rock and even if I have to be torn in two, that fact cannot be divided into half-truths. The pain is bad because I love C.G. and have given him all my loyalty, so that when he turns from me, as though all virtue had gone out of me, it is like an icy wind of December ... I think the only way is for us to talk it out face to face.

It was at this point that the subject of transference came up in the German seminars. The discussion raged around a paper given by a German analyst named Schmidt, from Basel. Peter spoke of a 'tremendous fluttering in the dovecotes' over this paper, which he described as 'a *durchaus* [absolutely] anima production'.

> Jung made a very fine contribution to appease the storm and got the thing on the level again. He told of how he had himself been

caught by a counter-transference to a beautiful aristocratic girl and how he had a dream in which she was enthroned very high on an Eastern temple, high above him. And this he explained was how all his knowledge and interest in Oriental ideas and feelings had developed out of his transference to the girl. He had, as he said, to cut off his head and learn to submit his ignorance to his patient.

I know that his case was Maggie and I have a feeling that his coldness to me now is very largely on account of her. He is very attached to her and feels her great value because it developed literally under his hand. I think he is entirely committed to the idea of Entwichlung – psychic development. Either you are developing or you are regressing. In this talk about transference he said a man deludes himself when he thinks that a woman is in love with him. A woman does not love him but loves the future she can bring to birth through him. She loves only the boy, the growing, developing immaturity in him and the man himself as he is, is often felt to be an almost intolerable interloper between her love and this grow-ing, incubating egg of the future. It was not quite as extreme as that but very nearly. I got the impression that he thinks the majority of women who marry are only willing to accept the man's sexuality in so far as it is conceived of as part of the generative yearning for the future being, whether as actual children or as the psychic child which she is mothering. If this is the case, it certainly would explain the disillusionment of the ego which regularly happens in marriage. But what I wanted to say was that I am beginning to feel more and more that all these people, who like myself have been caught up and swung almost off their feet by the ideas which analysis lives upon – well all these eager folk are just too hungry for this geistige Entwicklung; so that this is the sole interest that they seek, either in themselves or others.

Consequently, it is a great relief to go off to Lucerne and meet a whole pack of men who have not been inoculated.

So off Peter went to take part in a golf tournament between Zurich and Lucerne.

Perhaps these comments also indicate the beginning of the disso-lution of Peter's own transference to Jung. He was allowing himself to question the way of life in Zurich and to speak of the 'inoculation' of those who accept Jung and all Jungian concepts wholesale and unconditionally. On the one hand he was full of misgivings about

Jung's criticism of him and the inevitable separation from him, and on the other, he questioned his own transference to Jung, which had remained as strong as ever throughout their friendship and travels together. Was it time now for the gifted son, the one whom Jung had perhaps designated to be his successor, to begin to question and even to criticize the father? He projects these negative feelings onto Anne, when he refers to her 'alien' feelings towards Jung, but there is also an unconscious criticism towards his beloved 'friend' when he speaks of having discovered the truth, no matter what the 'experts' in Zurich might say.

However, he was still under the influence of these 'experts' while he was working in Zurich and he agreed to undergo another analysis with Jung; for, although he now believed that his love for Anne was beyond doubt, he wrote: 'I can see we ought to submit the question of our marriage to the elders of the tribe, as it were, because that is also a question of social ethic and in such things we have to submit to extra personal authority.' This seems like an about turn from his assertion that the 'social' ethic should in no way interfere with 'individual truth' Once again he is torn between the two.

Meanwhile, Anne had been having problems with a persistent sore throat and had to undergo surgery to have her tonsils out. Peter was concerned for her and longed to be with her. He was grateful to Anne's friend Ruth for ministering to Anne, visiting her with flowers, ferrying her to and from the hospital, and doing for her in many tender ways what Peter was unable to do.

He spoke of a delicate flower sent to him by Anne, which encapsulated for him her vulnerability and fragility: 'Delicate things move me so deeply because of the vast machinery of the world that destroys and pounds and clutters and snarls at beauty.' Were his friends in Zurich, at this moment, the 'machinery' that was trying to destroy for him this flower he had discovered of such infinite tenderness and beauty?

On September 19th Peter wrote to Anne to tell her that he would be starting his talks with Jung on the following day. He discussed at length the pros and cons of their union, as a preparation to talking it over with Jung. On the day following his talk with Jung, he sent Anne a most beautiful and passionate love letter: 'You have a very distinctive mana or power which evokes the best character in my anima and through that intercourse she becomes pregnant and brings forth her value with the light.' Then he continues to tell Anne about his talk with Jung:

> I had a very good talk with Jung, much easier than I expected, and the constraint I had felt in him before has entirely vanished. I did not tell him your dreams as I felt your objection was sound, but I told him the ones I sent you, except the pool with the children and ducklings which I feel is very clear and beautiful, and expresses the essence of my feeling almost like a poem. But there is a sensitive-ness behind the dream which does not want to explore it to analysis. There are things which should not be treated, but left as they are.

He wrote of a dream of Pat, the old pony they kept when he was a child. She was the pony on which he had learned to ride and which the family had used to pull their trap. She bolted three times and on one occasion they were unable to catch her. He told Anne that it was this aspect of his dream that Jung focused on:

> This is the crucial association. For it means there is still undisciplined libido that wants to break loose and throw every-thing to the winds, a kind of *animal* lust for freedom a tout prix, something in my *animal* character that must be tamed and disci-plined.
>
> This is the real test according to Jung, and my whole character and future depend on whether I master the undisciplined libido or whether it masters me. There is no escape from that problem and if I were to go into the marriage with you under the illusion that by doing so all would be well, I should be heading straight for disaster.
>
> He gave me no opinion and no counsel, as of course I knew he would not. But he said I have to weigh up and decide whether such a step will be more on the side of construction or destruction. He said in his view, I would have to pay a pretty heavy price, but it might be that the gain would be worth the price. His last words were, 'I can never advise a man in matters like this because in the last resort it is something you have to decide between yourself and your God.' He said this with great seriousness and with great love. I got the impression that he could say nothing now which I have not already taken into my reckoning. But if there rises new

material from the side of the anima which is very likely to happen, I shall take it to him.

Anyway, he realises now that I am not intending to repudiate my love for him in order to escape his criticism, or vindicate my own way.

It meant a final separation from Zurich and also the final chapter for Peter of acting as Jung's assistant. He had worked for seven years in the shadow of Jung. He wrote of Jung's 'contemptuous dismissal of my attempt at creation (which) made me lose all heart and courage.' The time had now come to distance himself from Jung and to discover his own individual voice. However, he saw this as the irrevocable loss of Jung's friendship. He wrote: 'I shall not recover his friendship, I think, because he could not agree with my ending my … marriage and my entrance into a new life with a new and young partner.' In a talk Peter had with Toni Wolff, she too had made it abundantly clear that she felt this marriage would end in disaster. She had said to Peter: 'I wonder whether Anne's woman's biological instinct is really very good in choosing you as her mate, because of the fact that owing to the development of an inner life which comes to a man of your years, you would not have so much interest and libido for young children, or be so completely in that phase as a younger man would be.'

Peter maintained that he had taken this fact into consideration. However, it was indeed a powerful factor for a man who was on the whole averse to domesticity and the shackles it imposed. After all he already had three children for whom he had only been present at infrequent intervals, never having lived with any of them for a significant length of time.

None of these arguments deterred Anne. She had unbounded faith in her feelings, in the power of love, and in the state of marriage itself. She knew with an absolute certainty that no one could disturb, that this marriage was the right thing for them both.

When writing of his doubts and misgivings in his journal, Peter compared himself to Jung, who had also found it difficult to remain loyal to one woman. He wrote:

> Jung … has also compromised with his evil side. But he did it with his eyes open and knew what he did. But you [he is addressing himself] created a rainbow illusion of fantasy in order not to see what you were doing. He chose to lame himself by the constant

burden of two women neither of whom could he satisfy. But because he chose to lame himself he also harnessed himself to the real human task and refused to climb to the heights of madness and illusion. He chose the harder way and therefore he has learned patience and humility. [I] chose the easier way of nature and therefore [my] patience is poor and [my] humility is not real.

Peter's doubts echoed the strength of the opinion around him, that of Jung, Toni and to some extent Emma. Also of course, Cary, and perhaps Ximena, who although she was only twelve, was a young girl who already possessed considerable charm and maturity, and she had become for Peter like a daughter. They were his inner circle and he was deeply fond of them all. These were the people who represented for him the way of wisdom, and also the possibility of living one's whole truth. He had now discovered his own truth, and his path was no longer the same as theirs. The time had come for him to create his own separate and divergent path.

His divided loyalties between Anne and Cary continued to torment him. Life in Zurich went on as before and in his letters to Anne, which continued until March 1931, Peter expressed his great longing for her. He had found in her 'a warmly lit chamber and a darling healing intimacy – in a word, a full acceptance.' He continues: 'I hardly knew how broken and unhappy I had been until I crossed the threshold of your little temple. I was in the dark, excluded from the communion of love … and the warring parties within gave me no hope of peace or reconciliation. Life at bottom was just a torment and there was no purpose that had any relation with happiness. I could heal others but myself I could not heal.' He ends this letter with the doubt, once more, as to how he can 'claim his love', and at the same time, deal the 'death blow' to Cary.

Peter's indecision and vacillation were, once more, causing Anne acute distress. Enclosed in a letter she had received from Peter, dated 1st February, Anne had written in pencil, on the back of a hand-written list of members of the Analytical Psychology Club in London, the following lines:

> Resolved – this 9th February 1931 never to hold Peter to account for the pain which I may suffer through him. To give him all the gentle love in my power – and to stand firm, and to bless him for his great gifts to me.

> To remember that deep and singular desire in Ruth's words: 'to be a good wife to a good man!'
>
> To follow the road leading to the star knowing the difficulties, yet with faith, courage and high heart.

There is an interval of respite at the end of February when he has a vacation skiing in the mountains at Parpan, at 1440 metres, together with Cary and another American colleague, Violet de Laszlo. In the mountains Peter writes that they found 'all the Junglings; Agi, Franz, Nannel (Marianne) and Lille and the two Fochs' and in addition, two very nice Swiss girls. So, in spite of his inner turmoil and anguish, it was a merry time for them all.

However, Peter wrote again on March 1st expressing his torment. The conflict between his love for Anne and his loyalty and sense of duty towards Cary had come to a head and had reduced him to a state of impotence and deep despair. He wrote:

> I was literally blasted by a storm of tears. I cried as I have not done since I was a child, except once when Hilda died. Cary was marvellously sweet to me and came into my bed and lay beside me. But I know nothing of why this had come upon me except this crucifixion between my love for you and my deep feeling for Cary. Those long deep breaths which came to me after the storm told me of the depth from which the whole storm had arisen. It was as though all the passionate misery of all the men of my race for generations who had forsworn their love in the name of duty was sweeping through me, as though the room was full of their spirits and adding their individual sadness to mine. I cannot describe it in any other way. It seemed as though the very sensitiveness which gave me a particular insight and feeling for the poignant loveliness and sweetness you were offering me at the same time made me impotent to cut the bond which holds me to Cary.

Anne had enabled Peter to experience his own inner feminine nature, and to acknowledge the value of this. This new awareness had put him in touch with Cary's unlived and unexpressed feminine side and his need to make things well for her also.

He was aware too of the conflict arising now from the fulfilment of his many years of work with Jung. His own individuation was causing him to find a separate path for himself. Yet, what he had earlier told Barbara Hannah was also true, that 'beyond doubt his true vocation was to be Jung's assistant'. In the same letter to Anne he wrote: 'It was my analysis with C.G. which gave me again the conception and the faith in my individuality as a function of life, as a link between the immemorial past and the endless vista ahead. Then again, I felt the meaning of being dedicated or rather of serving a goal which went beyond any personal programme I could devise.' He remembered the quote from Katherine Mansfield's prayer which had been so important for Anne: 'Oh God, make me crystal clear that thy light may shine through', and recognized this was his prayer also.

It was Emma Jung in her own deeply personal and feminine way, who was ultimately able to release Peter from this state of conflict and indecision. He was then able to follow his feeling and go the way that his desire and his own truth were leading him.

On March 4th 1931, Peter wrote to Anne with a new conviction, following a meeting with Emma.

> On Monday I spent the whole evening with Emma Jung alone at her house (C.G. was at Aarau lecturing to Christians). Emma was just lovely. We just seemed to get to a calm leisurely mood like a broad river where we found the most human understanding. She told me lots of things about herself and her deep feeling conclusions seem to me ever so true. So you see I was able to tell her about you and me … She said she would like awfully to know you. She got your spirit as a woman, I felt, and she said: 'You see Peter, I would never say that the way things are in our lives (meaning Toni and C.G.), is in any way a solution. She let me see how she had suffered and how she still suffers.

Peter goes on to describe a dream Emma told him which concerned Mrs Davidson and Christopher. Emma, in the dream, suffered a great thirst and the well she finds which slakes her thirst is behind the Davidson family's mausoleum. Peter continues that the dream was interesting but somewhat long to tell and concludes on a jubilant note:

> As I came home I felt simply wonderful and I danced and stamped my feet and blew kisses to you sleeping over there in your cot.

Could it have been that Emma's revelation to Peter about her own suffering finally released him from his doubts and convinced him that to be divided between two women causes intense suffering to everyone and is, finally, no solution for anyone? Choosing at last the way that had meaning for him released everyone from this impossible situation of stasis.

Peter returned to London in the spring of that year and once again took up his London practice. The divorce from Cary was finally settled and while this was in progress Peter shared a flat with Joe Henderson, close to Bart's hospital where Joe was doing his medical training. Peter and Anne were now able to see each other in London when she was off duty from the St Thomas' Baby Hostel, in Kennington.

In the autumn of that year, Anne and Peter went on a camping holiday together on Dartmoor. In the low autumn sun, in that ravishing landscape of rough moor land, with the wild ponies grazing about them, they realised their love and made the final commitment to one another. It was here that their first child was conceived. Here, beside a swift flowing stream, lulled by the gentle murmur of the autumn breeze, with the sweet autumnal scents and with the great blue arc of the heavens above them, they made love.

For Anne, it was the fulfilment of all her deepest longings, the realisation of herself as a woman, and the overcoming of her remaining anxieties concerning the consummation of their love. For Peter, it was to extinguish the last remaining doubts about embarking on yet another marriage. A marriage that was to create the final separation between himself and the Jungian world in Zurich. This was a time of wonder and magic that captured for both the essence of their love, which was to sustain them through the troubled times that lay ahead.

Chapter Sixteen

Marriage to Anne

Stay, stay at home, my heart, and rest;
Home-keeping hearts are happiest.
Longfellow, *Song: 'Stay, stay at Home'.*

Anne and Peter find the home where they can at last build a life
together. Within this home their lives can be creative and fruitful.
Their two sons are born, and Peter is able to write the book which
had for so long been taking shape in his mind.

Peter and Anne were married shortly before Christmas in 1931, at
the Registry Office in South Kensington. The only other person
present at their marriage was Joe Henderson. He had been living in
London for some months and had started his medical training at
Peter's training hospital, St Bartholomew's. The wedding was a very
simple affair and after the brief ceremony, the three of them went to
a nearby restaurant for lunch.

For the first months of their marriage Peter had rented a flat in
Cheyne Walk, on the embankment in Chelsea. While they were there
they house-hunted and Peter began once more to build up his practice
in Mansfield Street. It had been two years since he had worked in
London. Now he began in earnest to set things in motion again and
to bring the Jungians in London together in the meetings of the
Analytical Psychology Club. So these were busy months.

Peter was now well known in London and his unique experience
was increasingly in demand: there were several Americans in England
looking for a Jungian analyst and when Hitler began to gain power in

the thirties, a number of Jewish people came over to London from Germany to train as 'lay', in other words, as non-medical, analysts.

The Depression had left England, as well as all of Europe, in an unsettled state. Many of the wealthy had lost a fortune in the financial crash and no-one was in a mood to spend money. So it was at first a modest practice and the fees were necessarily low. An analytic session would cost one guinea and for those not so well off, it would be correspondingly less.

While Peter was building up his practice, Anne was driving round the countryside in Peter's Sunbeam looking for the house where they would make their home together. This house was to be a place of enormous significance to them both. For Peter, it represented a true home-coming. It was as though he had at last, in both his inner and his outer life, discovered the place where he really wanted to be. The 'runaway horse' was under his command and for the first time in his life he was happy and willing to be bound and contained by the constraints of a family, a home, and the whole domestic scene. His attitude to freedom had changed; he now felt free to be himself and to choose what he wanted for himself. He no longer felt the need to 'escape' from any situation or relationship that confined him. He quoted Nietzsche in relation to freedom: 'You ask to be free my brother. I ask you not what are you seeking freedom *from*, but what are you seeking it *for*. To what end shall your freedom fly.'[54] He was at last free to choose, and to discover that he was also free to have dreams of true happiness and to find a 'home' that could contain these dreams.

For Anne it was to be the first real home she had ever experienced. Her father's job as Vice Consular General had resulted in a cosmopolitan life style and they had never stayed for long in any one place. This home together was to contain her dreams of love, happiness, security and the family she had been longing for. She was bearing these hopes within her and was proudly and radiantly happy as she carried their first baby. This home was to be so important for Anne that she never left it for the rest of her life. It was her base, and within its security all of life became manageable.

Soon after their marriage Peter wrote, on March 13th 1932:

---

[54] Friedrich Nietzsche, *Thus Spake Zarathustra* (part 1, section 17), quoted by Jung in *Seminar on Zarathustra*, CW Vol. 1, p. 709.

Anne is my wife. This morning I felt the faint knock of the child against the wall of the womb.

Our boat has a keel and there is a steady breeze. In two weeks time we shall be going into our new home, Reed House. The dream is being realised.

And what of the book I am trying to bring forth? I have chosen the notion of attempting to describe the soul as a positive function of the autonomous psyche. Side by side with this conception there runs the reality of the anima as a negative destructive demon.

To write a natural history of the soul must involve both aspects. The soul has a daemonic nature and every daemon is potential god and devil. In other words out of chaos life emerges.

My own life nearly foundered in chaos and bitterness before I could trust myself to the slender promptings of the divine child. When I think, I lose my way, and the light goes out. But when I hear the voice of the child I believe again in simple truth and clear-eyed beauty.

The dream was indeed about to be realised, both in terms of the home that would become the outer manifestation of their love and of the book he was to write.

The home they eventually found together was a large country house in West Byfleet which was then in the depths of Surrey countryside. They had been looking at a house in Old Avenue and had continued on down the road to turn the Sunbeam. 'As they entered the Reed House drive to turn the car around they saw a notice pinned to one of the oak trees which said "House for sale, key in house opposite." They fell in love with it at once.

Reed House was a thatched house with six bedrooms built about 1910. It was owned by a young couple called Turnbull who had been given it as a wedding present. After a few years they inherited a large estate in Yorkshire and so put Reed House up for sale. This was the period of the Depression so the property had remained unsold for 18 months.' [55]

Reed House was the last house in a quiet cul-de-sac. The four acre garden was surrounded by a bank of towering rhododendrons and backed onto a woodland area. It was possible, in those days, to walk

[55] Reminiscences of John J. Baynes.

through the woods or along the tow-path of the Basingstoke canal which flowed alongside the wood, to the small town of Woking.

The house was architecturally very similar to others in the avenue. Its location near the railway station made commuting to London both quick and easy. More important still, it was near two fine golf courses!

On 22nd July 1932, Michael Godwin was born. Not only was he, for Anne, the longed-for child, the son of her dreams, but he was also her sun child, her baby Apollo, as she remembered the verse from the Hymn to the Sun that Peter had written for her from Arosa:

> Let man renew his love in thy pure rays.
> He shall fill the womb of his beloved,
> With the joyful seed of his loins in praise and wonder.
> For his joy springeth from the foundation of thy power.

Peter wrote to Bridget, announcing the birth: 'The boy was born this morning at 8:30 without any difficulty. Anne is splendid and he is fine too. Dark hair. $8^1/_2$ lbs and an oriental detachment.'

The baby was exceptionally beautiful with a fine, strong body, unusually large feet and by the time he was eighteen months old, he had a cherubic-looking head of golden curls. He had a serene temperament and unusual vitality. For Anne he was indeed a sun-child.

Unusually for those days, she didn't employ a nanny but preferred to nurse him herself. As a result of her training, she felt she knew as much as any nurse and felt confident in caring for her baby. She breast-fed him for nine months, in the accepted Truby King way, but did not stick so rigidly to the four-hourly feeding routine. She was prepared, as Peter had suggested, to be guided by her baby's needs.

Although at this stage there was no nanny, the household was beginning to grow. Anne had employed a woman called Violet to do the cooking and a house parlour maid to keep the house clean. Both of these women lived in the house. There were also two gardeners, one to maintain the large fruit and vegetable garden, and the other, Jackson, with considerable guidance and help from Peter, to maintain the flower-beds and the lawns.

The garden became Peter's passion. There was a magnificent herbaceous border, which he created himself, and a shrubbery which produced exciting new blooms at all times of the year. The rose garden had a trellis up which the ramblers grew to create an arbour where one could sit, sheltered and unseen. In the small coppice which bordered the roses, giant oak and beech trees grew. Sometimes grass snakes and adders were seen there. Once, Peter found a cluster of grass snake's eggs, which looked like a much larger, white and less slippery, version of frog's spawn. In the wild part of the garden, furthest from the house, a wide variety of rhododendrons and azaleas grew.

The French windows on the South West side of the house led onto a great lawn which was shielded from the road by an ancient oak tree. It was under this great tree that Mickey, as he was always known, rested in all weathers, between his feeds, in his large carriage-built pram.

Now, at last, Peter was able to think about the book he had been contemplating for so long. This was to be different from any book written by Jung and was to concentrate on the analysis of two patients with a schizoid personality disorder. The analyses centred upon a detailed study and elucidation of their dreams and paintings. It was to be a mammoth book which was to occupy him for several years and he decided to call it *Mythology of the Soul*.

This was a time of serene happiness and contentment for Anne and Peter. The troubles in Peter's turbulent life had now culminated in a sense of profound well being which affected all who visited them. Joe Henderson was a frequent visitor at Reed House. He would come there together with Helena Cornford (eldest daughter of Francis and Frances Cornford), whom he had met through Peter and Cary, and who two years later was to become his wife.

In his preface to the book Peter was to write, Joe expresses this sense of well-being:

> When Dr Baynes was writing *Mythology of the Soul*, I was a frequent weekend guest at his house in Surrey. Everywhere in the house or garden one felt the presence of this exuberant personality with his talent for creating an excitement of contrasts. The oars he had won as a Cambridge rowing blue and his herbaceous border were as appropriate an expression of his interests as the butterfly collection, the Chinese figurines, the antique furniture, or the masks and javelins of African tribesmen. Living there with his charming young wife and children he seemed to have reached as much stability and certainty as it is possible for human beings to find on this earth.

Joe Wheelwright, who together with Joe Henderson, was to introduce Jungian psychology to the West of America, was also in London in the early 1930's. He and his new wife Jane, who was expecting their first baby, had returned from their studies in China. They also had only recently been married. On his arrival in England, Joe decided he would like to become an analyst, perhaps influenced by Joe Henderson. So he began an analysis with Peter and also went to Bart's Hospital to study medicine. They stayed at Reed House for Anne and Peter's first Christmas together, in 1932, when Michael was still a small baby. With Joe's huge size and his American extraversion it was an especially lively time.

In September of that year the Bayneses were delighted to have a visit from Emma Jung, who came to stay at Reed House together with two of her four children, Franz and Lille. She was to be the guest of honour at the Analytical Psychology Club and the whole evening was devoted to the discussion of her paper on the animus. This was the first time Anne had met Emma. They liked each other at once and a strong friendship developed between them. Emma became an important person in Anne's life and the following year, when her baby was just eighteen months old, she went to Zurich for a month to work with Emma.

The time in Zurich helped Anne to make her own relationship with all those who had been a major influence in Peter's life and enabled her to be accepted as a person in her own right, not simply as an appendage to Peter. She wrote that her time with Emma was making everything seem extraordinarily clear and that 'we seem to have a fine understanding together.' Emma, with her woman's wisdom and warmth, could give Anne the affirmation she had never received from her own mother, and was also an important role model: 'I do love Emma', she wrote, 'She does symbolise for me the kind of woman I want to be.'

She attended Jung's seminar and sat next to Emma. Afterwards, everyone came up and spoke to her, including Cary who was, Anne said, looking splendid and younger and happier than Anne remembered her. The feeling between them was warm and friendly and Cary asked after Peter and baby Michael and of course, Christopher. Anne mingled with all those who had been a part of Peter's world in Zurich, many of whom she experienced, from her youthful perspective, as old-maidish, waspish and even witch-like! She met Dr Harding, Dr Barker and Barbara Hannah, as well as Cary and Ximena. She found herself sitting next to Toni who invited her to dine. She added: 'I said I would love to – but I'm full of doubts for I had always supposed we should not really like one another: but it will be great fun to see how it goes!' Best of all, she had been invited to dine with Emma together with two of her daughters, Agi and Marianne and about this invitation Anne was 'tremendously excited'. All those who had belonged to Peter's world now became real people for her and all were friendly and accepting of Anne, who was full of trepidation as she faced what she perceived to be this entourage of extraordinary women (referred to by Anne as the collective 'animi'), who surrounded Jung.

Anne wrote to Peter about his book which he had at long last embarked upon. It had been going well in her absence and he had been sending her each new handwritten instalment which she would then type during her spare moments in her hotel. She remarked that she was happy that Peter likes Michael Fordham so well [who was at that time a patient of Peter's] for she had 'always felt he would be such an excellent analyst one day, for he is sensitive, intelligent and "sympatica" and so few seem to combine all these qualities.'

This time in Zurich had been a baptism by fire for Anne. She had come because of certain 'resistances' (which she doesn't elaborate on), and because of problems 'with my Animus, who so badly needs a task, where his creative interest can flow.' Perhaps she went also, in part, to please Peter. But in spite of the warmth of her welcome, Anne was longing to return home. She wondered how her baby was faring without her and she was now nearly four months pregnant with her next baby and he was beginning to show. She commented that he seemed to be thriving on the Swiss diet but she was finding it rather harder to swallow!

She was delighted to be invited to attend Jung's seminars. Jung himself, she wrote, was in splendid form. The discussion was about imps and sprites. Jung described the imp as a 'lump' in the unconscious which, like a loose cargo in the hold of a ship, causes no inconvenience when the sea is calm, but in rough weather will roll about and become dangerous, so that in a crisis in life it may cause a person to do 'the fatal thing'. He spoke of never countering black magic with more magic or the laying of ghosts with incantations. He stressed the need to become conscious: not to combat a wrong situation with unconscious means, but 'to purify yourself and perhaps the situation may improve.'

He went on to speak of the need, when living in a city, to wear a persona, for all of nature is driven out. The more denaturalised a person becomes in their conscious aspect the more the *un*conscious-ness grows so that cities become the breeding grounds for the worst kind of superstition and perversity.

The pursuit of black magic is about using the power of the uncon-scious for ego purposes, which leads finally to the disintegration of so-ciety. But when one unites the conscious with the unconscious then life becomes full of meaning, 'and one needs to hold the conscious con-dition against the tremendous weight and power of collectivity. But one needs to do this going down into reality with a certain attitude, in a ritualistic way – neither casual nor flippant and *never* as though in a dream, but seriously, as though it were the Communion. You must be more conscious at this time than at any other.'

Jung spoke also of individuation. Individuation is about differenti-ation which also means consciousness. While one is identified with something (or someone), it is impossible to have a problem about it, to see it or to understand it. It is when one steps beyond the limitations of whatever one is identified with, that a person can achieve consciousness, 'and when consciousness is being extended, then one may expect visions or manifestations of the great, the powerful one, the old ape-man in us – who is best personified in Pan.'

The content of these seminars seems astonishingly relevant to the prevailing situation in Europe when one remembers what was incu-bating in Germany, in relation to unconsciousness and collectivity, in the early 1930s.

Anne returned home in early December to a rapturous welcome from her little son and she and Peter had much to talk about as she relayed her experiences of Zurich.

The following year, in April 1934, Toni came to stay. She was invited to give a talk at the Analytical Psychology Club and it is recorded that she gave 'a splendid paper on "Some Principles of Dream-Interpretation".' Toni stayed at Reed House for a while on her own while she worked with patients there and later Jung joined her. It was not a happy time for her. She seemed to be tense and critical and Anne reflected later on how different the feeling was between Jung and Toni at her first meeting with them at Bollingen in July 1930. She said that Toni used often to stay with Jung at Bollingen and she believed that the summer she visited them there was their happiest time together.

Toni's criticisms of Peter's book were not helpful. She felt that the drawings and paintings of the patient Peter was describing were too disturbed and that it was not possible to demonstrate the effectiveness of depth psychology with such disturbing material. Peter was cast down by her criticisms, but Jung seemed more positive about the possibilities for this book, and had himself been successful in working with patients who produced similarly psychotic material.

Peter wrote to Jung after this visit fearing that he had been influenced by Toni's negative comments in relation to this material.

> As regards myself I felt for a week that you had completely taken the wind out of my sails, because I sensed that you had concluded from Toni' s account that my whole work on those drawings was practically valueless. Then I said to myself, 'C.G has not read it and Toni is temperamentally averse from (sic) pathological material. I am a doctor, and it is precisely because the case was schizophrenic that I undertook the demonstration of the therapeutic evolution. The case is valuable and I stand for the value I put into it.' From that point I got right again and can appreciate the cogency and soundness of your criticism of the presentation.

One sees how vitally important Jung's opinion still was for him and how easily he could be cast down by a sense of Jung's disapproval.

The correspondence between Jung and Peter continued at frequent intervals about mainly practical concerns. Peter was arranging for Jung to talk to various societies; he was helping to initiate the Tavistock lectures,[56] discussing the content of these lectures as well as the potential audience. These lectures were arranged with Dr Rees and Dr Hadfield[57] and the audience was to be mainly made up of medical people and psychotherapists. The title of the seminar was to be: 'On Basic Conceptions of Analytical Psychology'. The letters between Jung and Peter discuss the format and content of these important seminars for a year before the event in October 1935.

Jung's visit was an unqualified success. Peter wrote expressing his delight: 'I let a little time flow for the sake of perspective and to see

---

[56] The Tavistock Clinic was founded in 1920 and was the centre in London for Psycho-analysis. These were a series of lectures Jung gave to doctors, psychiatrists and psychotherapists at the Tavistock Clinic in 1935 and 1936.

[57] Dr Rees and Dr Hadfield were two of the senior Freudian psychoanalysts working at the Tavistock Clinic.

the more distant effects of your visit as well as the near. You have changed the whole aspect of things in the various circles of medical psychology. It is as though you had put a burning log under the pot and made it boil. Wherever I go I sense an atmosphere of a new enthusiasm among people who are there, but also among people who apparently listened in.'

As early as November 1935, Peter was writing to Jung to inform him that 'Hadfield told me there was a powerful movement afoot to invite you again, and I feel tremendously happy to hear that you could manage it after your American visit.' Peter suggests the subject for the second Tavistock lecture should be Dream Psychology, 'so that you could elaborate your whole theoretical structure from a dream sequence.' Jung is happy to accept this second invitation but is doubtful about the content of the talks: 'of course dream-psychology would be a good subject ... but I don't know whether my audience is already quite up to the tricks of dream interpretation.' Later he adds: 'People as a rule understand nothing of dreams, they don't even know why dreams are important.' He is concerned with the problem of pitching the content of his talk to suit his listeners. He feels anxious about being faced with an audience that is bored and uncomprehending, within the psychoanalytic walls of the Tavistock Clinic.

In the same letter Peter speaks of a letter he has received from the secretary of the medical student society of St Bartholomew's Hospital, where both Joe Henderson and Joe Wheelwright were at that time studying. The letter was 'asking me to invite you to lecture to them on your next visit.' He adds that Wheelwright and Henderson 'tell me there is an extraordinary keenness among the students to have a regular tuition in psychotherapy and the idea of getting a special endowment for a psychological department there is on the tapis.' Peter suggests that 'you give a kind of outline of the value of the psychological conception in medical practice and your views as to how the teaching of psychology can best be introduced into the medical curriculum.' ... 'Your experience with the university students in Zurich, differentiating the instruction as regards general principles on the one hand by lectures etc. and personal tuition and instruction by means of small seminars and experimental classes on the other, would be most helpful. The whole problem of psychological education is very much alive over here and your experience and counsel would be of enormous value.' Peter suggests to Jung that he write to the secretary, Fairlie-Clarke, saying that he would like to accept the invitation. It seems that the attitude to psychology must have been more open within the corridors of traditional medicine at that time than it is today.

Peter had also been thinking further about his own writing. He had written a paper on the Archetype of the King and the origin of Divine Kingship, which he had given to the Folklore society in London and he was hoping for Jung's criticism of the paper. It contained 'certain ideas I have been working out in regard to the renegade or atavistic tendency of the libido.' He had also been rethinking his approach to *Mythology of the Soul* and was 'rewriting the book as a psychiatric contribution and I feel better about it. On surer ground.' He continues that he had had 'a fortunate attack of the mumps which gave me time to do the necessary reading and hunt for references.'

The household was growing and on May 21st 1934, another son was born: John Jeremy. He was a fine strong baby and weighed over 10 lbs, a huge weight for Anne to carry in the latter months, with her light and slender frame. A nurse was engaged now to look after the two little boys, but again, Anne insisted on nursing the baby herself. Mickey was a gentle older brother and the two boys later became inseparable.

Peter was an unusually present father. He enjoyed being with children and involving them with his activities, gardening and golf, sledging and skiing in winter. Because he was working at least three days a week at home, he was around and was a constant visitor to the nursery. He would laugh and joke with the maid or the nanny: he did not believe in the distance and formality that was usual at that time between employer and those engaged to do the household tasks.

There was also a great deal of entertaining to be done. Peter still loved to be surrounded by people: among the many visitors who stayed with them at Reed House, there was J.B. Priestley, Joe and Jane Wheelwright and the Cornford family including their brilliant son, John, who was later to be killed in the Spanish Civil War. The Jungs and Toni Wolff came to stay and of course, Joe Henderson and his wife Helena were frequent visitors. The friendships at this period of his life were altogether different from those of his youth and apart from occasional meetings with Arnold Bax, he had lost touch with the rest of the Bax circle.

Joe Henderson has given a description of Peter at this period of his life and of the effect he had on those who went to see him. It is the portrait of a man who has at last found the place where he wants to be.

This large warm-hearted man had none of the calculated reserve of the traditional psychiatrist or analyst, and he shared with his friends his innermost thoughts and feelings. I often wish I could find such an evocative influence for students as he was for me. His was the psychology of action, and he confronted his patients in his study or in his consulting room in London, with the same informal immediacy that he received his guests in the sitting room. But action also gave way to careful, thoughtful consideration of words and images. He had a genuine writer's response to language and an artist's sensitivity to form and colour.

But as the pressures on Peter at home were increasing, his own enthusiastic plans for establishing a base for Analytical Psychology in London created an extra strain. He wrote to Jung of his plans

> to start a Jung Medical Society in London. We have the makings of a team and we have had two palavas about it. The plan boils down to a Consulting House or clinic in the university district in the personal care of Mary Barker. The functions of the society are threefold; 1. Therapy, 2. Education, 3. Research. Therefore the house will contain several rooms suitable for Club meetings. And a flat above for the Barkers to live in. There should be a good library and a staff common-room. We badly need a headquarters and an accessible corporate existence. The only means of income would be the rents for the consulting rooms and lecture fees.

Peter speaks of the need for more funding and of the possibility of Wheelwright obtaining a donation from the Rockefeller Foundation. Jung, the introvert, is cautious in his appraisal of these ambitious plans! He replies to Peter's request for ideas about funding the project: 'You have big plans I see. Don't you think it is a bit early? For the time being I know no fat money-bag or a fish with the stater in its mouth.' He adds that he would hate to be asking for help in a project 'in which I would be suspected to have a personal interest.'

Peter also had ambitious plans for educating those who attended the Analytical Psychology Club meetings. He had begun a series of seminars based on the principle of Jung's seminars in Zurich. He made careful preparation for the demonstration of clinical material and was disappointed to find only a handful of people turned up. In addressing a Club meeting after these seminars, he says, with a crie de coeur: 'Whether we like it or not these demonstrations were prejudiced beforehand by an inevitable comparison with Dr Jung's original fertile seminars in Zurich, and by the same token I was inevitably compared with or measured by him ... Obviously I cannot swim with that millstone around my neck.' Finally, with characteristic honesty he tells his audience that 'It has taken me many years of painful effort to detach my own individual psychology from the tendency to identify with Dr Jung. It is a terrific problem for any man who follows in the steps of a great leader and I do not claim to have solved it. But the presence of an animus mechanism in members of the club which constantly measure me and my work by a comparison with Jung, multiplies my difficulties and also minimizes every attempt I make in the sphere of individual work.' Establishing his own separate school of Jungian Psychology was proving to be uphill work.

Peter was now experiencing increasing discomfort and misery from his duodenal ulcer, which he had become aware of when he first began working with Jung. He refers to this in a letter to Jung who writes of his concern, adding that he has,

> seen ... similar ailments in psychological conditions where people were living beyond themselves, driven by certain unconscious contents. Particularly intuitive individuals are inclined to disregard the reality of their body, of themselves and of the surrounding conditions. An ulcer looks to me like the psychological blind spot that begins to ache in the body. For intuitive people it is hard to grip reality. They never can touch the thing in the right spot nor say what they really want to say, being intercepted on the way by all sorts of volatiles. An intestinal affection can be instead of a contemplation of inner life. We seem to be more apt to stand strain and hurry imposed upon us by external circumstances than when we apply that poisonous whip to ourselves.
>
> My very best wishes,
> Cordially yours, C.G.

Peter replies to this letter, acknowledging his 'intuitive blindness concerning the actual bodily condition', and adding that the Jung Medical Society is to be started on a small scale and that he will have his consulting room there in order to bring in a small income at the beginning. But in order to realise the full scope of his dream, he must hunt for a millionaire!

In Jung's reply he congratulates Peter for beginning the Jung Society on a small scale 'as we did years before we founded the Club. Every beginning is, as you know, a small germ. Such things grow like plants, if a plant refuses to grow no pressure will help it.'

At this time in the history of psychological medicine in London, the psychotherapists of different orientations were still meeting and working together. Peter discusses the forthcoming Copenhagen Congress for international psychotherapists where he will be seeing Jung. He has been having a discussion with members of the Institute,[58] Rees and Crichton-Miller, about holding the Congress in England, either the following year (1938) or the year after.

Holding the balance between his involvement with the development of analytical psychology both at home and abroad, as well as maintaining the continuity in relation to his patients at home, was an increasing difficulty for Peter. It was perhaps in the work with his patients and the art of healing that he was at his best and it was this aspect of his work he most enjoyed.

One of Peter's early patients, Mabel Weiss, remembers her sessions with 'Daddy Baynes' with astonishing vividness. She spoke of the warmth of his personality; his interest in her and of his sensitivity. Above all, he gave her a very profound sense of being totally accepted just as she was. She referred to the description of the middle-aged singer, Sebastian, in Willa Cather's book, *Lucy Gayheart*. Lucy remembered him as a man who 'would be equal to any situation in the world. He had the simplicity that must come from having lived a great deal. If you brushed against his life ever so lightly it was like tapping on a deep well. You felt all that you could not hear.'

Lucy found when she heard the 'Singer' sing that she experienced a powerful sense of the completeness of things. Mabel commented that Peter also had this quality. 'He didn't understand the transference as we do today, and had little interest in working with childhood issues, but he gave one a sense of something beyond oneself.'

For six years, all went smoothly for Peter. Life flowed on serenely at Reed House. While he spent his days seeing patients and his evenings writing, Anne was taken up with managing the large and busy household. Perhaps, after all Peter's wandering and searching he had found, with the help of his 'soul guide' his own inner home at last.

---

[58] The Institute of Medical Psychology later became known as the Tavistock Clinic.

Home is linked to our core, and when something is brought home to us it is understood with our whole being … When the house is transformed into a symbolic centre the individual may find free-dom to explore, go out and go within, attuning to the dreaming mind … the ground plan forms a mandala. This permits encoun-ters with the unknown or terrifying through a prevailing sense of grace.[59]

Peter wrote of this time in his life with profound contentment in his journal, *The Book that Groweth*. This surely had something to do with his own growth, and the fact that in his present life with Anne he is no longer straining at the bit. This entry was written on April 6th 1935, when Michael was nearly three years old and John Jeremy was soon to be one. Christopher was with them at Reed House and he was devoted to his little brothers.

These years with Anne have been full of rich content. I can never frame in words the inexhaustible treasure she has revealed to me. She cares deeply about all the essential goods of which human happiness and well-being consists. She has the most gracious art of companionship. She is a loyal friend and eager lover. In her motherhood she is frugal and disciplined and wise. She has shown me the healing power of woman. Above all she is tender in her beauty and never arrogant. It is more than my heart dreamed of.

The home we have made together holds our treasure. We have put our best into it and it grows fairly in tune with the seasons.

My personal inner cup is full and I ask nothing more. But it could only grow at the expense of a certain detachment from Jung and his circle. My identification with him had to end. It was having a dreadful effect.

The Archetype of the Wise One became projected upon him and thus his will and personality became almost the absolute arbiter of my fate. Cary has always been in love with him. My own anima was in love with him and held me up in a contemptuously disparaging comparison. It seems now that I had to do something which would force him to repudiate and reject me in order to sunder myself from his enthralling influence. But it was the archetype of the Wise Man which caused the spell. I was possessed by it just as Nietzsche was, only because it was projected upon Jung I could not realise it.

[59] Ann Colcord, *Harvest;* Home Sweet Home, 1998.

I was caught up by this archetype of the Logos and thus my body with its earth-nature was neglected and inert. I had to come down and find my body again and strike roots in my own native soil. Through Anne, my children and my home, my nature made a covenant of peace with the primordial mother which I abide by and fully sanction.

Now, last week in Nauheim, I have been with Jung again. I felt the grip of the old spell. But now I belong only to Jung's past. I have no place in his present world. There came the old anima insistence to get near him and be accepted as of old as the favoured son. But this was not my real self, but a poor weak effeminate clinging like a man clings to an old faith ...

But now I no longer work to placate, convince or influence Jung. I have experienced a draught of life altogether deeper and more refreshing than anything that came to me through his acceptance of me. I have learned now to create out of my own being and to follow my own law and this was the truth that he gave me.

As long as Peter identified his spiritual being with Jung, as though he were God, his own creative energy was unable to flow. He continued, observing that now the projection from Jung had been withdrawn, he was free to realise this aspect of the archetype from within, no longer finding it only in Jung, the man. It was the discovery and realisation of the Self, which Jung had enabled, but which could never be realised while he worked within Jung's shadow. Moreover, the compulsive sexuality which had seemed to control him was, perhaps, because in his identification with Jung, he had placed too great a value on the spiritual and intellectual values, so that his physical nature, which he neglected, simply ran amok. He wrote that since his marriage to Anne, this compulsive character in relation to his sexual libido had entirely disappeared. In this new marriage a true home-coming had taken place in both his inner and his outer life.

Reed House is a plastic living mandala. Anne and the three boys are like the four gateways of the house. There is an instinctual completion in this natural design which was not *designed*.

Woman shall create in the power of love. Man shall create in the power of logos. This is the simplicity of married life. Thus only can a marriage be fruitful.

Chapter Seventeen

A New Chapter

Don't listen to what the world says about religious experience.
Whoever has been vouchsafed it, treasures up a source of life,
meaning and beauty. He sees people and things in a wholly new
light …
Is there any greater truth regarding the ultimate than that which
helps a man to live his life?

C.G. Jung

Having found his own separate path within the Jungian world, a
new relationship develops between Peter and Jung. Together with
their wives they are able to enjoy holiday time together.
The Baynes family's lives are suddenly disrupted, first by the loss
of their house, which is burned to the ground, and then by the
outbreak of war.

Now that Peter had truly created his own home base and had
found his own separate path in life, which was independent of Jung,
they were able to become colleagues on a more equal footing. It was
no longer necessary for Peter to see in Jung the father figure, against
whom he must always measure himself, or to perceive Jung as the
arbiter of his own validity.

He maintained a close contact with Jung during the years that
followed and Jung showed concern in relation to Peter's well-being,
both physical and psychological. Jung wrote to Peter on June 8th
1936, after receiving a paper Peter had written, to be given at the

Analytical Psychology Club in London. Jung thanked him for the paper which he said looked promising, 'but I haven't yet thoroughly read it. As soon as I have a spare moment I shall have a thorough look at it.' In this letter he is concerned about Peter's health and warns him against allowing himself to be too over-burdened. He writes:

> Thank you very much for the thorough information about your condition. It has worried me a great deal to know that you suffer from such an ulcer which I know is a hellish nuisance on account of its chronic character. I'm pretty sure that it wants a careful observation from either side, the psychological as well as the physiological. I think you ought to train yourself in the observation of the sokalled [sic] 'strain'. You often have that expression on your face, namely of being 'strained'. It would be good if you could learn the art of clinical relaxation. A course of proper breathing is not inadvisable, as I have seen intuitives who were merely possessed by the idea of their body without having a friendly contact with it. This is of course only symptomatic, the deeper cause is an uncontrolled striving after fictitious goals.

Peter was still sending all he wrote to Jung for his comments and approval and Jung was still giving his opinion and advice. The duodenal ulcer had become a chronic problem by 1936 and was to continue to give him pain and discomfort for the rest of his life. Although he had resolved much of the inner conflict that had pursued him for so long, the strains in his outer life were increasing. His three young children (a daughter, Diana Mary, was born on June 5th 1937) added to the expense and worry of the three he already had, created a growing financial and emotional burden. In his new home he had an ever larger household to support. The energy needed for the running of his practice and the growing Jungian Society in London was also demanding. All this in addition to his writing was taking a considerable toll on his energies and sometimes the strain was too much.

Since his return to London on a permanent basis the meetings of the Analytical Psychology Club had been more frequent and were now taking place on a regular basis. A variety of speakers were invited to give talks including Emma Jung, Toni Wolff and Jung himself. The talks Jung was to give when he returned to London in October 1939 were outlined in a letter from Peter. He was to lecture to the Club on the collective unconscious; he would also give his long anticipated address to the Abernethy Society at Bart's Hospital and finally he was to give a paper on the Grail and Mediaeval Alchemy for the Warburg Library. It was to be a full and exhausting programme.

During Jung's third visit to London in 1939, Jung and Peter attended the International General Medical Society for Psychotherapy which was to be held in Oxford that year. Jung was the president of the society and during the conference the university conferred on him an honorary doctorate. It was possibly the first time a psychologist or psychotherapist had received such an honour. It was after their visit to Oxford that Jung was to give a talk to the Analytical Psychology Club in London.

A list of the members of the Club dated November 1930 included sixteen members. Heading the list are Peter, Cary and Peter's sister Ruth. After this come Elsie Beckinsale and at the bottom of the list is J.M. Thorburn. The list includes a Mr and Mrs Kitto and four Miss Taylors. The address at this time for Mr and Mrs Baynes was Psychologischer Klub, Gemeinde Strasse, Zurich 1. The addresses of other members were mostly in London with four exceptions who lived in Huddersfield, Reading, Birmingham and Cardiff. There is no indication of how often the Club was meeting at this stage, nor of how many members attended the meetings, especially those members who lived out of London. By 1939 the membership had grown to more than twice that number and it was a considerable gathering of enthusiastic Jungians who looked forward to Jung's visit.

Peter suggests, in the same letter, that it would be fine if the Jungs could enjoy a short holiday with him and Anne after the lectures. He continues, after outlining the programme:

> That will be about enough I should think. Now on the other side I would like to take you and Emma to Glastonbury and Camelot and Salisbury and that country. How about a weekend at Glastonbury? The vicar there is a strange being. He has been caught by the Grail and the Joseph of Arimathea tradition. He actually had the sarcophagus of Joseph in the church, a beautiful thing and he has an immense amount of lore and scholarship about it which would interest you. The Chalice Well where the Grail was supposed to be hidden is still flowing and is built by megalithic workmen of the Stonehenge time probably. I am pretty sure you would be tremendously interested. So will you come?

He takes up this theme in a later letter and emphasizes the importance to himself of this West Country trip. It is about his need to get his relationship to Jung on another footing and to persuade him that he is, in a profound sense, now free of him in relation to the overwhelming aspect of the transference. Because of the person that Jung was – the depth, breadth and the power of his personality – it was a problem for many of his close associates to become free of the powerful projections that he aroused in them. Peter writes that a holiday together with C.G. and Emma,

> would be a wonderful thing. I have found my own true centre now and there is no expectation in your direction. You will feel this. I don't say I am free of you for that can never be, since you are the source of the tree which has its grip of things under the earth and yet grows towards the light. But I am free of dependence upon you. And I want to be easy and clear with you again. That is the one thing needful. If you can trust me then let us have a holiday together. There are no dark spots that have to be guarded and watched. I know we cannot leave this holiday to chance, because when you arrive the flies will be buzzing and so I put it to you now as a frank proposition. I know also from dreams that the time is favourable for me to make a move ... At bottom I am the same as I have always been. But with a difference and it is the difference that I want you to believe in.

Peter continues with a reference to a friend of his called Ashton-Swatkin who is working in the foreign office and who is also passionately interested in the Grail. He has recently been in Berlin negotiating with Hitler. Peter says he lent Ashton-Swatkin a copy of Jung's paper on Wotan which he has translated into English and is now circulating round the foreign office. He suggests that Jung might like to meet him during his time in London.

Initially, when Peter returned to live permanently in England, it was he who gave most of the talks at the Club. These talks were sent to Jung who read them when he had the time to consider and comment on them. They were later collected into a book that was published posthumously called *Analytical Psychology and the English Mind and Other Papers*. In these papers, Peter describes his own personal experience of psychology and conveys the Jungian concepts in a language and context that is relevant to his English audience. Jung himself wrote the Foreword to this work and in his appreciation of the papers he also wrote a warm tribute to Peter as a human being, remembering the friendship that had been so important for them both.

By 1937 Peter was already deeply engrossed in the book that he had been contemplating for so long; the book he described in his journal in March 1932 as an attempt 'to describe the Soul as a positive function of the autonomous psyche.' While working on it he wrote frequently to Jung to ask his advice on certain points. It was particularly important for Peter that this work should represent his own individual contribution to Analytical Psychology but that it in no way diverged or negated any of the main tenets of Jungian Psychology, to which he always gave his entire and life-long support. Peter was keen to make it known to Jung that his separation from him was not a split or a conflict in any way with what Jung stood for, but that it was a necessary and inevitable part of Peter's own development. For this reason, he maintained a close contact with Jung throughout the writing of the book.

Peter's seminal work describes the subjective material of two patients, expressed in a series of their dreams, paintings and active imagination. Through his examination of this material he was able to prove that the method of depth psychology employed by Jung could be effective in the treatment of psychoses. It was generally maintained at the time that only neuroses could be treated with depth psychology. This opinion was held within Jungian circles, even though Jung himself had achieved successful results in the treatment of schizophrenia and delusional states. However, none of these results were being published. Henderson writes:

> Ironically, he (Peter) then became for Jung's School what Jung had been for the Freudian School twenty-five years earlier, the one to show how material apparently of irreducible pathology could be understood and treated by analytical psychology. When he showed this new work to one of his Zurich colleagues, suffering the familiar rebuff from the orthodoxy of his school, he was told that the material was far too pathological to merit Jungian interpretation. Persisting in his belief in the new approach (which Jung himself later acknowledged as perfectly valid), he lived with his own loneliness creatively ...

Peter wrote to Jung as his plans for the book began to develop and crystallize. He became dissatisfied with his initial attempt and told

Jung that he was 'rewriting the book with the drawings, adding material from another case and presenting it as a psychiatric contribution from the standpoint of Complex Psychology.'

Mythology of the Soul was to be a valuable contribution to Jungian thought and was the first significant book on Jungian Psychology to be written in England. It became an inspiration to a wide circle of Jungians and to those who were interested in Jungian psychology and was also on the reading lists of all Jungian training programmes.

In Joe Henderson's introduction to the second edition of *Mythology of the soul* in 1953, he writes of

> Baynes' masterly demonstration of the emergence and development of a hero myth together with its therapeutic effect upon the patient as an inner personal experience of death and rebirth. The hero-dragon battle became the decisive image by which the patient seemed to become engaged in a struggle on his own behalf for deliverance from the psychotic threat. This was followed by a period of restoration in the formation of a new, stronger and more desirable ego-structure.

Perhaps this hero-dragon battle had some relevance for Peter himself. His personal dragon had been his own father's neurosis, which haunted and pursued him throughout his life. His fear of this had made him afraid of any kind of restriction and Nietzsche's words: 'What are you seeking freedom from?' aptly describe what had been the motivating force of his life. He was running in order to find 'freedom from' his father's neurosis, and perhaps what he referred to as his 'erotic charger', the run away horse in terms of his libido, which had seemed to be out of his control, was at last contained. He had mastered his own personal dragon and was truly free to discover 'to what end shall your freedom fly', and to harness his own creative energy.

Peter also felt free at last to engage Jung in his own personal creative quest instead of subsuming himself in the work of 'The Master'. He had in a profound sense now grown up and no longer needed a father's guidance to direct his life. This enabled him to write to Jung for his help in what was now his own work.

Jung wrote to Peter on March 6th 1937 in answer to a question from him about the nature of traumatic schizophrenia. Peter was particularly concerned about the interpretation of insect drawings in relation to psychosis. Jung wrote in reply:

Concerning the question of traumatic schizophrenia you are free to use this term in as much as you have sufficient evidence to substantiate such a term. It is quite possible and indeed even probable that a specific disposition consisting in a congenitally fragile tissue can be fatally upset by an emotion. It is even a wide spread experience that a psychosis can be acutely produced by overwhelming emotions.

The insect drawings you mention don't necessarily prove that there is a psychosis. They only show that there is a certain tendency towards a basic schizophrenic dissociation, the insects representing autonomous (Mendelian?) units that have a certain tendency to autonomy. In the same way as the cave dweller has filled the remote corners of his caves with drawings of hunting animals, so your patient tries to catch his autonomous units by drawing them. He tries to keep them in association with his conscious mind, decreasing thus the danger that they all run away in different directions and disappear altogether. The fact that he can draw them shows that his conscious mind is synthetic enough to control these little beasts which, if the control should fail, would reappear as those well known schizophrenic personality-frag-ments or insulae. The insects that appear on the tree show that he succeeded in establishing the proper hierarchy in his unconscious. At least the picture points out that positive possibility. You know the schizophrenic disposition is rooted much deeper than the neurotic one. It really starts in the sympathetic system. I have seen the results of certain researches which are carried on by a chemist in the psychopathic hospital in Boston about schizophrenia. These results show that the physiological coordination of vegetative processes is just as much and in the same way disturbed as the mental coordination. The vegetative factors also go by themselves.

The writing of this book was to absorb Peter's thinking and working time for several years. The days were so full that Anne soon felt that she was the last one in line for his full attention. His patients came first, and any time over was spent in researching and writing this mammoth book. His children absorbed his time when he wasn't working, and Anne received what was left over. This was difficult for her so they finally reached a solution by including Anne in his appointment book! Each week she had a one hour consultation with Peter in his consulting room, in which they talked together about their intimate concerns and not about household or family matters. This tradition was maintained until the end of Peter's life. It became sacrosanct and was an essential time for them both. It was respected by the rest of the family in the same way as any other hour of consultation.

Although Peter was absorbed at this time in their lives with his own writing at last, having spent so many years in translating Jung's, it was still difficult for him to formulate what he had to say. In this Anne was able to help. He spoke to Anne of his difficulty in deciding how he should write the book. She suggested to him that he should imagine himself talking to someone outside the profession, as she expressed it, 'talking to one sympathetic lay-mind'. She said of herself that she was 'the perfect Leay-figure'. Peter wrote that 'according to her I am always more clear when I am talking to one person than to a group.' So this is how the book began. Peter would speak to Anne about what he intended to write, then he wrote down what he had spoken, and as soon as he had written it, she would make a typed copy. So it was an enterprise in which she felt she had a vital part to play. In his inscription on the flyleaf of Anne's own leather-bound copy Peter pays tribute to her for the debt he owed her during this difficult creative process: 'To Anne my gentle collaborator through the years, from Peter.'

On November 28th 1937 the writing of the book was interrupted by a cataclysmic event. It was exceptionally cold for the time of year: frost had formed on the insides of the windows in Anne and Peter's bedroom; a fire had recently been lit in the hearth and Anne was lying in bed, her breakfast tray still beside her. She had been unwell for some days and was still feeling tired and depressed. Peter was working in his consulting room. Mickey and John were with nanny in the nursery and Diana, the baby daughter who had been born in June, was outside in her pram.

The maid had gone outside to hang up the washing. She looked towards the house and saw smoke rising, not just from the chimneys, but also from a section of the thatched roof, where a spark from Anne's fire had set fire to the thatch. The maid left the clothes in the basket and ran to the house. She found Nurse Marie, who was with the two boys in the nursery, and told her to alert the family. Nanny ran up the front stairs to Anne's bedroom. 'Hurry, Mrs Baynes', she said, 'I believe the house is on fire.' Anne was disbelieving. She

DOCTOR'S HOME DESTROYED.

AIRMAN GIVES FIRE WARNING.

FIREMEN INJURED IN STRUGGLE WITH FLAMES.

A blazing roof thatch, seen from the sky above by a Brooklands airman who gave the alarm, began a disastrous house fire on Sunday at mid-day which defied the combined efforts of the Woking and Byfleet firemen and left the occupiers of the house, Dr. C. H. Baynes, his wife and three small children, and three servants, homeless.

The fire completely gutted the upper storey of Reed House, Old Avenue, West Byfleet, the home of Dr. Baynes, a London brain specialist. It had a thatched roof, which caught fire near the chimney and the outbreak was first noticed by one of the servants. In the meantime Capt. Bremridge, an instructor at Brooklands who had been flying over West Byfleet, had noticed the fire and returned to the aerodrome and gave the alarm.

Mrs. Baynes, who had been indisposed for some days, was resting in her bedroom when the outbreak was discovered at the house and quickly removed the three children, the youngest of whom is less than a year old, to the homes of nearby friends. The Woking Fire Brigade and the Byfleet detachment fought the outbreak strenuously—and with considerable gallantry according to eye-witnesses—helped by the willing efforts of employees of neighbouring residents who joined in the effort to save some of the valuable property. The flames, however, had taken so fierce a hold of the upper part of the building that the firemen were able to save little of the first floor, on which was Dr. Baynes's study and the bedrooms containing clothes and other property. The men were at times in considerable danger from the collapsing roof, from which showers of burning thatch were constantly falling and two of the men were injured, both of them being taken to hospital. A witness states that a fireman ran from the house just after a part of the roof collapsed with burning thatch piled on his shoulders and the back of his neck. A number of Scouts of the West Byfleet group were among those who attempted to salvage the property in the house, and a grand piano, which it required six helpers to move was one piece of furniture which was removed from the ground-floor of the building. Little of the servants' property was saved from their bedrooms.

The Woking fireman who suffered injury from the burning thatch was Driver W. Phillips, of Knaphill, who was taken to Woking Hospital and treated for burns on the neck and back and was then allowed to go home. Fireman J. Denyer was burned on the arm and hand, also by falling thatch, but was not detained in Hospital. The Fire Brigade was in charge of Major C. H. Hudson, who has expressed his appreciation of police co-operation on the site. The Brigade was, however, handicapped by water shortage and could operate with only two small jets. They left at 8.55 p.m. to go to another fire at Mimbridge.

Dr. and Mrs. Baynes and their household were made welcome at the houses of neighbouring residents of Old Avenue when it was found that the home was unoccupiable.

The fire was the second outbreak at the house within recent years. About seven years ago the Fire Brigade were called to deal with a garage fire at Reed House when a previous occupier was in residence.

FIRE ALARM GIVEN BY AIRMAN

Flying Officer G. Bremridge, of Brooklands Flying Club, was flying over West Byfleet about noon yesterday when he noticed smoke and flames coming from a house. Immediately on landing at Brooklands he rang up Byfleet fire station. The fire was at the house of Dr. H. G. Baynes, in Old Avenue, West Byfleet, where, in spite of the efforts of the Byfleet and Woking firemen, extensive damage was caused.

Reed House ablaze (1937)

"Septem Sermones ad Mortuos"

One of Jung's paintings done during his confrontation with the unconscious, and presented to Peter as a gift together with a copy of The Red Book.
See back flap of book jacket for a colour rendition.

stepped out onto the balcony adjoining her bedroom, and there, sure enough, she saw flames that were now leaping from the thatch immediately above her room.

The whole household was alerted. Nanny ran to the nursery and handed the two boys out of the nursery window. They were taken to the Strachen's, who lived in the White House immediately opposite. There, John remembers standing on the lavatory seat and watching through the window as the flames rose higher and higher, leaping into the sky to form a forty foot crimson inferno, the dry thatch creating a wonderful opportunity for the fire to spread.

Peter, who had been working at his desk, had by now dialled 999 and the fire brigade were on their way. Meanwhile, the entire household had been evacuated. Anne had thrown a coat over her thin nightdress, and ran outside to Diana, where her pram stood under the giant oak tree.

The fire had also been spotted by a pilot, a captain Godfrey Bremridge, as he flew overhead. He landed his plane at Brooklands aerodrome and also alerted the Byfleet Fire Brigade who rang the larger Fire Brigade in Woking. By the time the fire engines arrived the whole roof was ablaze along its entire length.

Now everyone worked hard to rescue the most valuable items before the flames consumed all that had belonged to both their past and present lives. Anne rescued the money, her jewellery, and Peter's letters to her which were locked in her safe. Peter first looked for the manuscript of his book. From the drawing room downstairs it was possible to rescue Hilda's Bechstein piano and Peter's beautiful Persian rug. Apart from these few things, and the antique furniture from downstairs, everything else was lost. For Peter what most distressed him was the loss of his typed copy of Jung's *Red Book*, the book which contained a record of the dreams and fantasies which came to Jung at the time of his confrontation with the unconscious. Jung had presented Peter with this gift together with one of the beautiful paintings he had done at the same period, while Peter was working in Zurich as his assistant.

By the time the fire brigade arrived it was too late to put out the fire and being the last house in a cul-de-sac, it was discovered that the water pressure was too low for the firemen's hoses to be effective. All the family could do was to stand, with the gathering crowd, and watch while their beautiful home, so significant and symbolic of Anne's and Peter's love for one another, was reduced to a pile of ash.

Still burning as night fell – the flames leaping and dancing, sending sparks like a myriad stars soaring above the tree tops, lighting the winter sky, spreading its warmth to all the neighbouring houses – the fire seemed to devour all before it like a monstrous dragon. It was only towards dawn that the fireman were at last able to gain control of the flames and the weary onlookers finally departed to their beds.

Jung heard about the fire while he was in India. He wrote a letter in February expressing his concern for what he called 'the regrettable event of your house burning down.' He added: 'I wanted to write to you at once, but I had no address with me and thus forgot all about it.'

Jung was also writing to Peter about the imminent event of an international congress in Zurich and he was eager that Peter should come as soon as possible to Zurich to discuss plans for this congress. In the arrangements of the extrovert aspects of Jungian psychology, Jung still relied on Peter's practical abilities and his gift for bringing people together. Peter was concerned at this time, just before the outbreak of war and when the situation in Germany was becoming difficult for the Jewish people, about the increasing number of Jewish refugees who were pouring into both Switzerland and England. Many of these refugees were becoming interested in analytical psychology and in March, Jung wrote to Peter about the Jewish question:

> I'm glad you brought up the question of the German refugees. In the 'Statuten' of our International Society I took care to bring in the statement that German Jewish Doctors, whether living in Germany or abroad, could join our organization immediately without being members of the German "Landesgruppe". This paragraph naturally only refers to Germany, because in all the other countries (with the exception of Austria) Jewish members are admitted in the "Landesgruppe". It is therefore evident that any German refugee has a perfect right to attend our Congress and to read a paper, as any other member of the Congress. I should not advocate the exclusion of such names. If certain of the German delegates should feel uncomfortable, they have the individual right not to be present when the paper is read. It is of course understood that all political allusions should be avoided as it would be not only discourteous but also of exceedingly bad taste to make use of a scientific organization to fight over political follies. As Strauss himself is a Jew, I should like him to have a private chat with such refugees that want to read a paper.

The letter ends with the hope that there will be no ill feeling caused by the discussion of this sensitive issue and with Jung's comment that, 'I shall follow your suggestion to inquire with Göring[60] about the official attitude to which they are expected to adapt and I will let you know as soon as possible what his reply is.' Göring was the leader of the German group of the International Society of Psychotherapists of which Jung was at the time the president.

It was not a good time for Peter to assist in the organization of a congress so soon after losing his home and he was suffering once again from ill health. The duodenal ulcer was causing him a continual and quite disabling pain. There was much to think about in re-housing his family and all the appendages to that family: nurse, cook and house parlour maid. A house was rented nearby in a village called Pyrford and for a year Clare Cottage became the Bayneses home. A new Reed House was designed by the architects Amoury and English, with larger proportions and more generously sized rooms. It grew from the foundations of the old house. In almost exactly one year the house was completed. It was built with all the finest materials; the doors, floors and the stairs were all solid oak. The cost of this generously sized nine bedroom house was £3,000, which was roughly the sum claimed from the insurance after the fire.

The loss of their home in addition to the storm clouds gathering over Europe as another war threatened, took too great a toll on Peter's energy and in June of that year, before the Jungian Congress in Zurich, Peter went for a cure which included rest and diet, at the sanatorium Kurheim, under Dr Bircher-Benner in Berchtesgaden. Here the patients were encouraged to eat nothing but Bircher muesli, made of grated apple, oats, fruit and natural yoghurt. Exercise and cold showers were also included in the regime. It was an opportunity to have a complete rest away from his family and to have time to reflect on his own psychic and physical needs.

While he was in Berchtesgaden, in June 1938, Peter wrote to Jung about Freud's arrival in London to escape the Nazi persecution in Austria: 'I expect you have heard that Freud is now living in London and the question occurred to me whether it would be a favourable opportunity to invite him to the International Congress [which was the following year being held in England]. He is of course very old and

[60] Psychiatrist Matthias Heinrich Göring, cousin of Marshal Hermann Göring.

frail and almost certainly could not come, but I think it would be sound from every point of view to ask him to be a vice-president. I am sounding you about it unofficially, but I think it will quite likely be raised at the next Council Meeting.' Later in the letter he adds: 'My feeling is that, particularly in view of the special circumstances which account for his presence in England, we ought to offer Freud this honourable welcome and do it with generous warmth ... what do you think about it?'

Peter wondered whether Jung could tender this invitation to Freud, as the President of the Society.

Jung's letter in reply to Peter's is guarded:

> I have no objection against inviting Freud. It will be a well meant gesture of which I'm sure he will not avail himself. If he did, he would deny his own principle on which he has always lived ...

To the typed letter is added a p.s. in Jung's own handwriting:

> Concerning Freud's invitation I think it would be enough if the English Committee would send him a letter inviting him. You must realise that it was an awful trauma to him, to have lost my collaboration. If you call on him you confront him with this trauma. I should spare him.

Peter thanks Jung for his letter. 'I shall certainly take your advice about that. I am told he [Freud] is going to practice in London and Anna Freud too and I believe there are six or seven other analysts who have come with him from Vienna, so there is more or less a flood-tide in London. They have had a terrible time, I believe, in Vienna.'

In the end, it turned out that the Freudian Society declined to have anything to do with the Congress, which was a disappointment to Peter, 'although this merely means that [Ernest] Jones[61] is a dictator and enjoys these tedious displays of power.'

Whether Peter met Freud is not recorded but Freud's son, Ernst, was an architect, and Peter had at one time invited him down to West Byfleet with a view to asking him to design the new Reed House. However, Peter found that he had 'no feeling for these Surrey woods' and another architect was employed.

For a time after Peter's stay in Berchtesgaden his health improved. It was a complete rest for him and a relief from the pressures of his

---

[61] Ernest Jones was the head of the Freudian society in England.

professional and his personal life. He wrote that he was feeling fitter than he had for several years after three weeks rest and a course of 'biological medicine'. He had been free of pain for a whole fortnight. He looked from his bedroom window in Berchtesgaden to the mountains towering above,

> where Hitler is building a sort of guest house for visiting diplomats on the very summit of the Salzberg. It looks huge from below, and the people call it a tea house! But it looks to me like a cosmic fantasy. The light in it at night adds another star to the galaxies of heaven. He has 3000 workmen working up there on his mountain and a huge Kino and wooden barracks. Something terrific. The people are very nice about it. They laugh good naturedly at him, but he is undoubtedly secure in their loyalty. He must be a queer mixture. All the people here want to talk politics. It is like an obsession. However, you know all about that.

He finishes the letter with a further suggestion about the holiday they will have together the following year:

> When you are in England … I would like very much to take you off … in the Studebaker away from the crowd to a good place. It would be grand just to be with you again, without any business or pressing problems or anything! Even without a plan.

When Peter's treatment had come to an end, Anne went to join him in Berchtesgaden and they had a brief holiday together, returning home on June 19th via Munich and Heidelberg, visiting Meyer[62] and staying with the Zimmers[63] on the way.

The family had not long been in the new Reed House when war broke out on September 3rd 1939, although that did not immediately affect the family's life style. During the 'phoney war', which continued during the first six months of the war, life at Reed House carried on as before.

In the autumn of 1938 Peter had written: 'We are back in our new house and it is gradually being tamed in. The news from Germany is over the whole land like a pall, and one feels it is the beginning of the end. Either they will collapse, or it will soon lead to war. The feeling of people everywhere is so deeply outraged.' He comments in his next

---

[62] A colleague from Zurich days.
[63] A close friend and collaborator of both Jung and Peter.

letter to Jung 'It looks as though the acceleration of the whole movement [in Germany] had dispensed with the last brake. It really is as though Hitler had been swallowed by a whale.'

At Easter, in 1939, Jung and Emma came to stay. It was a particularly beautiful spring that year and the warmth brought the trees into early leaf. The garden at Reed House was bright with cherry and apple blossom and the meadow and woodland along the drive were a riot of golden daffodils. There was a sense of well-being and contentment, now that the family were established in their newly built home. The only room that had not been burned to the ground in the fire was the nursery, so for the children their surroundings were unchanged, but all other rooms in the house were now enlarged and modernized and had the appearance of a typical light and airy 1930's house.

Jung and Emma stayed at Reed House for two or three days before embarking, together with Anne and Peter, on a pilgrimage to Glaston-bury because Emma was at that time doing research into the Holy Grail.

This was a good time for them all. Jung was entirely at ease with small children and delighted in their company. As Ximena remembered, when she was so often at the Jung's house as a young child, 'Jung was a very friendly person of imposing stature. He inspired confidence and trust in me, as a child. Perhaps this was because he was very real, and in his own skin, not just giving off hot air.' Michael was now 7, John Jeremy 5, and Diana was not quite 2. Jung became a warm and familiar figure to all three and enjoyed playing football and tenniquoit with the boys on the big lawn, and bouncing Diana on his lap.

Christopher was also at Reed House that Easter. He remembered coming down the front stairs one morning and hearing a noise like thunder that seemed to rock the house. At first he had no idea what it could be. But then he realised that it was Jung's laughter coming from the dining room! He had an exceptionally loud laugh, and when Jung and Peter were together their laughter had an infectious quality. Christopher had spent much of his early childhood in Zurich when Cary and Peter were living together in Kilchberg. Like Bridget, he too had spent time in the Jung household and as Jung's godson, he had a special connection with the family. Christopher also remembered Jung as a warm, huge and friendly person who was entirely on the same wavelength as a child.

This time with Emma and Jung was the first opportunity for Anne and Peter to meet with them as a foursome. It was especially important for Peter who was still unsure whether his marriage to Anne had created a barrier between himself and Jung. Although Emma had, ultimately, wholeheartedly supported their marriage, Jung still had reservations about it. It was during this two week holiday that Jung was to accept Anne unreservedly as Peter's wife. Perhaps it was because of his full affirmation of Peter's new life that this time together was remembered as an outstandingly happy time for them all. Jung became a friend to Anne and the acceptance of one another was mutual.

After three relaxed days together at Reed House the four set off to visit Glastonbury and Camelot, being the places most closely connected to the Grail myth. As they drove into Salisbury they found posters in the town saying that the Germans had invaded Czechoslovakia. Their general mood of gaiety was interrupted and for a moment the four felt a great gust of cold wind, forecasting coming disasters. The Jungs wondered whether they should return at once to Switzerland. It was difficult to assess how serious this invasion was and what the international implications might be. They finally decided that it was all right to continue.

They visited the lake villages surrounding Glastonbury; the sites of ancient villages which had been built on wattles in the marshes to provide safety from enemies. After this they went to a village called Camel, which was traditionally thought to have been the original Camelot, but had not yet been excavated.

That Easter morning was an unforgettable time for them all. It was a spring day of extraordinary freshness and brilliance. The sky had a depth of blue and a clarity more reminiscent of the Swiss mountains than the South of England. It was as though the weather echoed the sense of increased awareness and the sharpness of vision that sometimes comes before a time of crisis.

The four friends were in excellent spirits. As Anne recalled later: 'It was an extremely happy time for all of us, I think, for Emma was doing what she most wanted to do. Everybody was extremely carefree, somehow; I suppose partly in contrast to the international situation.' There was a sense of great merriment among them which spilled out wherever they were. Anne remembered Jung's wonderful sense of humour and how, while they were staying in the hotel in Glastonbury, 'Other people in the hotel just couldn't make out how four people could rock with laughter every morning at breakfast, because it isn't an Englishman's best time for laughter, as a rule. They were all having their quiet breakfasts.'

She goes on to describe a small village in the Cotswolds which they visited after leaving Glastonbury, where 'There was ... a little village square with a butcher, baker and a little shop with rather sophisticated hats in it with a name over the door, "Madame Soul". This appealed to C.G. very much – the idea that he should find the anima in such a place.'

During such a holiday, with friends he was happy to be with, Jung was able to cast off all care. He used, in later years, to take similar trips into the mountains of Switzerland with Ruth Bailey (who had joined Jung and Peter on their African expedition and who looked after Jung when Emma died), and also the American Fowler McCormick (who had been unable at the last minute to take part in the expedition).

The holiday continued in this vein, with all four in great high spirits as they continued their journey into the past. They visited Avebury in Wiltshire, a monument and place of worship created in ancient Britain by the Druids. This giant stone circle is like Stonehenge only considerably larger. On the way home through Dorset they saw the old man of Cerne, near to the monastery at Cerne Abbas. Jung was fascinated to see this tremendous figure which has been cut into the limestone on the hillside, holding in his hand an enormous club; a great fertility figure dominating the surrounding countryside.

When Anne had tried later to recall their conversations during this time together, she found it difficult to remember specific things but was more aware of the general atmosphere. They were pursuing the myths from the ancient world which fascinated them all and these were the things that absorbed their interest and attention. Anne remembered no mention of 'shop' talk, of things psychological, patients, lectures or psychological terms; these were never mentioned.

However, the way of being and of experiencing things was, because of their understanding of the unconscious, enhanced and gave to each experience another dimension. Anne spoke of the archetypes always being there. 'This is why it is so hard to speak of it, because it is the atmosphere really and what is happening all the time. It is almost impossible to retell interestingly, somehow.'

Peter wrote to Jung after the holiday: 'I cannot tell you what a pleasure it was to have that holiday with you and Emma, and I hope you enjoyed it in the same way as I did.'

Jung wrote to say how much he too had enjoyed it: 'Our trip through all those interesting places was a great treat for me and I must tell you how much I enjoyed the adventure.' In March 1940, when the war had made their meeting again an impossibility, Emma also wrote with appreciation, as she remembered this holiday. After thanking Peter profusely for sending her her own individual copy of *Mythology of the Soul,* she went on to say:

> I have been thinking of you both often these days, and of our lovely trip last year at Easter-time, which was to me something quite marvellous and the impressions I took home with me are still fully alive and most dear to me. Doubly treasured through the nefarious circumstances in which our world finds itself at present, it won't be possible to see you probably for a long time, nor to repeat anything of the kind, as we had planned then.

Emma adds, at the end of her letter that Jung is well but that he

> has to be careful not to work too much, which I think he is learning by and by; it's exceedingly difficult for a psychotherapist to limit the demands to a reasonable amount. You know that too. He sends you greetings and special appreciation, being actually vertieft [deeply engrossed] in your work.

After this holiday Jung and Emma returned to Zurich, and that September war was declared. It was the last time Jung and Peter saw one another. The holiday the Jungs had planned together with Anne and Peter in Scotland the following year had to be cancelled. Nevertheless, the correspondence between Jung and Peter continued until Peter's death.

The letters they exchanged after the war began had to be written with the censor in mind. As early as January 1939 it was necessary to be careful in relation to the situation in Germany. Jung wrote to Peter expressing his concerns:

> I am glad you have cut out the allusions to Germany. We have to be careful, of course, when it comes to any observations as to the present German conditions. The general mood in Germany is not just brilliant. The great progrome [sic] has caused a terrific

revulsion in all decent Germans. I have heard very interesting details concerning the attitude of the army during the Tcheque crisis. Below the surface there is a division in the German mind which goes very deep. I think we have to reckon with the possibility of internal trouble, particularly in case of war.

The letters exchanged until 1940, the date when *Mythology of the soul* was published, are principally concerned with aspects of the unconscious and relevant mythological and alchemical texts relating to this book. There are references to the 'seven eyes of the Lord', to Sabina Spielrein and the *Egyptian Book of the Dead*, and to alchemical texts relating to attempts to make artificial gems from glass: the text 'Vitro insignes' is used meaning 'gems brilliant with glass'.

There was a lighter moment in the summer of 1939 when Jung, in a handwritten letter to Peter (the handwritten letters had a sense of informality which was not so evident in his typed letters), described a procession in the streets of Zurich which had clearly delighted him.

We recently saw the Lord Mayor of London in a marvellous state procession in full regalia in the streets of Zurich. Our cavalry had donned their uniforms of 1770. Everything was in perfect style. Enormous success; people cheered wildly!

With the outbreak of war, life carried on unchanged for a time. Peter was taken up with the completion of his book. As soon as it was published in 1940 he sent a copy to Jung and Emma and received a warm response from them both. Jung wrote:

Forgive me that I did not react immediately. But what can you do when such an avalanche rolls over you unexpectedly? Your book is not only most unforeseen as regards volume but also as to contents. I already got drowned in it. Your foreword is almost overgenerous – at least such a thing has never happened to me – most unexpected, most unforeseen! You will forgive me, if I say nothing about the contents yet. But I must give you my most hearty praise for the excellent way, in which your book is written. I wonder how your contemporaries will swallow this mighty pill. It may do something to them however. Well, the war will be a welcome excuse. I think the title of the book is aptly chosen, since the knowledge of the myth producing soul will be, or is already, a new and transfigured mythology.

[text continues p. 305]

Agnes Sarah Leay (Anne) at the time of her marriage to Peter (ca. 1931)

Anne with Michael (1932)

Reed House, newly built after the fire

Peter with Michael (1932)
In the meadow at Reed House

Peter and Michael at Corfe Castle (1937)

Anne, holding baby Michael (1933)

Nanny with Michael and Christopher (1932)

Peter with Diana (1937)
outside the original Reed House

Peter with baby Diana and John Jeremy

John and Diana and their red engine

*Peter, holding Diana with John and Michael
on Reed House lawn*

Michael, John and Diana,
playing on the big lawn at Reed House (1940)

Photo of C.G. Jung,
which hung above Peter's desk in his consulting room

John planting bulbs on Peter's and Michael's grave

John and Chloë (2003)

Peter's grave

I beg you not to be impatient, as I have to read the book conscientiously. It will take a while until I can say more about it. I have been a bit ill lately, which is the reason why I am so slow.

God, what a time! We all hope and pray for England's victory – St George slaying once more the dragon.

Many thanks!

Yours cordially, C.G.

Although Jung had not at this stage read all of *Mythology of the Soul*, this letter was like a benison for Peter. It was the affirmation from Jung that he had needed for so long and which could only be won when he was able to stand alone; to acknowledge his own ability to think and to create, independently. It was this, which Anne with her feminine warmth and wisdom – the quality that Peter referred to as 'the healing power of woman' – had enabled. Peter's earlier comment in his journal about what he felt to be Jung's 'contemptuous dismissal of my attempt at creation [which] made me lose all heart and courage', was no longer true.

In Peter's reply to Jung's letter he writes:

I was enormously pleased to get your letter and thank you with all my heart for your generous acceptance of it. There is absolutely no trace of courteous overstatement in my acknowledgement of you. It was as near as I could express it, the literal truth, and if the work is viable and has its own living merit it will only have these because it marches with the tradition or at least does its honest best to do so.

The book received enthusiastic reviews but it was Jung's opinion that counted more than all public acclaim. Peter wrote to Jung acknowledging his debt to him as the source and inspiration of the work:

I am glad you were interested in my book. I must confess, I scarcely expected you would be, since you would have treated the stuff so differently. And yet a good deal of my life went into it and you must naturally feel a stir of spiritual paternity in your bones when you read it.

Peter goes on to say that he would like, 'if I survive this idiotic war' to write a primer on Analytical Psychology for beginners. It would have the title *The Dynamic Psyche*. It would cover all the basic concepts of analytical psychology and deal with it in a practical way. It would be 'a readable introduction to dynamic psychology'. Alas, this book was never to be written.

He sees the conflict between science and the 'dynamic psyche' as an insuperable one. In the same letter he writes that 'since ... the goal of science and the goal of individuation are not only different but incompatible, we do a kind of injustice to the introverting quest when we present our material as though it was mensurable by scientific criteria.' The 'Eternal Art' of individuation is, Peter maintains, 'intrinsically alien to the rationalistic attitude of science. That is the difficulty in a nutshell.'

Peter records in his journal his thoughts about the internal conflict which continued to pursue him. Once again, it was the inner conflict between spirit and the whole world of nature, as well as the eternal conflict between science and psyche. The unbridled longings that had torn him apart he could now accept and acknowledge without needing to act them out. He saw this as his own crucifixion, as the need to be at one with both God and nature. But he felt that these two are incompatible, the inevitable result of this conflict being death, just as it was necessary for Christ to die. He wrote that it was 'so with the new ideas that were being launched two thousand years ago. If they were to bring life to mankind, someone had to give his spirit to those ideas in order to make men know that their ideas had tremendous life. Therefore Jesus Christ was killed as the foundation stone of the Christian Church.'

He wrote of this sacrifice in relation to the spirit: 'This truth is a cruel teaching. But it had to be so as long as man was so unconscious of the reality of the spirit that he could only see it under the aspect of human sacrifice. The Spirit is cruel to man just so long as he cannot know its power in his life.' Peter's deep admiration for Jung was in part founded in Jung's courage at having encountered the Spirit, of having met his God, as it were, face to face; the direct experience of the absolute power of God. Peter saw his own experience of 'The Spirit', as that of 'a disciple'; in other words, it was second hand. He had not yet encountered the reality of God as a direct experience.

This inner conflict, which seemed to mirror the conflict in the outer world, was echoed again in a letter Peter received from the close friend of his youth, Arnold Bax. Arnold had, in 1941, been appointed Master of the King's Music having already received a knighthood in 1937. Arnold wrote to Peter, a letter in reply to 'a grand' one from him which he describes as; 'the most interesting screed I ever had and I shall always keep it.' Arnold expresses his torment at having lost his inspiration at the very moment when he is at long last receiving public acclaim. He professes his doubts about the efficacy of 'psycho-analysis' which he does not see as a possible solution for himself in his present dilemma, seeing it rather as the reduction of all conflict to a state of stasis which destroys the urge to create.

Storrington, Jan 20th (1941)

My dear (as you say, very rightly) oldest friend.

I was much moved by your letter and the fact that you have been thinking of me and feeling solicitous about me. (Curiously enough, I had to go to Buckingham Palace on Thursday to be offered 'The Master-ship of the King's Musick', – how excruciatingly mediaeval – and dropping into the Bolivar afterwards was prompted to ask about you).

I certainly do not feel any inclination to 'ridicule' your profession, but I admit the subject still arouses antagonism in me. For years I have been bored almost to insanity by uninstructed P.A. talk, with especial reference to the Aedipus [sic] Complex which apparently accounts for every peculiarity in the psychic make-up of every little boy alive (whether Liberal or Conservative).

Now, as to my disinclination to write at the present time, this, as I now believe, has nothing to do with war-conditions, though every creative artist was stultified by them during the first few months. I am pretty sure that if I chose to seek solitude I could write as well as ever I did – and technically perhaps better, for I have thought a deal – and maybe too self-critically – about technique during this fallow period. But is there any more to say? You remember the French philosopher who maintained that every artist learned all that was really essential to know of life between the ages of eighteen and twenty-five and went the rest of his life in an endeavour to co-ordinate and express his experiences.

I was until quite recently about as instinctive [an] artist as could be found. I passed unperturbed during the last war, turning out my romantic stuff in an unending stream, and it was only very gradually that I realized that I was marooned upon a lonely rock with scarcely a companion. I do not believe that anything of true worth can be achieved by the artist when he is filled with an intoxicating and fiery impulse which will (?)brook us denial of expression. Heaven knows when I last felt seized by the Daimon! And surely the history of art shows that with few exceptions the artist in later years is inclined to dry up – the imagination loses its pristine vitality just as the body does. It is only to be expected. Elgar wrote nothing in the last fourteen years of his life, and consider the arid rot produced by Wordsworth and Coleridge in their (even early) middle age. You will say perhaps that they all should have been psycho-analysed; indeed I daresay you hold that everyone should be analysed. In that case it might happen that everyone would become so damned healthy that there would be no impulse to art at all. I have always thought that art may be a disease of the soul, like the pearl in the oyster.

Anyway, I am sure it is useless merely to repeat oneself – preying upon one's own technical learning. I know I should be stimulated by such public interest in my work. In spite of these outward honours it is very low at present, and increased appreciation might goad me to start again where I left off, if it is not a cul-de-sac.

Not one of my longer works is in the orchestral repertoire – even 'Tintagel' and 'Fand' have only very occasional performances, though they always make a direct appeal to the public when they are done. This is, I know, partly due to war-conditions and to a time when only the classics are considered 'safe'. But it is discouraging to the stranded romantic, already ten years ago struggling self-consciously. It must have been whilst writing Symphony 5 that I last felt the necessary incandescence, now I think of it. As a matter of fact, I have not been altogether idle since 1939. I enjoyed myself writing a somewhat frivolous memoir[64] two years ago. This affair came very easily and I am thinking of continuing it.

As to dreams, I do not usually remember them except as an atmosphere. I have never dreamed anything so portentous as the 'old horse-dream' since. It interests me that you remember it, and your interpretation of it struck me in the midriff, as it were. But to me the trouble about analysis of dreams is that it all seems very arbitrary. It would not be difficult to allegorize such a vision in twenty different ways. On the whole the dream world – mostly erotic – is a much pleasanter place than it used to be for me.

Well, I have never written so ego-centric a letter in all my days, but you asked for it, didn't you?

---

[64] ref. to Bax's autobiography *Farewell My Youth.*

I have written even these few lines with difficulty. I detest talking about myself; of being the subject of conversation and therefore I doubt if I could ever submit willingly to analysis, apart from the results of the very dreary and morbid conversations it [?] does for me. All the same I want you to know of the affectionate gratitude I feel for your letter, my dear Tiny. I should love to see you soon to talk of this and that. What days do you go to the Bolivar?

Love from

Arnold – Hand too cold to write properly!

The two men had taken very different paths in life; Arnold had devoted his life to music and Peter to the healing of souls, but their friendship remained close and they dined together from time to time at the 'Bolivar' club in London. Perhaps both were at this time in their lives suffering the unpredictable torments of the creative artist; Peter, in his first attempt at serious writing and Bax, who was nearing the end of his creative life as an artist whose personal crucifixion, now, was his loss of inspiration and his inability to create.

The year 1940 brought with it the first real experience of being at war, for England. Early in 1940 Russia invaded Finland, marching with her army across the ice, in an attempt to conquer (together with Germany, with whom they were at the time still allied) the states surrounding the Baltic Sea. However, the Finnish army was well armed, their defence was well-planned, their morale was high as they fought against the Big Bear, and amazingly, they defeated the Russians. Jung wrote to Peter on January 25th 1940 commenting, 'Finland's resistance is a moral tonic for the whole decent part of the world. It has done a lot of good to the general mood of Switzerland too. Switzerland is slowly transforming herself into a real fortress. We are grateful that nothing has happened yet. This has given us a precious time for thorough preparations.' He ends the letter: 'Let us hope for the Fins and for everybody on the human side of the world and anathema(!) to the peoples of the Great Monster!'

This was now the beginning of the real war. Peter was too old to take part but he shouldered a great burden of work with a growing caseload as one by one his colleagues, Dr Eddie Bennet, Dr Brown[65]

---

[65] Jungian analysts working in London. Dr E.A. Bennet had analysed with Jung and was also a close personal friend of the Jungs.

and others, were called away to serve in the army. He was also continuing to write. At the same time, there was an escalation in the bombing and very often the family was suffering disturbed nights. Commuting two or three times a week to London, to his consulting room in Mansfield Street where the bombing was becoming intense, was also an added strain.

In 1940 Peter was commissioned by the publisher, Gollancz, to write a book about Hitler. Peter had many contacts and was able to obtain material for this book of a private and intensely personal nature – information relating to Hitler which was not generally known at the time. There was, while he was writing this book, a very strong threat of a German invasion of Britain. Hitler had a list of all the people who were going to be liquidated when he reached England. A book had recently been published which included this list. Gollancz was of course himself a Jew, and it was known that he was on this list. He recognized that it would be foolish for him to be involved in the publication, so the book was eventually published by Routledge, and had the title *Germany Possessed*.

This book gives a remarkably perceptive psychological portrait of Hitler himself. It also gives a psychological appreciation of the German zeitgeist, which led to Germany being taken over by what Peter described as a daemonic spirit, which he likens to the god Wotan.

It was a powerful phenomenon, which affected the unconscious of the whole of Germany and acted like a river in flood, taking the whole country with it. Hitler, who activated this flood of unconscious energy, was caught up in it as the one representing this daemonic spirit, but he was no more able to contain or stop its momentum than anyone else. He too became a victim of its terrible and intractable energy.

Hitler was a totally inferior personality who was himself acting out some powerful unconscious experience. This experience for the German people, Peter maintained, was contained deep within the German psyche, and was linked to ancient German, pre-Christian mythology. It was linked with Nietzsche's writing in *Thus Spake Zarathustra* in which Nietzsche reasoned away the possibility of God's existence which led, inevitably, to the deification of Man. (Nietzsche's own identification with God may have been the cause of his eventual madness). This was linked in turn with the Wagnerian concept of a Superman, in the journeys of Siegfried in *The Ring Cycle*. These were concepts that had powerfully influenced Hitler, and Wagnerian operas became inevitably linked with the ideas contained in Hitler's philosophy, recorded in *Mein Kampf*. The concept of the 'superior man' was a powerful one for Hitler, personally. Peter maintained that there was certain evidence pointing to the possibility of Hitler being the illegitimate son of a wealthy Austrian Jew, which had contributed to a deep-seated sense of his own inferiority.

Germany Possessed was published in 1941. Peter said that the title of this book came to him because he recognized what he perceived as

> Germany enfolded in a terrible dream, with Hitler, the medicine man of the German unconscious, bent on realizing this power-dream in concrete form. From this standpoint, Germany appears like a colossal somnambulist carrying out machine-like activities and overcoming every obstacle, as though compelled by an unconscious will.[66]

Considering the time that it was written, when so many people were still unaware of what was really happening in Germany, at least on a psychological level, the book shows impressive insight as well as prophetic awareness.

In August 1940, while Peter was involved in the writing of this book, he received a letter from Jung who perceived the present international situation as the fulfilment of his own intuitive forebodings. This letter was written from Bollingen, and like many of his more personal communications, it is handwritten.

> My dear Peter
> This is the fateful year for which I have waited since more than 25 years. I did not know that it was a such a disaster. Although since 1918 I knew that a terrible fire would spread over Europe, beginning in the North East. This year reminds me of the enormous earthquake in 26 B.C. that shook down the great Temple of Karnak. It was the prelude to the destruction of all temples, because a new time had begun. 1940 is the year where we approach the meridian of the first star in Aquarius. It is the premonitory earthquake of the New Age.
> Up to the present moment, Bollingen has escaped, together with Switzerland – the general destruction, but we are in prison. You

---

[66] H.G.B., *Germany Possessed*, 1941, p. 15.

don't see the walls, but you feel them. The newspapers are hushed and one hardly cares to read them, except for doubtful informations about the war. For a while, just when I started your book, I went with all my grandchildren to the West of Switzerland, because we expected an attack. Afterwards I was very busy, because all doctors were with the army.

It is awkward to write as the censor reads the stuff. But I must tell you how often I think of you and all my friends in England. I often complain that Mr Chamberlain has not read my interview with Knickerbocker [an American reporter].

Your book is quite interesting and it seems as if your interpretations were hitting the nail on the head. Certain points would need some discussion. But one should talk, writing is too clumsy.

It is difficult to be old in these days. One is helpless. On the other hand one feels happily estranged from this world. I like nature but not the world of man or the world to be. I hope this letter will reach you, and convey to you all the wishes the human heart can't suppress, despite of censors. They are human too, after all.

In autumn I resume my lectures at the E.T.H, about the individuation process in the Middle Ages! That's the only thing with me one could call up to date. I loathe the new style, the new Art, the new Music, literature, politics and above all, the new man. It's the old beast that has not changed since the troglodytes.

My dear Peter, I am with you and with old England.

The effects of the war were escalating, and everyone, in their different way, was becoming affected. At Reed House, even though it was twenty-five miles from London, the bombing was coming close and doodlebugs were seen sailing overhead. These were watched anxiously in case they should choose to descend in the neighbourhood, although the sighting of a doodlebug was always an intense excitement for the children, who were unaware of the implications.

In his letter in answer to Jung's, Peter gives a picture of the daily reality of the war:

The boys are just coming in with toy-carts full of bomb splinters and chunks of metal casing. We had a streak of bombs straddle the house last night; one fell among the trees just beyond the ditch at the bottom of the field and one in the wood the other side of the road. But the only damage was a couple of window casements blown out by the blast in the summer-house, and some glass in the greenhouse. That was at 8:30 in the evening. So now we all sleep down in the hall. Christopher is the only one of the children who shows signs of nervousness, although of course they all awoke with the blast with beating hearts and cried a bit. They were all asleep again very soon each holding the hand of a guardian angel.

It was a lucky escape. But Peter goes on to describe the grimmer realities of the war where, 'invisible hosts have brought into play an indomitable courage.' He writes that 'a patient of mine, a flying officer in the RAF, told me of a sergeant-pilot. In a fight at 10,000 ft flying a spitfire, he had his leg shot off somewhere just below the knee. He "bailed out" and as he was coming down in his parachute he made a tourniquet fast round the leg and this saved his life. He is now recovering.'

Jung wrote on December 9th 1940, thanking Peter for the news from England and adding: 'I can't tell how glad I am that you and your family have escaped the danger of getting bombed that came so close to your house.' He continues that things are all right for them at the present moment but they are concerned about the future, and also about shortages in food. As a result, he is spending every spare moment in the garden preparing a field for potatoes for the following spring. He says they are practically cut off from all food supplies and are having to live on their wits. His daughter from Paris is with them together with her children, which is a great happiness for him and Emma, although her husband has remained in Paris.

In his letters, Jung shows intense awareness and concern in relation to the current events in Britain. He writes: 'We are following the exploits of the R.A.F. with the greatest admiration and we marvel at the way the British people is carrying on. It is at least a light in the darkness which we feel very much being so close to it.'

This was the time of the Battle of Britain. The Germans, having won the land battle in France, and having occupied the channel ports and airfields, had started to make plans for an invasion of Britain, with attacks from the air.

Although the outcome of the war was far from certain at this stage, the Battle of Britain changed a situation where Germany had undoubted superiority both on land and in the air, to one in which the British now held the trump card. The morale in Britain was profoundly affected by this stunning victory in the air.

This was a time of intense outer conflict which seemed again to correspond to a similar state of inner conflict for Peter. He was still a man in search of his own individual path in life. He dreamed he was at a crossroads, wondering which path to take. He must go on alone and he chooses the road that is eminently suitable for a bicycle and for light traffic. This road has only just been opened and he inspects the surface carefully to see if it is ready. This is the route that has been suggested by Anne. Christopher, the little boy, sits waiting while Peter makes a decision about the path to follow. Peter now perceived Christopher as his puer aeternus[67] which he must take with him on his own creative path; it is he who can show Peter the right path to take and who can help in Peter's writing. This will enable him to include the child as the spirit of pleasure and joy so that the creative act need not become a dreary labour. The dream also refers to John Buchan's *The Green Mantle,* and this brings to mind for Peter the idea of the Verdant One, El Khidir, or in other words, 'the living presence of the living God'. He speaks of 'the soul who burgeons with life and desire when one is on the right way'. He recognizes that the way he is searching corresponds to the book he has been absorbed in writing: 'So I am really at bottom hunting for my soul and the soul is also the right way that life needs to go.' It is his own, intensely personal, mythology of the soul which he has been seeking for so long.

---

[67] Figure representing eternal youth.

Chapter Eighteen

The War and Death

O death, where is thy sting?
O grave, where is thy victory.

1 Corinthians xv vv.55

As the war gathers momentum help in house and garden is no longer available. The family is under great strain and Anne nearly dies. Peter becomes overburdened with work and with financial and emotional demands. Finally he succumbs to the illness from which he dies on September 6th 1943.

It was towards the end of 1940 that the war began to have a real effect on the Baynes family and to create major changes in their way of life. There was still a full complement of staff at Reed House up to this time. But soon the regular cook, the house parlour maid and the two gardeners were called away for war service. The house staff were replaced by refugees from Belgium.

This was now the beginning of the real war. At fifty-seven Peter was too old to take part but he shouldered a great burden of work with a growing case-load, as one by one his colleagues were called away to serve in the army. He was also continuing to write. At the same time, there was an escalation in the bombing and the family regularly suffered disturbed nights.

Peter's practice was full to overflowing. He practiced for two days a week at his consulting room in London, at Number 11 Mansfield Street, and the rest of the week he worked in his beautiful consulting room at home. This room was situated very close to the nursery which meant that when they passed by to go up stairs, the children had to be mousey quiet. They were only allowed into this room on rare occasions.

The room had, for his children, an atmosphere of strange and important happenings. At the far end of the room was Peter's large, oak, knee-hole pedestal desk. There he would sit, on his blue swivel chair, writing and puffing away at his pipe, which was quite often out or even empty, but it seemed nonetheless to aid his thinking.

On the wall just above his desk hung a signed photograph of Jung. When asked who this distinguished looking man might be he would reply: 'That is a picture of my teacher.' It seemed strange to his children that he should need a teacher.

Behind his desk was the fireplace with its surround of Dutch tiles and an oak mantelpiece that contained on it many treasures from antiquity. Next to his desk were some small oak cabinets which were always kept locked, and on a shelf there were busts of Akhnaton and Nefertiti. To the right of the fireplace was a French window leading out onto a big lawn, across which Peter could often be seen strolling with one of his patients.

On the wall to the right was a fine secretaire, the bookcase of which was filled with his more esoteric books on subjects such as mythology and religion; there were also books on Chinese wisdom and antiquity as well as books on psychology, including all Peter's and Cary's translations of Jung's books. These were all the reference books Peter needed for his own writing.

Books of a more general nature were kept in a floor-to-ceiling oak bookcase, which covered the entire wall opposite to his desk. Here could be found books on every subject under the sun. On the floor was a beautiful Chinese carpet of deep blue. It gave to the room a sense of quiet and meditative introversion.

On the east side of the room was a bay window with a seat along its entire length. This was a lovely place to sit, looking out over the lawn where the giant oak tree grew. Beneath this the children (up to the age of two) would have their afternoon rest in the large carriage-built pram. From here, Peter could also observe his patients when they arrived, for it looked up the driveway towards the quiet cul-de-sac avenue at the end of which the house was situated.

In those days there was no clear division between Peter's patients and his private life: many of them became close family friends. They would be invited to parties and to dine with the family. Sometimes

they would come after their session to sit and talk with Anne until
they felt ready to face the outside world again.

By now the demands of Peter's practice and his large household
were becoming overwhelming. In his letters to Bridget he expresses
his sense of being both over-burdened and exhausted: the severity of
the bombing was increasing; his shares and his income had dwindled
as the stock market crashed and at the same time the financial
demands seemed to increase.

Bridget was married now to an Irishman called Brian Coffey. He
was an academic and a poet and was completing a PhD so was unable
to support his wife, who in 1941 had given birth to a son, John.
Bridget's constant demands for financial assistance together with
Christopher' s school fees were an increasing burden. Peter wrote to
Bridget about Chloë, now married to John Green (a pilot officer who
had joined the RAF soon after their marriage): 'Chloë is afraid she will
want help from me too, so you can see why I get rattled.'

The situation at home was increasingly tough. In September 1940
he wrote to Bridget 'There are bombs and gun fire all around us so
that the house simply staggers and rocks ... We all sleep downstairs
in the hall, the two boys in the cloakroom. Diana and Anne in a bed
just beside the boys. Rosaline [the governess] further down the hall
and me in a bed just outside my study door. The morale is really
excellent. No fuss or terrors. Only tempers a bit shorter perhaps.'

In addition to his practice, his writing and the increasing domestic
pressures, Peter also had a busy schedule of lectures. On 7th April
1941 he writes of having lectured during the past three months in
Liverpool, Edinburgh, Oxford, Cheltenham, Bryanston (where Christopher was at school), and at an Anglo-Catholic conference in Angle-
sey. He writes: 'I have to talk a lot these days on the liaison between
psychology and religion. It is very much in the air. I am very keen to
start an Institute for Psychological Research in some university near
London. I hope it may be Oxford.'

The relationship between psychology and religion fascinated Peter
increasingly and in November 1941 he was writing to Jung about his
collaboration with Archbishop Temple:

> During the last weeks I have had long and pretty intimate talks
> with the Archbishops of both Canterbury and York ... I have been
> proposing to the Archbishops a kind of college or centre be
> established for the treatment and training of men in the analytical

way. Archbishop Temple responded to the idea very warmly and he is corresponding with me about it now.

In response to this letter, Jung wrote: 'Your lecturing activity is really astonishing. But I can understand that the public realises a certain need to compensate the onesidedness of organized activities. And I can well imagine that the great cataclysm has knocked over many prejudices and false values.'

Peter had given a series of religious broadcasts together with Archbishop Temple on this subject and he was later to collaborate with Dr Winifred Rushforth, the Edinburgh psychoanalyst, who was also fascinated by the close link between the goals of psychology and religion: both are concerned with 'health' in its deepest sense, and in the quest towards becoming whole (the words 'whole' and 'holy' both derive from the same Greek root). Both Peter and Dr Rushforth saw the teaching of Christ as absolutely in tune with profound psychic well-being and health. In Christ's teaching ('love thy neighbour as thyself') it is essential to learn first of all to love oneself before it is possible to truly love another.

It was in 1943 that Winifred Rushforth wrote to Peter to come with his family to Edinburgh, to escape the bombing in London, and to help her set up the Davidson Clinic for which she later became well-known. It was an attractive idea but was not in the end a possibility.

Peter wrote to Jung on the publication of *Germany Possessed* early in the summer: it had achieved considerable success. Henri Zimmer, a brilliant man and close friend to both Jung and Peter, had given a fine paper at the Analytical Psychology Club and Peter goes on to say:

> The AP Club is vigorous and growing aware of itself in a new way. Our old rooms were bombed and we meet now in the Welbeck Hotel. Flora Bennet is secretary and is a splendid support to me ... It really does seem that the new sun which can light our world is the healing work of individuation and you are the first clear voice of this principle in our Western culture. That is the whole truth of it in a nutshell ... A word from you would be almost like a beam of the Sun coming in.

Peter adds a final paragraph to this letter asking Jung if he has another typed copy of the Red Book that he could spare him: 'The thing I miss the most from the burning of my house was the loss of the typed copy of the Red Book which you gave me.' To send a copy in the conditions of war would have been impossible so Peter suggests he should wait to send it to him until the war is over, adding, 'if I survive this idiotic war.' However, that was not to be.

In response to Peter's letter, Jung wrote on 22 January 1942 a handwritten letter that was to be his penultimate communication, and a letter that Peter particularly cherished.

> My dear Peter,
> It was a great pleasure to have your letter of Nov. 23rd. It took its time in arriving, but it gave me at least an idea of what you are doing. I appreciate your letter all the more as I know how difficult it is to write letters at all. Your dealings with the clergy are interesting. What will become of the Christian Church? I will try to send you a MS of the Mass and one about the Trinity. It seems as if one or the other will be included in the English edition of an Eranosbook launched in America. At the moment I am unable to give you sufficient information: there is such a turmoil of publications, translations etc. that I have lost control. I will try whether I can procure another copy of the Red Book. Please don't worry about translations. I am sure there are 2 or 3 translations already. But I don't know of what and by whom. A little book about Paracelus is about to appear. This "religio medica" might interest you. I will send you a copy. I have given up lecturing at the E.T.H. It became too much of a strain, with everything else minus the auto, which has facilitated so many things. I have done a lot of research work within the last years besides my practical obligations. A certain slowing down seems to be indicated. I cannot get reconciled to the stupidity and shortsightedness of man, nor to this world in general. We are in for a new "Katakombenmentalität" ["catacomb mentality"] the only German invention or article "made in Germ." of lasting value. The devil has been seriously underrated within the last centuries. And the Church has played along with him in an irresponsible way. God, things are so very much worse than one likes to admit. No reason for any optimism: this world will never be better as it is already "le meilleur des mondes possibles". But it has an almost uncanny faculty of deteriorating into something infinitely worse. The Church insists too much on faith and far too little on insight and judgment. Thus the Church preserves a general credulity which the devil can make use of and *he does use it!* Childishness has been favoured, propagated

and nurtured. Its result is Socialism, the *political infanti-lism*...which is always the first step toward the Leviathan. The future might easily be so bad that the Church could be forced by circumstances to give up all her childish worldliness and socialism and to turn to the spiritual problem of man, which she has so sadly neglected. I would say of the *Catholic church* – "criminally neglect-ed." (More sins are forgiven to the great sinner than to the petty one.)

It is all like talking about the weather in a howling storm at sea or in a snowstorm on a glacier. It does not matter and nobody hears it. The shrieking of the demons is the stillness of the spirit. It means a withdrawal unheard of, until one hears the great silence.

Hoping you are in good health and that the same is true of your family, I remain,

Yours cordially, C.G.[68]

This was a letter full of pessimism and despair in relation to the total lack of understanding at all levels in the world; a despair that was matched also by Peter's own sense of overwhelming exhaustion at the time.

By April 1943, all the staff at Reed House had left. Peter writes to Bridget: 'We have no ... cook, no nurse and no regular gardener. But we are thriving under it and I find the garden work tremendously interesting, though of course there is always more to do than we can really manage.'

But as his burdens increase he writes to Bridget despairingly: 'Everyone assumes that they can rely on me even though my income is about halved. Even the money I hope to get on this new book [*Germany Possessed*] is already bespoke for Christopher's school bill. I can't run away from my responsibilities, but one day I shall have a lovely long sleep when nobody can reasonably expect me to do any more.'

As early as 1941 Peter was having a premonition of his death. He continued to suffer debilitating pain from his duodenal ulcer. He wrote in his journal, on Good Friday of that year:

The sea is cold, turbulent and forbidding. Dissolution prevails. I stand on a rock. The sea swirls below me. Is this in fact the end? Am I secretly desiring death or am I just fascinated, spell-bound by

---

[68] C.G. Jung, *Letters*, Vol. 1, p. 311-312.

the unconscious. No I am cool and sane and detached. Only this constantly recurring pain which gnaws my vitals. It is like a cruel hand clutching at the most exquisite sensitivity. I have dreamed and wondered about the descent under the sea. I am the old westering sun going down into the mouth and stomach of death. When God has finished with me then I shall know and I will be willing. He is the very centre and germ of my desire for life. Therefore He is the centre of my desire for death. I would not die just to escape pain of melancholia.

As the end of his life approached, Peter seemed to become more preoccupied with his relationship to God, but this was not the God of his father – it was a god who seemed to have little to do with church worship.

We have lost the reality of God as He appeared to the Jews and to our forefathers as a Power over against us. He now seems to come quietly out of the Earth-darkness into the circle of the single human flame and He calls this man or that man to His service. Not visibly in the churches or along the old trodden paths, but severally from within, drawing a man or a woman from their familiar ways and giving them a task to do, which they accept without knowing who it is that commands. Jesus appeared to John who was His friend and He drew his sorrowing eyes away from the scene on Calvary, where all the concourse of followers and persecutors were gathered together, and showed him the real cross which extended from earth to heaven and which provided a contained way for the human soul to ascend and descend. Thus Christ gave to man the symbolic means by which the terrifying opposites of Heaven and Earth could be reconciled. The man of the earth wants to extinguish the light of heaven because it binds the soul too closely to necessitous striving and cruel lust. But partisanship is in itself a spiritual calamity since it divides mankind into sheep and goats and the soul of man into irreconcilable opposites. We must not identify with either principle but belong faithfully to both. Through serving the Mother we gain realism, strength and nourishment. Through serving God the father we gain the light which shows us the Way and the Task. The energy and fire of the earth-nature needs the light of heaven or it expends itself in the machinery of power and life destroying lust. The light of heaven needs the fire and realism of the dark earth nature or it wastes itself in the upper spaces and cannot create beautiful objects. Earth generation without light is machine like productivity. Spirit without earth is a *fata morgana* [mirage], the illusion of beauty without concrete reality. Spirit and earth combined is creation. 'In the beginning God created the heaven and the earth. And the earth was without form and void and darkness was upon the face of the deep. And the Spirit of God moved upon the face of the waters. And god said, "Let there be light", and there was light.' As I began to read the story of Creation a spider came and lay half concealed in the middle of the book's binding in between the opposites. Then he came to life and ran across the page of creation and back again. The spider symbolizes the irrational activity of the psyche that will not be contained in any purely rational form. He is the primaeval associative industry of the psyche which weaves everything which comes within the psychical realm into an integrated structure. Therefore, in actuality the psyche-spider is the creator of our world. This is the miracle. But what is that germ or jewel by which this ceaseless activity of the mind is illuminated by revelation and meaning. In the moment that we detach our minds from the spider's web or system and ask what is that light which makes the web radiant with rainbow brilliance we are in the presence of the Boddhisattva who first manifested himself in the World-lotus and filled the world with unimaginable radiance ... The primordial irrational core of human nature by which Man is able to embrace both earth and heaven within his soul and reconcile Spirit and Sex, is beyond the limits of rational explanation, and here psychology must remain devoutly agnostic and humble. By means of analytical therapy, the way is made clear for the primordial religious experience and the doctor is able to show the patient, by reference to examples in the whole field of religious experience, the nature of the healing, religious process. But the inner context of the experience is always beyond our grasp. 'He who does not see the Grace of God as a great Wonder has never seen it at all ... Let not him who seeks ... cease until he finds, and when he finds he shall be astonished, astonished he shall reach the kingdom, and having reached the kingdom he shall rest.'

Peter sees a striking correspondence between the aims of analytical psychology and the Christian way; the need for what was in the dark to be brought into consciousness:

As Jesus taught, 'Jesus saith, everything that is not before thy face and that which is hidden from thee shall be revealed to thee. For there is nothing hidden from thee shall not be revealed to thee. For there is nothing hidden which shall not be made manifest nor buried which shall not be raised.'

As the escalation of the bombing made life at Reed House seem increasingly perilous, it had been suggested by Christopher' s grandmother that the three children should be evacuated to Edinburgh, to be looked after by Christopher' s nurse, Brownie. There had also been a possibility of sending them to America. In a letter to Jung, Peter speaks of,

> a gruelling time deciding whether to send the children to America or perhaps to somewhere safer in this country. We consulted the Yi [*I Ching*], and were told categorically to stay quiet and cultivate our garden. So that is what we did and I don't believe any bombs will touch us. But in case I am wiped out and we go to sleep every night to the sound of enemy planes overhead … this brings you, CG, my undying affection.

With no staff to run the large household, Anne was up at dawn each morning to light a coal fire in the dining room (there was of course, no oil to run the central heating), so that Peter and the houseguests could eat their bacon and eggs in warmth and comfort. It would be a tall order for anyone brought up to perform household tasks, but this was quite new to Anne and she was having to learn the basic elements of cookery! Peter wrote in a letter to Jung that 'Anne is simply indomitable. Her morale has never cracked for a second. She holds to the pact and her finest quality has come out during this long strain of work and responsibility.' Later he writes that 'Anne is magnificent … and she too has developed splendidly from her own inner core of quietness.' He continues that 'all are well and thriving'.

> The spring is ravishingly beautiful, long drawn out sweetness, and the season promises well, abundant blossom. This state of daemonic possession of the mass has certainly had the effect of making more people aware of the Golden Flower. I wonder if it is ever possible to realise the Star without first being broken by daemonic powers.
>
> Now I send you my love as bright as ever and please give my love to Emma and to Toni, Yours Peter.

These were to be Peter's final words to his beloved 'teacher', the man who had been his guide, friend and inspiration for nearly a quarter of a century.

In the spring of 1943 Anne became mortally ill with septicaemia. The surgeon who looked after her said he would need to amputate the offending leg, where the infection had entered (it was thought to have occurred when she was cutting her toe-nails). Anne refused to accept this mutilation and for a time it seemed certain that she would die. Peter was distraught.

At that time penicillin was known about but was available only for the troops. However, the sulphonamide drugs were just beginning to enter into general use. Anne was treated with M & B and this, together with her total determination to live, was able to save her. She remained in hospital until August, having celebrated her fortieth birthday (on June 9th) in hospital.

She was still very weak when she returned home and could only manage to walk with the help of crutches. One may imagine what rejoicing there was for the children when she returned.

The war was at its height, and help, in Anne's absence, had been almost impossible to find. A Mrs Bennet was procured, with the help of Mrs Evelyn D'Oyly, always known to the children as 'Midiboo'. Midiboo was a dear, loyal friend to the family and in the absence of any surviving parents for Anne and Peter, she acted as a grandmother for the children. Her daughter, Ingaret, was later to become the wife of Sir Laurens Van der Post. Midiboo was a tower of strength to the family at this difficult time. However, Mrs Bennett was not a success.

Meanwhile, Peter's health was deteriorating. He was suffering from mind-blowing fatigue; it was becoming increasingly difficult to work and he was having a problem with speaking. He blamed himself for becoming neurotic and he soldiered on. In a photo taken of him at this time the exhaustion is apparent in his face and he looks much older than his sixty-one years. The 'sad eyes' he spoke of years before, in 1924, are especially noticeable.

It was a time of unimaginable stress for all of England, and Anne and Peter had had their share of this. Peter was landed with a practice that was more demanding than at any time in his life. He had been trying to manage a large and busy household without help, except that of an unsatisfactory housekeeper and the occasional help of a nineteen year-old youth, Christopher. He had the care of three young children, as well as needing to comfort and reassure them in the absence of their mother. The bombing was at its height and doodle-bugs were often seen going over the house. The sound of the air-raid alarm and of German planes flying overhead was a nightly occurrence, followed by the wail of the all clear. Diana remembers climbing into her father's bed for comfort and reassurance while the sound of bombing could be heard all around.

Finally, not long after Anne's return home, it was recognised that Peter was seriously ill. The doctors could find nothing wrong and it was the district nurse who suggested that he might be suffering from inter-cranial pressure. The modern techniques for brain scans were of course not available, but it was ascertained that he did indeed have an inoperable tumour in the speech area of the brain, hence his increasing difficulty with speech that had made it so difficult for him to do a job that entirely depended on speaking.

In August, Peter was taken to St Thomas' Hospital and was under the care of the well-known physician, Dr Evan-Jones. Anne, who was still walking with crutches, went into hospital with him. He was ill for exactly one month. Anne spoke of Peter's time in hospital and of 'how tremendously impressed they were with him there. They had never seen anyone like him. They used to say to me that he must be a very remarkable person because apparently most people when they have this haemorrhage lose consciousness. This he never did.' He continued to communicate with her with his eyes, or by clasping her hand, but he never lost awareness of himself. Anne said how valuable this final month had been for him. He no longer felt he had to struggle to do things and the month of immobilization was like a wonderful preparation for death. Anne said: 'I think that only in this way was he able to accept death, by having a month when he could slowly relinquish his hold on life.' Peter died on September 6th 1943, with Anne by his side.

For the children, who had been cared for during Peter's illness by Evelyn D'Oyly, it was a sad home-coming. There was little help or support available and the outcome of the war was still very uncertain. Finances, without Peter's salary, were stretched to the limit and at that time there was no government support for widows. But in spite of difficult circumstances, Anne's spirit was indomitable. She let half of Reed House, and the family lived on the proceeds. Somehow, the three children were not aware of financial privation, perhaps because everyone in the war was in the same boat. There were food shortages and rationing and only doctors were provided with petrol to drive their cars. So the Bayneses situation was like that of everyone else.

Anne remained for the rest of her life in the same house and somehow managed to keep Peter's spirit alive there. It never seemed to his children that he was absent from their lives. Anne spoke of him every day and things that belonged to him remained in every room. There was always laughter and Anne managed to give the three children a sense of freedom and a long rein to find their own paths in life. However, perhaps at some level she never recovered from his death. She had opportunities to re-marry, but she felt that no-one could take Peter's place. She remained a widow for the next 40 years.

Peter's death left a yawning gap, not only in the lives of his immediate family and his children by three different wives. It was also a catastrophe for the growing world of Jungian Psychology in London. There was no obvious person to take over from Peter. Many of the analysts had gone away to fight in the war. It was considered necessary in the early days of analytical psychology to be a doctor and preferably a psychiatrist, before being accepted for training as an analyst (although there were exceptions, especially amongst those analysts who came to England from Germany during the war).

Eventually, the small group of Jungian analysts practicing in London wrote to Michael Fordham, who had gone with his wife Frieda to work in Nottingham to escape the bombing. Fordham was still young and as an analyst, relatively inexperienced, but he was a qualified doctor and psychiatrist, and therefore the most suitable person to lead the Jungian Society.

Fordham wrote:

> 'In 1943 Erna Rosenbaum, a Jungian analyst and a founder member of the Society of Analytical Psychologists, telephoned me in Nottingham asking me to come down to London to help organize a group of analysts who wanted to form a professional institute ... During the earlier efforts Godwin Baynes had been the leader but now he was dead. I assumed that an Englishman with sufficient status to act as a persona was required, especially by the analysts who had migrated from Germany and did not have English medical degrees.'[69]

---

[69] Fordham, 1993, p. 9.

Although Fordham was the obvious person to be Peter's successor, and Peter had possibly hoped that he would be the next person to lead the Jungian society, their relationship had at times been problematic. Fordham had been Peter's patient and had also been the subject of one of the case studies in *Mythology of the Soul*. Fordham had agreed to have the material used, but at that time, with so few people involved in the Jungian world, it was not difficult to identify him as the patient about whom Peter was writing. This later caused Fordham to feel antagonistic towards Peter and as he eventually took a very different direction in his work from that of either Jung himself or Peter, his leadership finally led to the splitting of the Jungian world in London. So often, when the original pioneer leaves the field, his or her successors take different paths and splits occur, so perhaps these divisions, which now number four or five different Jungian groups in London, would have occurred whoever had taken over the leadership. However, there is a sense that after a short time, Peter's contribution – his early commitment and pioneering work – was largely forgotten.

Fordham has at times acknowledged his debt to Peter and this was so at the meeting of the Analytical Psychology Club that followed Peter's death, on October 14th 1943. The meeting began with an introduction from Culver Barker who opened the discussion by saying that, 'All of us present have at least one close and intimate bond with all the others present and that is the memory of a great, warm-hearted and wise friend – Dr Baynes – and it is under his inspiration that we meet here today as an informal gathering of those people interested in the pratice of analytical psychology in England.' He went on to propose Dr Fordham as Chair. In reviewing the events and developments of the previous years, Fordham said that the credit for these developments 'is really with Dr Baynes who worked alone for a great many years in England and he really fought for analytical psychology and made a place for it. I remember when I started to be an analyst he was really the only one of any calibre in England at all. And I think it is worth remembering that it was not till the continental members came over to England that there was any co-operative body which made it possible to combine together and try and work out something which one could play on for the future.' He went on to describe Peter's plans to form a centre for Analytical Psychology and his proposal for a training centre or institute 'whose aim was partly educational, to give lectures, partly to treat patients, to have a clinic and partly to do research.' All these plans were brought to a halt at the onset of the war. He added that at the instigation of Dr Baynes a great deal of work had already been done towards the establishment of a clinical centre.

However, perhaps as a result of having been used as a clinical case, Fordham's feelings about Peter were ambivalent. He had left Peter to analyse with Hilda Kirsch[70] because of these ambivalent feelings. The ambivalence veered between feelings of idealisation and intense antagonism.

His idealization of Peter had begun when he was a child and he remembered Peter's visits to the Fordham's home in the village of Steep, in Hampshire. Fordham remembered: 'There was a very large man who used to visit us. I believe he came to sing with my mother, but he impressed me very much because of his size. He seemed a sort of giant; his name was Godwin Baynes. Subsequently he became my Jungian analyst but he had no connection with psychology or Jung when I knew him as a child.'

At first, in his analysis with Peter, Fordham admired Peter's vast knowledge and his capacity to unravel profound meaning from the prolific unconscious material which had been evoked. Fordham spoke of his 'idealization' of this giant personality who had worked alongside Jung. While his analysis was in full flood, there came a time when he was unable to pay for his sessions, so Peter agreed to see him without payment and in return he asked for Fordham's permission to use his material in the book he was writing. Fordham readily agreed to this.

The negative feelings arose as a result of the complications caused by having his rather disturbed material used in a published work. He wrote: 'My work with Baynes had become further complicated because it gave rise to gossip.' Fordham knew that Peter had shown the material to Jung who had felt uneasy about it being published. Peter had consulted Fordham about this and Fordham said 'he should not drop the project as Jung wanted him to do; it was part of our agreement anyway and I thought he should fight off Jung's views. Baynes thought that "peculiar", if I remember the word he used. This state of affairs got around and I received condolences, especially at being a published case, which it was said would be used against me.'

---

[70] Hilda and her husband, James Kirsch, were both Jungian analysts in London.

Although the publishing of the material had Fordham's whole-hearted consent, he held it against Peter in later life. He writes of his tendency in later life to publish clinical material that came largely from his work with children: 'There was ... I now think, an unconscious reaction deriving from my material having been published by Baynes.'[71] The use of his material was later to become as Tom Kirsch expresses it 'a lifelong albatross'[72] for Fordham, and it was this that somewhat soured his attitude towards Peter in subsequent years.

Fordham acknowledges his 'quite serious mental disorganisation' at the time. He writes: 'I must correct the impression that work with Baynes was unproductive. I have mentioned the "breakthrough" which took place almost at once. That released my imagination and I painted pictures almost every day. In addition I studied dreams and held conversations with imaginary figures.' However, he adds that 'most of this activity went on in my spare time on my own.'[73] He gives the impression that this outpouring of unconscious material which enabled his recovery had very little to do with his analyst. Perhaps he also under-rated Peter's contribution in relation to the Jungian community when he claimed, later in life, to be the 'founder' of Jungian psychology in London. Kirsch quotes Fordham, when asked why he had remained a Jungian since his theories were more consonant with those of the object-relations school.[74] Fordham replied: 'It wouldn't look good if the founder of analytical psychology in England defected to another school, would it?'[75] In making this claim he was forgetting the debt owed by the Jungian community to Peter's pioneering activities during the twenty-one years prior to Fordham's leadership. However, this happened much later, and at the time of Peter's death, Fordham paid him both a generous and a magnanimous tribute.

Anne received letters from all over the world when news of Peter's death, under difficult wartime conditions, eventually reached people. Jung, writing of Peter in his introduction to Peter's posthumous book *Analytical Psychology and the English Mind*, refers to him in the

---

[71] Fordham, M., *The Making of an Analyst*, p. 130.

[72] Kirsch, T., *The Jungians*, 2000, p. 38.

[73] Fordham, M., *The Making of an Analyst*, p. 73.

[74] Object Relations is the term used to describe the school of psychology inspired by the theories of Donald Winnicott.

[75] Kirsch, 2000, p. 47 (Personal communication, November 1994).

following words: 'I write these few introductory words ... in affectionate memory of their author. The late H.G. Baynes was my assistant
for several years, my travelling companion on our African expedition,
and my faithful friend till his all too early death, which has left a
painful gap in the circle of his friends and colleagues.' He ends with
'H.G. Baynes left us too soon. May this volume, which he has left to
us, become a milestone on the road of psychological research. C.G.
Jung.'

Letters came also from his circle of artistic friends, from so many
years before, whose lives had developed so differently, and who found
Peter's psychological outlook difficult to understand. Arnold Bax
wrote of him, 'He was a great fellow, the most all round man I ever
knew. I think he was friendly to all the world and with him went much
of the physical and spiritual vitality of England.' He wrote later,
'Godwin was a very rare man. If I could play the organ [for Peter's
funeral] I would of course have come to say goodbye to my oldest
friend, and I thank you dear Anne for asking me.' Arnold's brother,
Clifford, wrote: 'You must have loved Godwin very much – and he was
so easy to love. I cannot imagine the creature who would not like him.
He and I were friends for 35 years. I know that we must get used to
death. I know that it is better to have loved and lost than never to have
known at all: but very few deaths really upset the hearer's equilib-
rium. This one, my dear, has somewhat upset mine.'

There was a letter also from The British Psychological Society at
the Tavistock Clinic with a warm acknowledgement for his work: 'As
a fellow of the Society and the leading exponent in England of the
theories of C.G. Jung, Dr Baynes was held in high regard by his fellow
psychologists and his loss will be greatly felt.'

In his recent book, *The Jungians*, Thomas Kirsch pays tribute to
the pioneering role Peter played in relation to Jungian Psychology in
London. He writes: 'One can only speculate how differently analytical
psychology might have developed had Baynes lived longer. Baynes
was deeply devoted to Jung and his way of working with the psyche
and was excellent in presenting Jung to both professional and public
audiences. The *rapprochement* with psychoanalysis which began in
the 1940's would have taken on a different character if Baynes had
lived longer. A closer alliance with Jung's views would have been
more likely.' [76]

---

[76] Kirsch, T., *The Jungians*, p. 39.

Later in his book, where he discusses the splits that have occurred in the Jungian groups throughout the world, he comments that there has also been a hostile relationship between Freudians and Jungians in all but two places in the world. These exceptions are San Francisco and London. He explains the reason for these exceptions as being threefold: 'psychological types; the nature of the founders' transferences to Jung; and the fact that the founders were medical doctors. In both London and San Francisco, the extraverted Baynes and Wheelwright could relate to Freudians and made them feel comfortable with Jungians, if not with Jung's theory. Most of the founders had an extremely strong positive transference to Jung, seeing him as a charismatic figure.' Had he lived longer, Peter's more extraverted personality might have held the Jungian group in London together as a cohesive whole which could absorb and also be enriched by their differences, in personality, outlook and heritage. Perhaps also, as Tom Kirsch suggests, the Jungians and Freudians could have worked with one another, respecting each other's differences, yet remaining true to their own way of working.

Many tributes were paid to Peter and to his contribution to analytical psychology. An address given at his funeral service at Brookwood cemetery in Surrey, by a man whose name has not been recorded, but who had worked with Peter, speaks of his skill as an analyst:

> I could not help admiring the skill with which Dr Baynes wielded his analytical technique. In the interpretation of unconscious material, he would utilize not only his own scientific knowledge but also his comprehensive reading in anthropology, the mythologies of the world, and a comparative study of religions. He possessed a massive mind with a very wide range of interests and never lacking in depth. I have known scientific men, whose scientific training has been so austere that they lacked all traces of culture as ordinarily understood. In the case of Dr Baynes, his scientific training had been mellowed by knowledge of the humanities. There was an artistic creativeness about his personality as a whole, a quality which was very marked in his published works as well as in his practice of the healing art.
>
> Moreover, in some strands of his teaching there was, I now think, a prophetic note of an authentic kind. I believe it was Lord Acton who said that power corrupts, and absolute power corrupts

absolutely. The theme which Lord Acton maintained on historical evidence, Dr. Baynes would urge on psychological grounds. He held that the solution of the problem of power was not to repress the desire for it, but to use it in the interests of the ideal of service. Here, doubtless, is a creative principle we would do well to lay to heart if we are to build the new world on stable foundations.

His pilgrimage under conditions of space and time has come to an end. It has been interesting, exciting, full of enthusiasm and ardour. I am sure he continues his pilgrimage under different conditions in another dimension of reality. Today, we thank God for a very noble and courageous spirit.

Another tribute was written about him by Michael Fordham, who had by this time most courageously taken on the task of leading the Jungian world in London at a time when the future of Jungian Psychology as well the fate of England was very much in the balance. It was a huge undertaking which he embarked upon in 1943 with many misgivings and without the experience he would like to have had as an analyst, before being plunged in at the deep end. He wrote:

Everybody who knew him well will mourn the sudden death of Helton Godwin Baynes at the age of 61. His generous and vital nature enriched the lives of all who came across him, whether they belonged to intellectual and artistic circles or whether they were real enough persons with the simplicity to see into his real nature which contained such wide, loyal and genuine humanity.

His career is remarkable in several respects. In his earlier years he seriously considered becoming a professional singer, and his athletic record is one of which anyone might well be proud.

His sheer talents presented problems which others would not find because they opened up so many avenues to him, but in the end he became a doctor, thus laying the basis for his real life work. For two years he was in general practice and later on he was for a short time at the Maudsley Hospital.

I have heard him comment on the tremendous impression which a mass panic made upon him during the Balkan war and how all human values were cast aside in the mad rush to find the great mother who would succour her children but who in reality only sought their destruction. He was a surgeon at the time and it was he alone who stood firm amidst the collective cataclysm.

It was not until he went to Professor Jung in Zurich that he started along the line which then led him to realise the inner forces which corresponded to the outer experience. The whole of the rest of his working life was dedicated to the study of these inner forces arising from the depths of the psyche which has been called by Jung the Collective Unconscious. His work was more than just a cold interest for it sprang from the inspiration of a man to whom he gave his unswerving allegiance.

He became Jung's assistant in Zurich and it was not until 1924 that he settled in England. During this period he translated three of Jung's major works, he was the interpreter of Jung and his translations expressed this fact.

In 1925 there was no Jungian analyst of any calibre in this country but he was a fighter and he fought for the science to which he had given himself. The fight was expressed in his papers some of which, *Freud versus Jung, The Importance of Dream Analysis for Psychological Development*, etc., were published in this journal. In these he sought to widen the basis of medical psychology beyond the psychoanalytic conceptions which largely dominated the scene. He made a place for analytical psychology but until a number of analysts came from the Nazi occupied countries he was almost alone. During this time he was not daunted by what some might have conceived his small success, he simply served the ideas which had gripped him and placed them before his colleagues, and in so doing prepared the ground for a further development which it is the task of those who follow him to bring about.

In spite of his realisation that the human psyche could not be entirely embraced by scientific concepts, Baynes was above everything, a scientist. He had no respect for dogmatic doctrine and was always ready to throw over a useless concept. He went further than merely discarding theories, however, because he had grasped how the scientific intellect draws its life from the collective unconscious. This being so it was not possible to discard a theory without also changing the deep basis from which it sprang in the mythological substratum of the soul.

This depth of consciousness, if one may be permitted to express it in this way, extended into his personal relationships which consequently gained just because he was able to reach the sources of his views and feeling about people. It made him a man who aroused a love in his friends, it was a love that would stand the test of conflict and disagreement.

In *Mythology of the soul* he brought to fruition the result of many years' labour. He combined the vast experiences of his life with his clinical observations and mythological research. It is likely to be a classic work which will give him a permanent place amongst those who struggle with the depths of the psyche and the human problems, neuroses and border-line schizophrenic states which have their origin in these layers.

He died on September 6th 1943 at St Thomas' Hospital, an irreparable loss to his friends and his profession.

A generous tribute indeed from the man who was to become Peter's successor and who continued to lead the Jungian world in London and to put his own personal stamp on what is now known as The Developmental School of Jungian Psychology, for the next forty years.

The Obituary that appeared in *The Times* was written by the dear friend from his youth, Arnold Bax.

The death of Godwin Baynes has removed from a vast circle of friends and enthusiastic admirers one of the most all-round men of his time. When he was young he was almost idolised by many who came under his influence and not without reason. In every department of life he was a very gallant fellow, interested and proficient in all things except perhaps competitive games, for which he did not much care. A great mountaineer and mighty swimmer, he was also declared by Gustav Holst to be the best amateur singer whom that famous composer had ever met. Always out for adventure, he volunteered his medical services during the Balkan War of 1912 and took a strenuous part in the reorganisation of the army hospitals of Constantinople which had previously been in a very haphazard and ill-conditioned state. Later he performed hectic feats of surgery among Turkish refugees from the savagery of the Kurds. It is characteristic of him that he once found himself engaged in lonely combat with a golden eagle in the Persian mountains.

There had always been a deeply serious side to his nature, and when, after serving in the RAMC in the last war, he took up psycho-analysis this side became markedly more pronounced, possibly somewhat at the expense of the gaiety and ebullience of his earlier days. But to the end there was a fundamental and endearing boyishness about him. He was a generative mental force and everyone was the livelier for 'Tiny's' society and converse, whether his mood was irresponsible or philosophical, grave or laughing.

Chloë received a letter of condolence from Peter's old friend, Bertie Farjeon. He wrote:

> I don't think there is anyone for whom I had more affection and admiration than I had for Godwin when we were young. Rosalind will tell you that. I loved him very dearly and he opened my heart and the hearts of many of us then, and now I remember many things too deep for praise, but I have to write you a line, which is for Bridget too. But I write this not to comfort you, but to comfort myself, for one wants to say 'I loved him' in words, – thinking isn't enough.

Rosalind wrote a brief note to share her sadness with Anne:

> I must write and say how sad I am and how terrible it is to think that Godwin is gone. I do send you all possible sympathy. It must seem an impossible future – but to have found him as you say happy at the end, in his far away state, must be a living comfort to you.

Peter had lived with a rare intensity and had known extraordinarily rich and varied experience in his sixty-one years. He was tired, mentally, spiritually and physically, and a part of him was ready to die. The burden of his responsibilities had overwhelmed him and he longed for a rest that would last forever. Somehow, he had completed his life's journey: the search for his own soul was won, and what he experienced at the end of his life was, for him, a true home-coming.

List of Illustrations

Part Three

Glossary of Jungian Terms

Anima
The term used by Jung to refer to the feminine aspect within a man. The anima presents as an unconscious psychic image. She is not only the contra-sexual aspect to a man's maleness but also acts as soul-guide and inspiration. Anima in its negative aspect can present in a man's life as moodiness and irrational behaviour. A man's anima can also be represented by an actual woman. She may be embodied by a collective figure (like Helen of Troy or Princess Diana), or alternatively, as friend, lover or wife.

Animus
Similarly, this refers to the masculine aspect within a woman. Whereas, anima acts as a mans inspiration, animus, in its positive aspect, can give a woman confidence in her own ability to be effective and creative in the world. In its negative aspect, it can lead a woman to behave in a way that is opinionated or aggressive.
Jung referred to anima and animus as 'soul images'. He wrote that the animus is 'the archetype of *meaning;* just as the anima is the archetype of life itself' (CW 9, para. 66).

Analysand
The patient in an analysis is called an analysand.

Archetype
The universal language of primordial images, or pre-existing patterns of energy in the unconscious, which lie at the root of the symbol. Archetypes present as archetypal images in the world of dreams or fantasy. An archetypal image can be in relation to the universal aspect of Mother, Father, Old Wise Man, Trickster, etc.

Collective Unconscious
An unconscious layer of the psyche which lies at a deeper level than the personal unconscious. It is collective, universal and impersonal in nature and is identical in all individuals. It does not develop individually but is inherited.

Ego
A unique centre of consciousness which represents only a small part of the Self.

Father Imago
A subjective inner image of the father.

Individuation
Is the process of becoming conscious and is the search for integration and wholeness; it involves the 'union of opposites'.

Jungian Typology
Jung identified four functions that are fundamental to the human personality. Thinking and feeling, which lie in opposition to one another, and intuition and sensation, which are

also opposed. These four functions produce within the psyche the tension of opposites and if they are in perfect balance, a state of psychic wholeness is achieved. In most people, one function is less well differentiated and this is known as the inferior function.

Jung also formulated two further categories in his concept of typology. These categories are now included in common parlance. An extravert is one who is more in touch with outer realities whereas the introvert is more at home with his own inner realm.

Libido   Jung used the term to describe psychic energy.

Mandala   A geometric figure comprising a circle and a square which can represent a potential for psychic wholeness or the symbol for cosmic wholeness. The appearance of a mandala within a dream or unconscious representation can have a numinous quality. The word in Sanskrit means, 'magic circle'.

Numinous   That which pertains to religious experience; which relates to an experience of mystery and a meaning beyond conscious understanding.

Personal Unconscious   Unlike Freud, Jung did not regard the unconscious only as a repository for repressed material, but also as a rich source of psychic information.

Persona   Refers to the mask or aspect a person assumes with which to face the world, deriving from the Latin word for the mask used by actors in classical times.

Self   A psychosomatic unity comprising both the ego and the unconscious. It is also the transpersonal centre which seeks to restore balance and unity to the personality. The Self and the God-image within, are interchangeable.

Shadow   That which contains the hidden, repressed and less acceptable aspects of the personality. It tends to remain unconscious.

Symbol   Expresses a psychic fact that cannot be formulated exactly.

Transference   This occurs in the relationship that an analysand has with his/her analyst. It refers to psychic contents and attitudes (often relating to early childhood) which are (temporarily) transferred onto the analyst. The analyst 'holds' these projections until the analysand (or patient), is ready to integrate them into him/herself.

Transference is a central feature of analysis. It can be of great importance therapeutically and can also cause difficulty and resistance which can create obstacles to successful therapy.

Counter-transference is the experience of the analyst in response to the patient's transference. It can be a valuable organ of information, but can also at times become a hindrance to the work.

Bibliography

Bax, Arnold, *Farewell My Youth* – and other writings. Scolar Press, Hants, 1992.

Bax, Clifford, *Inland Far*. Heinemann, London, 1925.

Baynes, Chloë & Thornycroft, Rosalind, *Time Which Spaces Us Apart*. Private Publication, 1991.

Baynes, H.A., *Commonplace Book* (unpublished).

Baynes, H.G., *Journals and Letters* (unpublished).

    Mythology of the Soul. Methuen, London, 1949.

    Germany Possessed. Cape, London, 1941.

    Analytical Psychology and the English Mind – And other Papers. Methuen, London, 1950.

Baynes, John, *Reminiscences*. Unpublished, 2001.

Cabot Reid, Jane, *Jung, my Mother and I*. Daimon Verlag, Einsiedeln, 2001.

Cather, Willa, *Lucy Gayheart*. Virago Press, London, 1985.

Clayton, Ann, *Chavasse Double VC*. Pen and Sword, York, 1997.

Colcord, Anne, *Home Sweet Home*. Harvest, 1998.

Delaney, Paul, *The Neo-Pagans: Friendship and Love in the Rupert Brooke Circle*. Macmillan, London, 1987.

Farjeon, Annabel, *Morning Has Broken*. Macrae, London, 1986.

Farjeon, Eleanor, *Nuts and May*. Collins, London, 1926.

    Edward Thomas – The Last Four Years. Oxford, 1958.

Fordham, Michael, *The Making of an Analyst A Memoir*. Free Association Books, London, 1993.

Foreman, Lewis, *A Composer and his Times*. Scolar Press, Hants, 1983.

Garnett, David, *The Golden Echo*. Chatto & Windus, London, 1954.

Hannah, Barbara, *Jung, His Life & Work; A Biographical Memoir*. Perigree Books, New York, 1976. (New edition, Chiron, Wilmette, 1998.)

Henderson, Joseph, *Reminiscences of H.G. Baynes*. Unpublished, 1998.

    Preface to Mythology of the Soul. Rider and Co., London, 1962.

Hislop, Francis, Daniel, *Dr Jung, I presume*. *The Journal of Her Majesty's Overseas service*. Corona, London, June 1960.

Jung, C.G., *Memories, Dreams, Reflections by C.G. Jung,* recorded and edited by Aniela Jaffé, Fontana Press, London, 1995.

> *C.G. Jung Letters 1906-1950.* Routledge & Kegan Paul, London, 1973.

> *Correspondence with H.G.B.* (Unpublished).

> *Seminar on Zarathustra,* CW I, p. 709. (seminar of 20 November 1935).

Kirsch, Thomas B., *The Jungians.* Routledge, London, 2000.

Lawrence, D.H., *Lady Chatterley's Lover.* Penguin, Harmondsworth, 1960.

McGuire, William & Hull, R.F.C. (ed.), *C.G. Jung Speaking.* Pan Books, London, 1980.

Nicoll, Maurice, *In Mesopotamia.* Hodder and Starton, London, 1917.

Nietzsche, Friedrich, *Thus Spake Zarathustra.* Part One, Section 17, 'On the Way of the Creator', London, 1931.

The Oxford Dictionary of Quotations. Oxford, University Press, 1975.

Sassoon, Siegfried, *Letter to the Times.* Quoted from: Barker, P. *Regeneration.* Penguin Books, London, 1992.

Index

Index

Recent Titles from **DAIMON**

What is Death?

Three outstanding elderly Jungian analysts from Zürich, all of whom worked closely with C.G. Jung, addressed questions about dying and death shortly before their own departures from this world. They drew upon their lifelong analytic work in accompanying others as well as their own personal experiences in addressing this greatest of mysteries.

Endings and beginnings, renewal and transformation are reflected in the rich dreams and other material upon which they have drawn.

Aniela Jaffé writes about *C.G. Jung's View of Death*

Marie-Louise von Franz about *A Psychological Clarification of Experiences of Death*

and **Liliane Frey-Rohn** about *Archetypes Surrounding Death*

ca. 140 pages, ISBN 3-85630-621-8

Jung, My Mother and I

The Analytic Diaries of Catharine Rush Cabot
Edited by Jane Cabot Reid

Catharine (Katy) Cabot, a young American woman in Europe, was for many years a patient of C.G. Jung. She kept a diary, recording the details of her psychoanalytic sessions with Jung along with her inner and outer experiences. Jung became an integral part of her life and he, his family and their friends all figure prominently in her life story as it unfolds in these pages. The journals include interpretations of dreams, sketches, letters, fragments of dialogue and Katy's reflections on how her life was developing. There are stories from the famous Psychological Club of Zürich, the Eranos Conferences in Ascona and other historic occasions in the circle around Jung. This fascinating account provides a rare portrait of Jung's Zürich in those creative years between 1930 and 1950.

We see how doctor and patient worked with the stuff of her life, some of it specific to her, much of it universal and timeless.

640 pages, hardbound, richly illustrated, ISBN 3-85630-601-3

ENGLISH PUBLICATIONS BY **DAIMON**

ENGLISH PUBLICATIONS BY **DAIMON**

Laurens van der Post - *The Rock Rabbit and the Rainbow*

Jane Reid - *Jung, My Mother and I: The Analytic Diaries of Catharine Rush Cabot*

R.M. Rilke - *Duino Elegies*

Miguel Serrano - *C.G. Jung and Hermann Hesse*

Helene Shulman - *Living at the Edge of Chaos*

Dennis Slattery / Lionel Corbet (Eds.) - *Depth Psychology: Meditations on the Field*

Susan Tiberghien - *Looking for Gold*

Ann Ulanov - *Picturing God*
- *Receiving Woman*
- *The Female Ancestors of Christ*
- *The Wisdom of the Psyche*
- *The Wizards' Gate, Picturing Consciousness*

Ann & Barry Ulanov - *Cinderella and her Sisters: The Envied and the Envying*
- *Healing Imagination: Psyche and Soul*

Erlo van Waveren - *Pilgrimage to the Rebirth*

Harry Wilmer - *How Dreams Help*
- *Quest for Silence*

Luigi Zoja - *Drugs, Addiction and Initiation*

L. Zoja & Don Williams - *Jungian Reflections on September 11*

Jungian Congress Papers - *Jerusalem 1983: Symbolic and Clinical Approaches*
- *Berlin 1986: Archetype of Shadow in a Split World*
- *Paris 1989: Dynamics in Relationship*
- *Chicago 1992: The Transcendent Function*
- *Zürich 1995: Open Questions*
- *Florence 1998: Destruction and Creation*
- *Cambridge 2001*

Available from your bookstore or from our distributors:

In the United States:

Continuum
22883 Quicksilver Drive
Dulles, VA 20166
Phone: 800-561 7704
Fax: 703-661 1501

In Great Britain:

Airlift Book Company
8 The Arena
Enfield, Middlesex EN3 7NJ
Phone: (0181) 804 0400
Fax: (0181) 804 0044

Worldwide:

Daimon Verlag   Hauptstrasse 85   CH-8840 Einsiedeln   Switzerland
Phone: (41)(55) 412 2266   Fax: (41)(55) 412 2231
email: info@daimon.ch
*Visit our website: www.daimon.ch
or write for our complete catalog!*